Routledge Research in Human Rights Law

International Human Rights Law and Domestic Violence

This innovative book examines the effectiveness of international human rights law, through the case study of domestic violence. Domestic violence is an issue that affects vast numbers of women throughout all nations of the world, but as it takes place between private individuals it does not come within the ambit of the traditional interpretation of human rights law. Ronagh J.A. McQuigg questions whether international human rights law can only be effective in a 'traditional' case of human rights abuse or whether it can rise to the challenge of being used in relation to issues such as domestic violence.

The book focuses primarily on the question of how international human rights law could be used in relation to domestic violence in the United Kingdom. McQuigg considers recent case law from the European Court of Human Rights on domestic violence and whether the UK courts could use the Human Rights Act 1998 to assist victims of domestic violence. The book goes on to look in detail at the statements of the international human rights bodies on domestic violence, with particular focus on those made by the United Nations Committee on the Elimination of Discrimination against Women and the Special Rapporteur on Violence against Women. The book explores the impact that the statements have had so far on the UK Government's policy in relation to domestic violence and discusses how the statements made by the international human rights bodies could be used more effectively by non-governmental organisations, such as human rights groups and women's groups.

Ronagh J.A. McQuigg is a lecturer in the School of Law, Queen's University Belfast. Her research interests are in the area of the effectiveness of international human rights law, particularly in relation to violence against women.

Ensuring and Enforcing Economic, Social and Cultural Rights
The jurisprudence of the UN committee on economic, social and cultural rights
Marco Odello and Francesco Seatzu

Human Rights Monitoring Mechanisms of the Council of Europe
Gauthier de Beco

The EU as a 'Global Player' in Human Rights?
Jan Wetzel

Human Rights in the Asia-Pacific Region
Towards institution building
Hitoshi Nasu and Ben Saul

Vindicating Socio-Economic Rights
International standards and comparative experiences
Paul O'Connell

International Human Rights Law and Domestic Violence

The effectiveness of international
human rights law

Ronagh J.A. McQuigg

Routledge
Taylor & Francis Group

LONDON AND NEW YORK

First published 2011
by Routledge
2 Park Square, Milton Park, Abingdon, Oxon, OX14 4RN

Simultaneously published in the USA and Canada
by Routledge
711 Third Avenue, New York, NY 10017

Routledge is an imprint of the Taylor & Francis Group, an informa business

British Library Cataloguing in Publication Data
A catalogue record for this book is available
from the British Library

Library of Congress Cataloging in Publication Data
McQuigg, Ronagh J. A.
    International human rights law and domestic violence : the
effectiveness of international human rights law / Ronagh J.A.
McQuigg.
       p. cm.
    ISBN 978-0-415-58226-1
    1. Family violence—Law and legislation—Great Britain.
    2. Human rights—Great Britain.   3. Family violence—Law and
    legislation.   4. Human rights.   I. Title.
    KD7973.M37 2011
    345´.02555—dc22   2010041822

ISBN13: 978–0–415–58226–1 (hbk)
ISBN13: 978–0–203–81928–9 (ebk)

Typeset in Garamond by
RefineCatch Limited, Bungay, Suffolk

Printed and bound in Great Britain by
CPI Antony Rowe, Chippenham, Wiltshire

Contents

How international human rights law could be used in
relation to domestic violence: The litigation approach

How international human rights law could be used in
relation to domestic violence: Using the statements of
international human rights bodies

Table of cases

Table of statutes

Introduction

In this book the effectiveness of human rights law is assessed through the medium of a case study of domestic violence. This is an issue that affects vast numbers of women throughout all nations of the world. An examination of the potential of human rights law to make a contribution in this area therefore casts new light on the effectiveness of the discourse of international human rights law. Domestic violence takes place between private individuals and thus would not have come within the ambit of the traditional interpretation of human rights law. Nevertheless, the practice of domestic violence constitutes a clear violation of several internationally recognised rights, for example, the right to be free from inhuman or degrading treatment, the right to bodily integrity and indeed the right to life. Can international human rights law only be effective in a 'traditional' case of human rights abuse? How well can it rise to the challenge of being used in relation to such an issue as domestic violence?

For many years the issue of violence against women taking place in the home was largely ignored. As Kelly and Radford comment, the concept of domestic violence 'simply did not exist before the present wave of feminist activism'.[1] Although violence was certainly taking place against women in the home, there was no social definition for this behaviour. However, domestic violence is now widely recognised as being a massive problem. Nevertheless, as Dobash and Dobash state, problems of definition still remain.[2] For example, they comment that 'As descriptive terms, domestic, spousal and family violence obscure the gendered nature of the problem and ignore the nature of the relationship involved'.[3] Although there are cases in which men are the victims of domestic violence, nevertheless 'the available research suggests that domestic violence is overwhelmingly directed by men against women'.[4] In the United Kingdom, it has been found that 77 per cent of all victims of domestic violence are women.[5] In addition, violence used by men against female partners tends to be much more severe than that used by women against men.[6] Mullender and Morley state that 'Domestic violence against women is the most common form of family violence worldwide.'[7] It can affect women from any background and of any age.[8]

The opening chapter of the book outlines a number of factors that may create problems as regards the effectiveness of international human rights law in relation to domestic violence, that is, factors that may prevent human rights law from making a tangible difference as regards this issue. These are the way in which rights were formulated and the development of a public/private dichotomy; the fact that rights will often conflict; and problems surrounding implementation. The book will examine the issue of whether these difficulties can be transcended to such an extent as to enable international human rights law to have an effective role to play in the struggle to combat domestic violence.

The next chapter of the book examines the types of measures that academic commentators working in the field of domestic violence believe would be beneficial in this area. The remainder of the book measures the effectiveness of international human rights law in relation to domestic violence by assessing whether human rights law can contribute to the achievement of these measures.

In order to examine the question of how international human rights law can be used in relation to domestic violence, this book uses the United Kingdom as a case study. The possible use of human rights law through two strategies is assessed. The European Convention on Human Rights has been incorporated into UK law by the Human Rights Act 1998. The first possible route is therefore to take a litigation approach, based on the European Convention. In Chapter 3 the question of how the case law of the European Court of Human Rights in the area of positive obligations could be used in relation to domestic violence is therefore examined. Chapter 4 then assesses whether the UK courts could rise to the challenge of using the Human Rights Act to assist victims of domestic violence.

The book proceeds to consider whether international human rights law could be used more effectively as regards domestic violence through a strategy of using the statements made by international human rights bodies. In Chapter 5, the statements themselves are assessed, with particular emphasis on those made by the United Nations Committee on the Elimination of Discrimination Against Women and the Special Rapporteur on Violence against Women. Chapter 6 analyses the impact that the statements have had so far on the UK Government's policy in relation to domestic violence.

1 Potential problems for the effectiveness of international human rights law as regards domestic violence

International human rights law has accomplished a great deal since its inception. Nevertheless, it seems that there are certain factors that may stand in the way of human rights law reaching its optimal level of efficacy as regards the issue of domestic violence. In this chapter, these factors will be examined. The potential problems include the negative way in which rights were formulated and the public/private dichotomy; the fact that rights will often conflict; and difficulties surrounding implementation.

The achievements of international human rights law

International human rights law has undoubtedly accomplished much within a relatively short period of time. As Baxi comments, the twentieth century could be entitled an 'Age of Human Rights'.[1] The last century saw the emergence of all the main international human rights treaties, and these Conventions have certainly had a major impact throughout the world. For example, democratic government has emerged in Central and Eastern Europe.[2] Likewise,

> South Africa's transition from the racial authoritarianism of the apartheid era to the non-racial democratic institutions and entrenched constitutional rights of the post-1994 period is widely regarded as one of the great human rights triumphs of the post-Second World War era.[3]

As Robinson states,

> Starting with the Universal Declaration and carried forward in the body of international law that has been painstakingly developed over half a century, the world has expressed through human rights its shared commitment to the values of dignity, equality, and human security for all people.[4]

Cassel comments that 'international articulation of rights norms has reshaped domestic dialogues in law, politics, academia, public consciousness, civil society, and the press'.[5]

In various states non-governmental organisations are working with governments in preparing reports to human rights treaty monitoring bodies and are also preparing their own reports. Women's groups are using the international treaties to further their causes.[6] In most, if not all states, the international human rights treaties are available in the main languages.[7] Indeed the discourse of human rights now plays a major role in the development activities of the United Nations. Human rights experts are also regularly involved in UN post-conflict operations.[8] International human rights law has been used to establish standards that transcend national barriers and has opened up to external scrutiny atrocities that would otherwise have remained solely the concern of the states wherein they were perpetrated.

Human rights adjudicatory bodies, such as the European Court of Human Rights and the Inter-American Court of Human Rights, have been established. As Cassel states,

> As a result of judgments of the European Court of Human Rights, not only have individual plaintiffs been awarded damages, but European governments have revised legislation on such sensitive matters as media criticism of judicial proceedings, national security measures against terrorists . . . and criminal justice procedures.[9]

The judgments of the Inter-American Court of Human Rights also appear to have been effective. Orders for governments to take precautionary measures to protect the lives of witnesses have frequently been issued and in the majority of these cases, such measures were taken. All Spanish and Portuguese speaking countries in Latin America, with the exception of Cuba, now accept the jurisdiction of the Court and state compliance is increasing. The African Charter of Human and People's Rights has not yet had a great impact; however, it must be remembered that this Convention only came into force in 1986. The African system may well develop into an effective means of protecting rights.[10]

Essentially it is clear that 'human rights are now firmly on the agenda of the international community'.[11] International human rights law has served to outline the principles by which governments should act, and the governments of most states now generally accept these principles. Human rights are also being taken into account in the foreign policies of many countries. It is clear that international human rights law has accomplished much during the last century, and the rhetoric of rights is now frequently heard. As Risse and Ropp state, 'transnational human rights pressures and policies . . . have made a very significant difference in bringing about improvements in human rights practices in diverse countries around the world'.[12]

Problems

International human rights law has certainly been effective in some areas in that it has played a tangible role in changing situations. However, it is undeniably true that the rights of millions of people are still being violated across the world. For example, many national laws remain in force that discriminate against women or fail to recognise socio-economic rights.[13] In a survey of 20 representative countries throughout the UN, it was discovered that none of the states involved had fulfilled their duty of timely submission of reports to the international treaty monitoring bodies. Indeed the states were on average two years late with their reports.[14] One of the most common reasons for this trend was a lack of governmental commitment to the process. In states such as Canada, Finland, India, Iran, Jamaica and Zambia, it was said that the submission of reports was not a high priority for the governments.[15] When reports are submitted, they tend to be formalistic and insufficiently frank. Governments do not usually disseminate the concluding observations of the treaty enforcement bodies to the public.[16] Indeed, in many states there is widespread ignorance of the international human rights treaties.[17]

It is therefore clear that although the rhetoric of human rights has been firmly established with the creation of the international human rights treaties, this rhetoric is not being translated into reality in all situations. In many cases there are immense difficulties with the effectiveness of international human rights law. Nevertheless, as Cassel states, 'continued atrocities do not disprove the case for international human rights law; the fact that it has not triumphed everywhere does not mean that it serves no useful purpose anywhere'.[18] However, which factors may create difficulties for the effectiveness of international human rights law in relation to domestic violence?

The way in which rights were formulated and the public/private dichotomy

One potential problem for the effectiveness of international human rights law may be found in the way in which the rights themselves were formulated. Thomas and Beasley remark that, 'the concept of human rights developed largely from Western political theory of the rights of the individual to autonomy and freedom'.[19] The foundation of international relations is the idea of the liberal state. Romany comments that, 'liberalism constructs a social and political order which seeks to emancipate the individual from the oppression of political structures'.[20] International law thus has its basis in the liberal social contract theory, whereby states are regarded as individuals that should have equality, independence and freedom. Inherent to this theory is the idea of negative rights ensuring individual freedom. This concept is thus embedded deeply in the discourse of international law, and subsequently human rights law.[21] Essentially the concept of 'negative rights' means that the state cannot interfere with an individual in certain aspects of his or her life.[22]

Another main principle of international law is that only states can be subject to this body of law. Individuals are immune from this framework. A number of exceptions did develop. For example, pirates and international war criminals can be held individually accountable under international law. However, as Cook comments, 'These exceptions prove the general rule that private individuals and agencies are not directly bound by the provisions of international law'.[23]

The idea of negative rights ensuring individual freedoms emerged again during the fight against totalitarianism, which was a vital catalyst in the development of human rights law. The concept of human rights evolved to protect the rights of the individual from encroachment by the state. As Thomas and Beasley remark, 'States are bound by international law to respect the individual rights of each and every person and are thus accountable for abuses of those rights'.[24] However, the rights norms that emerged were generally formulated in a very negative manner, whereby the state was required only to refrain from violating the rights in question. There were no obligations on the state to take positive steps to ensure that the rights of the individual were not breached. The 'neo-liberal commitment to minimal state intervention'[25] resulted also in the situation whereby the state was not required to protect the rights of the individual from violation by another private party.

The implications of the theoretical underpinnings of human rights law can be clearly discerned from the practical developments in the field. The 'first generation' of rights was concerned primarily with civil and political rights. These were mainly rights possessed by the individual, with which the state could not interfere. As Romany comments, the ultimate concern was the separation and protection of the individual from the state.[26] The objective of the framers of the earlier human rights instruments was to ensure that there was a space wherein the individual would be 'left alone' by the state. Their aim was not to obtain positive entitlements from the state, and neither was it to compel the state to intervene in a situation whereby the rights of one individual were being breached by another private entity.

For example, arguably the most influential regional human rights instrument is the European Convention on Human Rights. This Treaty dates from 1950 and was formulated as a defence against totalitarianism in the aftermath of the Second World War.[27] As is to be expected, the Convention deals primarily with fundamental civil and political rights, and most of its provisions are framed in a negative way. For example, article 8, which is commonly known as the right to private and family life, actually prevents only an interference with the exercise of the right to privacy.[28] Again the emphasis is placed on the state's duty of non-interference. The European Convention provides one of the clearest examples of the negative formulation of rights that is found in many human rights instruments. Historically this negative formulation of rights has caused major difficulties for the effectiveness of international human rights law, as it served to limit greatly the types of situation in which human rights law could be used.

Rights were developed in such a manner as to create a public/private dichotomy whereby human rights norms were upheld in the public sphere where the state is involved, but were not applied in the private sphere. The public/private dichotomy may be formulated in several ways. Cook points to two possibilities.[29] First, the public realm can be seen as the area that is regulated by law and politics, and the private sector as the area where regulation is viewed as being inappropriate. Second, the public arena can be seen as the state and its agents, while the private sphere is constituted by non-state activities.

In relation to the first definition of the public/private divide, Charlesworth and Chinkin comment that 'the liberal account of international law rests on a series of distinctions between the "public" and the "private" that has long played a central part in Western legal and political philosophy'.[30] Even back in the time of the ancient Greeks, a division between the public sphere and the private realm of family and home was recognised. The general principle was that men were free to participate in the public sphere because they were supported by their wives at home in the private realm.[31] John Locke later used the distinction between the public and private spheres to deny the existence of the divine right of kings without criticising the patriarchal familial structure of the day. Locke claimed that the king's political power was accorded to him by those he governed, and fell within the public sphere. Patriarchal authority, however, fell within the private realm and thus was immune from regulation. Indeed it was regarded as being divine in origin.[32]

Charlesworth and Chinkin point out that an 'important function of the (public/private) dichotomy in liberal jurisprudence is to demarcate areas appropriate for legal regulation from those that come within the sphere of individual autonomy'.[33] The dichotomy divides a public realm of rationality where political activity occurs, from a private realm that is believed to fall outside the boundaries of regulation. For example, the 1957 Wolfenden Report on Homosexual Offences and Prostitution stated that 'there must remain a realm of private morality and immorality, which is, in brief and crude terms, not the law's business'.[34] Essentially the Report took the stance that the law should not involve itself with the private realm unless an adverse impact on the public sphere was produced.[35] There is certainly some degree of merit in this argument. Most citizens would be of the opinion that there are certain areas in relation to personal or consensual acts that must remain unregulated, in order to respect the right to privacy.

The public/private divide may also refer to human rights law binding only states. Hirschl comments that,

> Despite the open-ended wording of the constitutional catalogues of rights in Canada, New Zealand, and Israel, the national high courts of all three countries tend, by and large, to conceptualise the purpose of rights as protecting the private sphere (human and economic) from interference by the 'collective' (often understood as the state and its regulatory institutions).[36]

He points out that courts in the three legal jurisdictions in question appear to see state regulation as more damaging than the oppression that can result from allowing powerful private bodies to be immune from international human rights law. It seems that these courts are of the opinion that the role of the state as regards human rights is to refrain from violating rights, as opposed to taking positive steps to ensure that the rights of individuals are not breached by any party – whether by the state or by another private individual. It is interesting to note that constitutional rights are usually given a wide interpretation by the courts of Canada, New Zealand and Israel where negative rights are at issue, but are given a far narrower interpretation in positive rights claims.[37]

Analysis of the public/private dichotomy is certainly a recurring theme in feminist literature.[38] For example, Ewing states that, 'The public/private distinction in international law ... places many forms of violence against women beyond the protective scope of human rights instruments'.[39] Quite frequently, women's human rights will come into conflict with powers other than that of the state. These powers generally emanate from the private sphere, for example from within the family unit. These powers are, however, frequently just as strong as the state itself.[40] Indeed they may be even more effective as they are found within the sphere that is closest to the individual concerned – a sphere which is usually associated with safety and security. Women all over the globe suffer from human rights abuses in the private sphere such as domestic violence, female genital mutilation, dowry killing[41] and sati. 'Daughters, sisters, brides, wives, mothers, grandmothers, and caregivers – all are vulnerable to domestic violence, degradation, and devaluation.'[42] Under traditional principles, abuses perpetrated by these powers did not come within the ambit of international human rights law as they are not inflicted directly by the state. It has been argued that 'abuses, exclusions and constraints that are more typical of women's lives are neither recognised nor protected by mainstream human rights instruments'.[43]

For example, the right to be free from torture and inhuman or degrading treatment is regarded as fundamental. However, it was usually drafted in such terms as to apply only to situations where it is the state itself that is inflicting the prohibited treatment.[44] For example, article 1 of the United Nations Convention against Torture clearly states that to constitute torture, the pain or suffering in question must be 'inflicted by or at the instigation of or with the consent or acquiescence of a public official or other person acting in an official capacity'. The right to be free from torture was designed to prevent situations such as where a political prisoner is ill-treated in prison. Such a prisoner is usually male. Torture as it is experienced more frequently by women was not envisaged. Various feminist critics have likened domestic violence to torture.[45] They have pointed out that similar methods are used both by official torturers and abusive partners. However, until very recently, domestic violence has not been viewed as torture, or on the same level as torture, by the international human rights community. Provisions such as the European Convention's prohibition on torture were formulated in response to the atrocities of the Second World War and the Holocaust. It is essential to recognise that these provisions must be interpreted in such a way as to be effective in the circumstances that prevail in modern times. Nowadays, for women the reality is that when torture is encountered it is often inflicted by those closest to them. It is imperative that the right to be free from torture and inhuman or degrading treatment is applied in such a way as to be effective in protecting women.

However, does the public/private dichotomy still pose an insurmountable problem in international human rights law? It should be noted that human rights law has developed in such a manner as to create a range of ways in which it may now enter into the private sphere. First, human rights law can be made directly applicable against the private actor. An example of such an approach can be seen in the Constitution of South Africa.[46] Second, domestic statutes may be enacted that are protective of rights. One example of this is the anti-discrimination legislation of the United Kingdom. If an individual breaches these statutes he or she can be held liable under domestic law. Third, national courts may apply ordinary law in a manner that is protective of human rights. This approach has been referred to as an indirect horizontal effect or the interpretative obligation. One of the prime examples of its application is found in section 3 of the UK's Human Rights Act 1998. This provision states that courts must interpret statutes in accordance with the rights contained in the European Convention on Human Rights, so far as it is possible to do so.[47] Fourthly, a concept of state responsibility has been developed, under which positive obligations can be placed directly on the state to ensure that human rights standards are upheld in situations involving only private individuals. This strategy has been utilised by the European Court of Human Rights. Similarly the United Nations human rights bodies refer to the state's duties to respect, protect, promote and fulfil rights. In relation to domestic violence, General Recommendation 19 of the Committee on the Elimination of All Forms of Discrimination Against Women was extremely important as it officially interpreted the CEDAW Convention as prohibiting violence against women in both the public and private contexts. This Recommendation stated,

> that discrimination under the Convention is not restricted to action by or on behalf of Governments . . . Under general international law and specific human rights covenants, States may be responsible for private acts if they fail to act with due diligence to prevent violations of rights or to investigate and punish acts of violence, and for providing compensation.[48]

Therefore, in light of these developments, the public/private dichotomy may not now pose as great a difficulty to the effectiveness of international human rights law in relation to domestic violence as once would have been the case.

It should also be noted that cases involving sexual violence have come before the International Criminal Tribunal for the former Yugoslavia and the International Criminal Tribunal for Rwanda. For example, in 2001 the ICTY gave its judgment in the case of *The Prosecutor v Kunarac, Kovac and Vukovic*.[49] This was the first case in relation to the prosecution of international war crimes that was based solely on alleged crimes of sexual violence against women. The accused were found guilty of rape, enslavement and outrages on personal dignity, as war crimes and crimes against humanity. Dixon comments that in this judgment the ICTY 'challenged the "state action" doctrine in international humanitarian law, which, as a constituent element of the public/private divide in international law, has served to obstruct the recognition and prosecution of crimes against women'.[50] Similarly, in *Prosecutor v Akayesu*[51] and *Prosecutor v Musema*,[52] the ICTR found the accused guilty of genocide, based partly on charges of rape. These judgments certainly seem to represent positive developments. Also, under the rules of the Tribunals, witnesses can retain their anonymity and are entitled to protection. In a case involving sexual assault, no corroboration of a victim's testimony is necessary. The Tribunals have established victim and witness protection units and their rules of procedures limit the use of the sexual history of victims.[53]

Under articles 7 and 8 of the Rome Statute of the International Criminal Court, gender crimes are listed under the definitions of both crimes against humanity and war crimes. These include rape and sexual slavery. The Court should take appropriate measures to protect the safety of victims, particularly where the crime involves sexual violence. These measures may include the presentation of evidence electronically and the participation of victims at appropriate stages. The Statute establishes a Victims and Witnesses Unit to advise on the protective measures that should be adopted and to offer assistance to victims and witnesses.[54] The need to include judges who have expertise in the area of violence against women must be taken into account in the selection process.[55] Again these provisions represent very positive developments in international standards concerning sexual violence.

Conflicting rights

It is undeniably true that the rights of individuals will conflict in some instances. Therefore, although human rights norms are said to be universal, the rights of one party must nevertheless be limited in such cases. As McColgan states, 'Rights do not exist in a vacuum, but have to be balanced against other rights'.[56] This is an unavoidable problem with the discourse of rights, and the wording of various human rights treaties acknowledges this fact. For example, article 8(1) of the European Convention on Human Rights states that 'everyone has the right to respect for his private and family life'. However, article 8(2) continues,

> There shall be no interference by a public authority with the exercise of this right except such as is in accordance with the law and is necessary in a democratic society in the interests of national security, public safety or the economic well-being of the country, for the prevention of disorder or crime, for the protection of health or morals, or for the protection of the rights and freedoms of others.

Articles 9–11 of the Convention contain similar clauses. It was clearly envisioned by those who drafted the Convention that the rights would have to be balanced against each other in some circumstances.[57]

In order to deal with such cases of conflicting rights, the European Court of Human Rights has developed the doctrine of proportionality. Essentially, an individual's right may only be limited if the restriction is prescribed by law, pursues a legitimate aim and is proportionate to the aim being pursued. The courts of the United Kingdom must now apply a similar balancing process when dealing with arguments made under the Human Rights Act 1998.[58] A good example of the House of Lords entering into this process is found in *Campbell v MGN Ltd*.[59] In this case the defendant newspaper had published various articles concerning the claimant. These articles stated that she was attending Narcotics Anonymous and contained details of her treatment. Photographs of the claimant leaving the meetings were also published. The claimant brought proceedings under the Data Protection Act 1998. The main issue in the case was how a balance should be struck between the claimant's right to respect for private and family life under article 8 of the European Convention on Human Rights and the right of the newspaper to freedom of expression under article 10 of the Convention.

The House of Lords held that the interference with the claimant's right to privacy was unjustifiable. The private nature of Narcotics Anonymous meetings encouraged people to attend, and disclosure of the information in question had potential to cause considerable harm. The right to privacy had to be balanced against the right of the media to impart information to the public; however, no democratic or political values were at stake and there was no pressing social need to disclose the information. Any benefits achieved by publication were therefore disproportionate to the interference with the right to privacy.

Venables and another v News Group Newspapers Ltd and others[60] concerned two claimants who had killed a two-year-old boy when they were ten years old. They had been convicted of murder and the trial judge had imposed injunctions restricting publication of information about them. However, these injunctions were based on jurisdictions applicable only to minors. When the claimants reached the age of 18 they sought injunctions preventing the press from publishing details of their appearances and their whereabouts. They claimed that their right to life under article 2 of the European Convention and their right to be free from torture or inhuman or degrading treatment under article 3 would otherwise be violated. The newspapers relied on the right to freedom of expression under article 10 of the Convention. Under section 12(4) of the Human Rights Act the courts are required to have particular regard to this right.

The court stated that,

> The onus of proving the case that freedom of expression must be restricted is firmly upon the applicant seeking the relief. The restrictions sought must, in the circumstances of the present case, be shown to be in accordance

with the law, justifiable as necessary to satisfy a strong and pressing social need, convincingly demonstrated, to restrain the press in order to protect the rights of the claimants to confidentiality, and proportionate to the legitimate aim pursued.[61]

It was held that the law of confidence could extend to cover the injunctions sought and therefore the restrictions proposed were in accordance with the law. The injunctions would be granted to protect the claimants 'from serious and possibly irreparable harm'[62] and therefore the court held that the proportionality requirement would be met. Injunctions were thus granted protecting any information concerning the identity or future whereabouts of the claimants.

In *Re S (a child) (identification: restriction on publication)*[63] the question to be decided was whether the court could or should restrain the publication of the identity of a defendant and her victim, who was her son, in a murder trial, in order to protect the right to privacy of her other son. There was essentially a conflict between the article 8 right of the child and the article 10 right to freedom of expression of the press. The House of Lords held that an injunction restraining publication should not be granted. It was commented that the contemporaneous reporting of criminal trials promoted the values of the rule of law and that the granting of the proposed injunction would mean that informed debate about criminal justice would suffer. The article 8 right of the child was not sufficient to outweigh this consideration.

The fact that the rights of individuals will frequently conflict is an unavoidable difficulty in international human rights law. Fenwick comments that there is 'widespread judicial uncertainty' in the UK as to the proper means of dealing with cases in which rights conflict.[64] In relation to the issue of domestic violence, the rights of a victim may come into conflict with the right of an alleged perpetrator to a fair trial.[65] McColgan comments that,

> When it comes to the "balance" between the "right to a fair trial" and the complainant's interests in privacy, security of the person or the equal protection of the law, the accused's "right to a fair trial", understood decontextualised from the rights of the complainant, can operate to trump any other considerations.[66]

In order to attain the optimum level of effectiveness of international human rights law it is certainly necessary to ensure that rights are balanced against each other in a thoughtful and considered manner. If the balance between conflicting rights is not struck carefully, the human rights movement may be placed 'in the uncomfortable position of legitimating more injustice than it eliminates'.[67]

Implementation difficulties

It is clear that the implementation of international human rights law has been inconsistent, to say the least.[68] However, as Wallace comments, 'What is required is not more substantive human rights but rather more effective implementation of the existing instruments'.[69] The international treaties contain comprehensive lists of the rights that should be afforded to individuals. However, the simple fact is that in many situations these rights are being violated. There must be a political will among governments to implement human rights,[70] and frequently such a will is lacking. The essential difficulty is that human rights are still regarded by many as mere rhetoric as opposed to real legal obligations that must be observed,[71] due largely to the fact that human rights treaties tend to suffer from enforcement problems. There is a necessity for governments to realise that they must act on the commitments that they have made by signing the international treaties. Copelon remarks that 'the international human rights system still operates more in rhetoric than in reality'.[72] Although generally governments will acknowledge that human rights considerations should have a part to play in their decisions, nevertheless they may argue that other factors are of greater importance.[73]

One of the main problems with ensuring the effectiveness of international human rights law is the fact that it is somewhat difficult to compel states to comply with their duties. This is a difficulty that pervades international law generally. A number of states consistently fail to fulfil their international obligations.[74] As Byrnes comments, 'The limitations of international law generally when it comes to enforcement of binding standards are well known, and international human rights law is no exception in that regard'.[75] It seems that this failure may well be due at least partly to the 'lack of an international policing force that demands compliance with international edicts'.[76] For example, the UN has no real method of forcing states to alter their policies. It must instead attempt to persuade nations to comply with their international obligations.[77]

It seems that the enforcement difficulties surrounding international law are magnified as regards international human rights law.[78] It appears that states violate their international human rights obligations even more frequently than they do their obligations under other forms of international law. The human rights treaty bodies can highlight the shortcomings of governments in this field, thus bringing international pressure to bear on states and shaming them into compliance. As Risse and Sikkink comment, 'Countries most sensitive to pressure are not those that are economically weakest, but those that care about their international image'.[79] However, if a state still consistently refuses to act in accordance with human rights principles, there appears to be little that can be done. If a government is powerful on a global scale, it may tend to be somewhat impervious to international human rights law.[80] As Merry states,

> Countries are concerned about their reputations in the international community, but they clearly differ in their vulnerability to international pressure depending on their size, wealth, form of government, and dependence on the international community for trade, aid, and other symbolic and material forms of exchange.[81]

The United States is a case in point. The most powerful nation in the world has not ratified the Convention on the Elimination of All Forms of Discrimination Against Women or the Convention on the Rights of the Child and tends to ratify other international human rights treaties only with extensive reservations. It seems that the impact of the UN human rights treaties depends largely on the degree of commitment held by states to give effect to their obligations. It is, however, important that the duties that states have undertaken and the work of the treaty bodies be widely publicised in order to place as much internal and external pressure as possible on states to comply with their obligations.[82]

Ulrich states that the problems concerning enforcement are magnified in respect of treaties addressing women's rights.[83] For example, there are major difficulties as regards the enforcement of the Convention on the Elimination of All Forms of Discrimination Against Women. Every four years, states that are party to this Convention must present a report to the CEDAW Committee. Under General Recommendation 19, these reports should contain information on the prevalence of violence against women,[84] and the legal, protective and preventive measures that the state in question is taking to protect women from violence. Information should also be provided on the effectiveness of such measures.[85] In 1999 non-governmental organisations were invited to submit their own reports on the issues in question. These reports tend to adopt a much more critical approach, and often provide a more accurate and informative assessment of the situation of women living in the state in question. The state reports are reviewed by 23 independent experts. As Byrnes comments,

> The examination of a state's report under a treaty can provide an occasion for exerting international pressure on the state. If members of a supervisory body are strongly critical of a state or express the view that the state has not carried out its obligations under the treaty, this can serve to put some pressure on a government, particularly if the proceedings receive publicity internationally or nationally.[86]

However, the CEDAW Committee has been allocated insufficient time each year in which to review all the reports submitted. The delays caused constitute one of the factors that have led to problems as regards the enforcement of CEDAW. Schopp-Schilling remarks that 'many States Parties have often not addressed issues of legal reform or programmes to improve the material situation of women to enable and empower them to claim, exercise and enjoy their human rights, even if they ratified the CEDAW 15 or 20 years ago'.[87]

Interestingly, Merry outlines seven methods by which states can escape proper scrutiny by the CEDAW Committee.[88] First, the state may fail to write a report or do so after a long delay. Second, the state may write only a superficial report. As Fortin comments in relation to the Convention on the Rights of the Child,

The reporting mechanism relies on governments to subject their implementation programme to an objective and critical analysis before compiling their reports. The absence of any supervision or coercion over this can lead to reports painting an over-optimistic and complacent picture of governmental achievements.[89]

Third, the state may send only low-level government representatives to present the report. Fourth, the state may avoid answering questions directly. Fifth, the state may promise to make changes but omit to carry out these changes. Sixth, the state may enter extensive reservations to CEDAW. Seventh, the state may refuse to present its report even after submission. The fact that there are so many ways in which to avoid scrutiny is in itself clear evidence of the problems of enforcement that surround CEDAW.

A major difficulty with the enforcement of CEDAW is that it has no official 'teeth'. If a state refuses to comply with its provisions, the CEDAW Committee cannot impose sanctions; for example, no fines can be ordered. Ulrich comments that,

> Although the Women's Convention is significantly more enlightened with regard to women's rights than previous human rights documents and possesses some potential in quelling violence against women, CEDAW must be granted more authority and additional resources to foster substantive change effectively.[90]

Certainly being granted more authority and resources would greatly assist the CEDAW Committee in carrying out its role in an effective manner.

Essentially, as Vesa comments, when dealing with international human rights systems, 'one should remain aware of an overarching issue that straddles all human rights systems; enforceability is still a lingering weakness'.[91] It seems that this issue may well pose difficulties for the use of international human rights law in relation to domestic violence.[92]

Difficulties surrounding the implementation of socio-economic rights

Schneider argues that the most pressing needs of victims of domestic violence may be to receive social support measures, such as refuge accommodation, monetary resources and housing.[93] It seems therefore that socio-economic rights may be particularly important in relation to the issue of domestic violence. However, there are undoubtedly particular difficulties associated with the implementation of this category of rights. Oloka-Onyango comments that,

> Despite the statement in the Vienna Declaration of 1993 that proclaims all human rights as ". . . universal, indivisible and interdependent and interrelated", certain categories of rights within the international corpus

are marginalized. Civil and political rights are considered to belong to a first category, or "generation" of rights, while economic, social, and cultural rights have been relegated to a lower less important sphere. The marginalization of the latter category can be discerned not only from the level of international attention paid to them, but also with respect to the approach of governments, judges, non-governmental actors, and even academics to the subject.[94]

Johnstone remarks that, 'The focus on civil and political rights at the expense of economic, social, and cultural rights suggests both a male and a Western liberal bias that relegated the immediate needs of anyone who was not Western, white, adult, and male'.[95]

Nevertheless, during the nineteenth and early twentieth centuries, the concept of the state having a positive duty to provide certain services did emerge. For example, article 42 of the Irish Constitution of 1937 contains a right to education, while article 45 contains directive principles of social policy. In 1948 the Universal Declaration of Human Rights included civil and political rights, such as freedom of expression, and also socio-economic rights, such as the right to work, the right to housing and the right to education. However, Lyon comments that, 'although economic, social and cultural rights formed a significant part of the original post-war body of human rights doctrine, they were casualties of ideologically based Cold War politics'.[96] The Soviet Union supported socio-economic rights, while the United States supported civil and political rights.[97] Eventually two treaties were created – the International Covenant on Civil and Political Rights and the International Covenant on Economic, Social and Cultural Rights. McGregor states that,

> The price of this tandem progress, unfortunately, was a significant divergence in approach between the two treaties, with (socio-economic) rights getting what many people would see as an inferior degree of protection. The key difference . . . is the fact that while the ICCPR binds its signatories to immediate implementation, the ICESCR allows for an incremental approach. While both the initial framing of the covenants and the statements made subsequently by those involved in their administration support the view that the two sets of rights are not only of equal importance but indivisible, the fact is that the creation of two different regimes has allowed the various states to indulge their own ideological predispositions in deciding what is required under the various heads.[98]

Clearly the development of socio-economic rights had major ramifications for human rights discourse. One of the fundamental tenets of the concept of human rights was the idea that the state should simply be prevented from interfering in certain aspects of the life of an individual. The notion that the state would now be required to take positive steps to ensure that the individual was provided with his or her rights was disapproved of by many human rights theorists. Arguments against encompassing such 'socio-economic' entitlements in the definition of human rights included a belief that it is impossible to lay down universal standards in this area. Steiner and Alston state that such arguments were based on the opinion 'that economic and social rights do not constitute rights (as properly understood) at all'[99] and that,

> treating them as rights undermines the enjoyment of individual freedom, distorts the functioning of free markets by justifying large-scale state intervention in the economy, and provides an excuse to downgrade the importance of civil and political rights.[100]

Essentially, states should not be obliged to take positive, and potentially costly, steps to ensure an individual's access to his or her rights. However, Woods argues that,

> the negative rights/positive rights distinction poses a false dichotomy; all human rights potentially contain both negative and positive dimensions. The assumed dichotomy blurs the true dilemma that social rights pose for the liberal paradigm; that rights implicating the redistribution of social resources are collective in character and rooted in the common needs of human beings in society. The collective nature of social rights contradicts the liberal conception of rights, which presumes that social living requires the surrender, not the creation, of rights.[101]

Dennis and Stewart comment that 'shopworn opposition to economic, social, and cultural rights on "ideological" grounds should be abandoned'.[102]

Hirschl carried out a study of the interpretations afforded by national high courts to the bills of rights in Canada, New Zealand and Israel. Interestingly, he arrived at the conclusion that while the success rate of negative rights claims ranged between 38 per cent and 44 per cent across the three jurisdictions, positive rights claims were successful in between 17 per cent and 22 per cent of cases.[103] The very significant variation between the two results indicates that there is still much controversy over the issue of whether states should be obliged to take positive steps in the arena of human rights protection.

Oloka-Onyango states that numerous countries, in particular the United States, 'are still reluctant to accord (socio-economic) rights the same level of domestic recognition and enforceability'.[104] Steiner and Alston comment that, 'economic, social and cultural rights are often characterised as "mere" programmatic rights, in the sense that they require only a general programme of measures designed to promote realisation of rights'.[105] For example, in May 2002 UK Government representatives informed the UN Committee on Economic, Social and Cultural Rights that the government had no intention of incorporating the Covenant into domestic law. Likewise, in Ireland socio-economic rights are deemed in the Constitution to be non-justiciable principles, despite the fact that Ireland has obligations under the ICESCR.[106] Similarly, although states applying for membership of the Council of Europe are required to ratify the European Convention on Human Rights, which contains primarily civil and political rights, they are not required to give any undertakings concerning the European Social Charter.[107] As Steiner and Alston state,

> Although formal support for economic, social and cultural rights has been near universal, in practice no group of states has consistently followed up its rhetorical support at the international level with practical and sustained programmes of implementation.[108]

Essentially, 'the effective realisation of economic, social, and cultural rights remains a global challenge of gigantic proportions'.[109] Nevertheless, there is still the potential for the realisation of such rights.

The use of litigation as a vehicle for implementation

The law usually relies on a litigation approach to promote change; however, how effective are the courts as a vehicle for the implementation of human rights law? Epp comments that 'the judicial process is costly and slow and produces changes in the law only in small increments'.[110] Van Schaack states that, 'an overreliance on adversarial litigation . . . raises . . . concerns . . . about the efficacy of resorting to law and the judicial process to promote durable social change and the ability of the judicial process to address major social . . . problems'.[111] Scheingold argues that such an approach 'grossly exaggerates the role that lawyers and litigation can play in a strategy for change'.[112] Essentially, judges generally must confine themselves to dealing with the precise matter in the actual case that is before them. They cannot make sweeping statements on societal issues. This clearly places limitations on the role that litigation can play in promoting change. Also, as Chayes comments, it is much more difficult for courts to order that affirmative programmes be put in place than it is for them to hold that a certain practice be halted.[113]

Similarly, if a court were to state, for example, that financial resources should be given to victims of domestic violence, the judge may be entering into a debate on which it is simply inappropriate for him or her to adjudicate. If the government decides to accord resources to victims of domestic violence, it may be the case that fewer resources will be allocated to other areas. Chayes comments that, 'the court has little basis for evaluating competing claims on the public purse'.[114] One could argue that judges do not have the specialist knowledge and expertise needed to rule on such issues involving the allocation of public finances. If courts were to enter into such debates, they may also be entering into the political arena to an excessive extent. Rosenberg argues that 'litigation steer[s] activists to an institution that is constrained from helping them'.[115]

In addition, the effectiveness of the courts depends very much on the approaches and attitudes of the individual judges who sit on them. As Epp remarks, the decisions of a court may in theory 'become a matter of personal idiosyncrasy and historical accident – a matter of who is chosen to sit on a court and how long it takes the judge to retire or die'.[116] Palmer comments that,

> Rights are capable of being given a wide range of interpretations, not least because (human rights) charters are formulated at a high level of abstraction. In some ways this elasticity is an advantage, allowing flexibility in decision-making and adaptation to novel circumstances, yet there are times when consequential choices need to be made. Inevitably, these broad and open-textured guarantees can lead to uncertainty when these general rights are applied in specific contexts.[117]

If the judiciary is unwilling to use human rights instruments in a dynamic and imaginative manner, this will clearly create problems for the effectiveness of human rights law. Due to this reliance on judges to give practical effectiveness to rights, concerns have been raised in the United Kingdom 'about the lack of diversity of members of the judiciary . . . and the socially exclusive and secre-tive process of judicial selection'.[118] Nevertheless, it is also worth noting that there are particular judges in the UK who bring a great deal of potential to the area of human rights. For example, Baroness Hale of Richmond is certainly very much in favour of enhancing the rights of women and children.[119]

Even if a court does make a progressive and dynamic judgment, effective results will not always ensue. As Rosenberg comments, 'Legal victories do not automatically or even necessarily produce the desired change'.[120] For example, in *A v United Kingdom*[121] the European Court of Human Rights held that the UK was in breach of article 3 of the European Convention. The case concerned a nine-year-old boy who had been severely beaten by his stepfather. The latter had been acquitted by a jury of assault occasioning actual bodily harm. He had relied on the defence of reasonable chastisement. The European Court held that the UK had failed to provide an effective legal framework to protect rights. Following the decision in *A v UK* the Department of Health carried out what Fortin describes as a 'bizarre consultation over how to reform the law [that] demonstrated the Department's . . . reluctance to influence or change parental practices'.[122] The Department maintained that physical punishment should not be made illegal as any attempt to do so would be a 'heavy-handed intrusion into family life'.[123] The reasonable chastisement defence was therefore not to be abolished.[124] The possibility of prohibiting all physical punishment was not even considered. The only matter open for discussion was how to delineate the scope of the defence.[125]

The UK eventually adopted section 58 of the Children Act 2004, which states that reasonable punishment is no longer a defence in relation to certain offences, such as assault occasioning actual bodily harm or grievous bodily harm. However, it is still a defence to lesser offences. It seems therefore that although this legislation abided by the strict letter of the judgment of the European Court, it did not comply with the spirit of the judgment, which appears to have been to protect children. It may be seen therefore that even if progressive and praiseworthy decisions are made by the courts, there is no guarantee that they will be effective in achieving change, if the legislature is not in agreement. As Epp comments, 'There are limits to the social changes produced by judicial rulings, and those rulings depend on support from government officials'.[126] Rosenberg remarks that 'courts depend on political support to produce . . . reform'.[127] This is a major problem for the use of a litigation strategy as a way of implementing human rights law.

Using litigation in relation to the issue of domestic violence raises a further problem. Domestic violence is an 'unseen' crime which victims are often too frightened or too ashamed to report. The British Crime Survey found that the police come to know of less than one in four of the worst cases of domestic violence.[128] Many victims simply may not want to take cases to court. This may constitute a major difficulty for the effectiveness of human rights law in relation to domestic violence. As Epp comments, 'Judges . . . cannot make rights-supportive law unless they have rights cases to decide'.[129] Indeed, such problems lead one to consider how human rights law may be implemented in ways other than through litigation.

Conclusion

International human rights law has accomplished a great deal since its inception. However, there are particular factors that may stand in the way of human rights law reaching its optimal level of efficacy in relation to the issue of domestic violence. These are the public/private dichotomy, the fact that rights will often conflict and difficulties surrounding implementation.

However, do these factors constitute insurmountable obstacles to the effectiveness of international human rights law? This book will examine the issue of whether the difficulties can be transcended to such an extent as to enable international human rights law to have an effective role to play in the struggle to combat domestic violence. The next chapter will consider the types of measures that commentators working in the field of domestic violence feel would be beneficial in this area. The remainder of the book will assess the potential effectiveness of international human rights law in relation to domestic violence by examining the question of whether human rights law can contribute to the achievement of these measures.

2 What measures may it be beneficial for human rights law to achieve in relation to domestic violence?

There are certainly a number of factors that may cause difficulties for the effectiveness of international human rights law. The previous chapter highlighted problems surrounding the public/private divide, the fact that rights will conflict, and difficulties surrounding implementation. However, can these problems surrounding the effectiveness of international human rights law be overcome to such a degree as to enable human rights law to play an effective part in the fight to combat domestic violence?

In order to examine the ways in which international human rights law could be effective in relation to domestic violence, it is first necessary to investigate the question of what changes it may be beneficial for this body of law to achieve in the area of domestic violence. This chapter will thus examine the views of academic commentators working in the field of domestic violence on the measures that would be beneficial in this area. The taxonomy of the chapter has been constructed by consulting the work of many domestic violence advocates and drawing out the main types of measures suggested. The remainder of the book will assess the effectiveness of international human rights law in relation to domestic violence by examining whether this body of law can contribute to the achievement of these measures. What measures therefore do domestic violence advocates feel are needed in this field?

Improving the criminal justice system

Domestic violence advocates have remarked that there are substantial problems with fitting the issue of domestic violence into the criminal justice system as it stands. For example, in the context of the United States, Freedman comments that, 'the criminal justice system is best at dealing with relatively straightforward examples and easily categorised domestic violence, with recognisable story lines and sympathetic victims'.[1] Such paradigmatic examples are emphasised to the detriment of cases that do not so easily fit the mould.[2] Merry comments that in cases of domestic violence, the concept of 'good' and 'bad' victims seems to come into play.[3] A 'good' victim is one who is entirely innocent and who does not drink, take drugs or fight back. The United Kingdom cases of *R v Ahluwalia*[4] and *R v Thornton*[5] both concerned women who had been victims of domestic violence and who killed their abusive husbands. The characters of the defendants were subject to much comment during their respective trials. In *Ahluwalia* the defendant was painted as a dutiful wife and a good mother. By contrast, in *Thornton* the defendant was portrayed as a calculating woman who drank and used drugs.[6] Nicolson comments that the treatment of these women depended 'on a judgment, not so much of their actions, but of their character and the extent to which it accords with social constructions of appropriate femininity'.[7] As Merry remarks, if a victim of domestic violence shows ambivalence about pursuing her case, she may be defined as a 'bad' victim, and thus receive a far lesser degree of assistance from the police and other actors in the criminal justice system.[8]

Freedman comments that in many instances of domestic violence the imposition of criminal law measures is inappropriate. For example, some victims are faced with a degree of coercion that has not yet reached the level at which the criminal law can be applied.[9] Diduck and Kaganas point out that emotional abuse, such as severe and continuous criticism, does not fall within the ambit of the criminal law.[10] Many victims of domestic violence simply do not trust the criminal justice system. Others may want to continue the relationship, while the involvement of the criminal law assumes that the relationship has come to an end. James comments that,

> Coming into the open with domestic violence is an extremely difficult thing for a victim to do. There is an inherent belief common among victims that what they are suffering is not serious enough to trouble the police and the courts with. In fact, quite often, they are convinced that to do so will make a bad situation worse.[11]

Essentially, the criminal justice system does not take account of the many complexities and variations at work in the issue of domestic violence.[12] Freedman remarks that,

> The criminal justice system concentrates its resources on the most serious, urgent and unambiguous cases, then labels one or both parties as deviant, and administers simple and easy to understand remedies, thereby providing a safe social distance between "normal" families and those afflicted with domestic violence.[13]

Maguigan comments that in the United States, an excessive reliance on criminal justice measures to deal with domestic violence has also led to difficulties for victims from ethnic minorities. These communities may have had experiences of police brutality and such victims may therefore be extremely reluctant to enmesh themselves in the criminal justice system.[14] Merry draws attention to the fact that the involvement of the criminal justice system can be a very humiliating experience, even for the victims of domestic violence.[15] Also, the victim is not legally represented in a criminal prosecution and has no control over how the case proceeds.[16]

The difficulties involved in fitting domestic violence into the criminal justice system are reflective of the problems surrounding the role of the victim more generally. It is clear that the victim is a key actor in the criminal justice process. As Zedner remarks, 'Without the cooperation of the victim in reporting crime, furnishing evidence, identifying the offender, and acting as a witness in court, most crime would remain unknown and unpunished'.[17] However, up until relatively recently the criminal justice system has largely ignored the experiences of the victim.[18] As Shapland states, 'So, there is the paradox. The criminal justice system depends heavily upon victims for the reporting and detection of offences and for the provision of evidence in court. Yet, it does not appear to value the victim'.[19] Elias comments that 'law enforcement definitely does not serve one group: victims'.[20] Even though the criminal justice process needs victims to report crimes and provide evidence, it nevertheless largely abandons their interests once the process has begun. Elias remarks that, 'victims play a minor role in law enforcement, mainly affecting decisions and behaviour only marginally'.[21] Essentially the case is taken entirely out of the hands of the victim. Nevertheless it is questionable whether this should be so. In the UK victims are simply regarded as a source of evidence. This may be contrasted with the situation in France and Germany, where victims have substantial rights to participate in prosecutions. In UK jurisdiction, 'the victim as witness remains in a position of some vulnerability – at the mercy of questioning by defence counsel *and* prosecution alike'.[22]

Zedner states that, for the victim,

> insensitive questioning by police, inadequate provision of information, delays, or unexplained decisions by the prosecution service to drop a case each entail further suffering. At worst the impact of the criminal process is tantamount to secondary victimization . . . Failure to recognize the burdens placed upon victims can also lead them to withdraw from the criminal process and limit its ability to pursue cases effectively.[23]

Up until quite recently, the notion that the police force provided a service for victims was rare. If the police are insensitive in their approach to victims, this can leave the latter feeling very dissatisfied.[24] There is 'little reason to believe that [the police] primarily conceptualize their role as protecting individual victims, much less as caring for them after victimization'.[25]

Another difficulty is that victims are often not kept informed during the criminal justice process. They want to know if the offender is in custody or out on bail, whether the victim has to give evidence and finally the outcome of the case.[26] As regards domestic violence, the Crown Prosecution Service is adopting a policy of ensuring that victims are kept informed at every stage of the process. It is to be hoped that this will increase the victim's trust of the criminal justice system.

The criminal justice process tends to be long and drawn out. For the victim this means that an incident that lasted only a few minutes may, in effect, be prolonged for several months or even years.[27] Also, the initial court appearance itself may prove to be very intimidating for the victim, especially if she is subjected to aggressive questioning from the defence. Elias states that 'participating in law enforcement further victimizes most victims'.[28] Zedner lists the arguments for and against greater victim participation in the criminal justice process. She states that the arguments in favour are,

> recognition of [the victim's] status as a party to the dispute . . .; reduced risk of inflicting further psychological harm on the victim; greater victim cooperation, and thereby the improved efficiency of the system; and better information about harms suffered, and thereby closer proportionality in sentencing.[29]

The arguments against increased victim participation include,

> the intrusion of private views into public decision-making; limitations on prosecutorial discretion; the danger that the victim's subjective view undermines the court's objectivity; disparity in sentencing of similar cases depending on the resilience or punitiveness of the victim . . .; and, lastly, that to increase their involvement may entail further burdens on victims while raising their expectations unrealistically.[30]

Elias also puts forward the point that victims may not, in reality, want to bear the burdens of increased participation.[31]

Roach comments that, 'the future of criminal justice will largely depend on how victims' rights evolve'.[32] At present, the criminal justice system does not hold victims in any great esteem. This is problematic in that victims are thus discouraged from entering into the criminal justice process. Victims are needed, both to report crimes and to supply evidence, and therefore it would seem that more attention should be paid to their needs.[33] Jones and Brown remark that, 'Taking proper account of the needs of victims and witnesses is critical to persuading them they have a meaningful role in the criminal justice system and in helping them to understand better what that role is'.[34]

Nevertheless, despite the difficulties involved in using the criminal justice system in cases of domestic violence, most commentators still believe that the criminal justice system has an important role to play in relation to this issue. For example, Mullender and Hague state that the police 'frequently top the list of agencies contacted by domestic violence survivors for help'[35] and that 'most women favour a strong criminal justice stance'.[36] They also comment that, 'survivors think domestic violence should be responded to as a crime, but need support and protection in order for this to be a viable option'.[37] However, domestic violence advocates have argued convincingly that improvements are needed in relation to the responses of police, prosecutors and the judiciary to cases of domestic violence.

Police responses

Commentators have argued that unhelpful police attitudes constitute a very significant problem in relation to domestic violence. Armatta states that, 'police throughout the world often fail to enforce criminal assault laws where violence occurs within an intimate relationship. Traditionally, police simply do not intervene, or intervene only to mediate on an informal basis'.[38] Sullivan remarks that the police cannot be relied upon to arrest the perpetrator.[39] However, Stanko comments that it is indisputable that the police have an extremely important role to play as regards the protection of victims of domestic violence. She states that 'In cases of acute violence, police intervention is crucial – a woman's life depends on it'.[40] One advocate speaks of her decision in the mid-1970s as to where to allocate financial resources in relation to the problem of violence against women in the home.[41] She comments that,

> What was clear to me was what a battered woman needed most immediately was for someone to come in with a gun in the middle of the night, stop her from being killed and take her violent husband away. Until she could count on that, nothing else mattered.[42]

The advocate in question decided that the resources should be used in training the police.[43] Likewise, Armatta remarks that,

> Police occupy a pivotal position in any criminal law strategy to address domestic violence. In most places, police are the only institution with twenty-four-hour and comprehensive geographic accessibility. They also bring the coercive power of the state to bear on volatile and potentially lethal situations.[44]

Hague and Malos state that,

> the police role in combating domestic violence is . . . essential, and their handling of violence cases is of key significance to abused women . . . because of the traumatic and crucial point at which they are being asked to intervene on women's behalf.[45]

Nevertheless, despite this vital part that police officers must play, they have historically been reluctant to intervene in situations of domestic violence. Hughes comments that, 'Police forces may be unresponsive to requests for assistance from women on the receiving end of domestic violence, or they may adopt a non-interventionist approach, considering that it is a "private" matter'.[46]

Various studies carried out in the United Kingdom during the late 1970s and early 1980s show the unhelpful attitudes of the police towards victims of domestic violence. For example, in the report of research carried out by the University of Bradford in 1979, it is stated that,

> Although a man's home is his castle, and very little short of murdering his wife will make people feel justified in violating its privacy, the position is quite different if he has broken the law in some other way; if he is suspected of burglary, grievous bodily harm to an acquaintance or harming his own child, we forget his rights to privacy. It seems reasonable enough that if someone is breaking the law, they lose some of their rights to privacy at home, and that search warrants, for instance, are available. It is therefore very striking that the police, who are the group most often authorised to bypass social rules about privacy, show such respect for them when it comes to violence to wives and cohabitees.[47]

This quotation serves to make the point that violence against women taking place in the home was viewed as being unlike other types of criminal behaviour, and even not truly 'criminal' in nature. The study found that the police were extremely reluctant to violate the privacy of a perpetrator of domestic violence by intervening in the situation to protect his wife or partner. A study carried out by the Research and Planning Unit of the Home Office in 1989 uncovered similar findings.[48] In the report of the study it was commented that 'the single most common police response is non-intervention, that is, officers state that there is nothing they can do and leave the incident to which they have been called'.[49] The report stated that a common occurrence in the UK was for the victim to be told that the abuse she had suffered was a matter for the civil and not the criminal law. This was in line with general attitudes whereby domestic violence was regarded as being not truly 'criminal' in character. Other responses remarked upon by the Home Office study included attempts to defuse the situation and the removal of one of the parties from the scene for a period of time. Notably, it was often the victim who was removed.[50]

The view of domestic violence as not being criminal in nature was, as the Home Office study pointed out, based on the idea that 'domestic violence is almost exclusively a "family matter" or a "private affair" in which State intervention has no business since it would constitute not solely an intrusion into a private relationship but also an erosion of individual liberties'.[51] Goodmark makes the point that in the United States also, 'police officers frequently told abusive spouses to take a walk around the block to cool down and attempted to mediate between abusers and their victims'.[52]

The UK police, like their US counterparts, therefore have a history of being reluctant to respond to domestic violence as a crime. They have tended to adopt the attitude that violence against women in the home would more appropriately be dealt with by social services.[53] There was very little change in police policy until the late 1980s.[54] However, in 1987 a Metropolitan Police force order emphasised the necessity for positive intervention rather than mediation in domestic violence cases and stated that an assault occurring in the home is as much a crime as one occurring in the street.[55] In 1990 a Home Office circular was distributed[56] which recommended that the police adopt pro-arrest and pro-prosecution policies with regard to domestic violence. It also advised that domestic violence units and domestic violence liaison officer posts should be established to support victims, and that the police should engage in multi-agency initiatives on violence in the home.[57] This guidance stressed the obligation to protect victims from further attack, the necessity of treating domestic violence seriously, the use of the power of arrest, the dangers of mediating between the perpetrator and the victim and the need to keep full records.[58] In 1993 the Association of Chief Police Officers' evidence to the Home Affairs Committee said that, 'the Police Service [had] changed its focus from one of conciliation to intervention'.[59] Another Home Office circular on domestic violence, issued in 2000, again emphasised that arrest should usually occur when an offence is committed and that charging should occur in all but exceptional cases.[60] In 2008 the National Policing Improvement Agency issued guidance on investigating domestic violence which stated that, 'Proactive investigation will always be required in cases of domestic abuse as the victims, children, neighbours and other witnesses may be reluctant to disturb the perceived privacy of family life. They might also fear threats, emotional pressure and violent reprisals from suspects'.[61]

Nevertheless, there are still major problems with police responses to domestic violence. It is possible to criticise pro-arrest policies as actually endangering victims.[62] Mullender and Hague comment that not all victims want to see their partner arrested.[63] This may be because they love him or depend on him; however, 'Very frequently . . . the hesitation springs from fear of reprisals and repercussions from the perpetrator . . . because women simply do not feel safe'.[64] Hanmer and Griffiths state that, 'a major unresolved issue for policing is how to combine "victim sensitive" approaches with proactive strategies'.[65] Nevertheless, Mullender and Hague comment that, 'Survivors generally prefer a proactive interventionist response provided it is combined with attention to safety and a believing and supportive approach'.[66] They also state that survivors of domestic violence need 'non-judgemental attitudes; an early response; proactive and sympathetic questioning and offering of help; prompt, effective, co-ordinated action; and respect, sensitivity and confidentiality'.[67] Essentially, 'Discretion is an integral part of policing. In best practice, responses are tailored to individual circumstances within broad frameworks of policy and good practice guidelines'.[68] Hanmer and Griffiths also point out that,

> Arrest is a factor in identifying future chronic offenders as well as a response to common law offences and criminal assault. Arrest is a means of identifying men who are more violent and is useful in assessing the risk of future calls for assistance. Understanding the full potential of arrest as a policing strategy and integrating this into police work are major issues.[69]

Hester and Westmarland state that 'up to 50 per cent of incidents reported to the police may remain unrecorded'.[70] This appears to indicate that domestic violence is still not being taken sufficiently seriously. 'Policies and guidance on policing domestic violence remain to be fully implemented'.[71] Mullender and Hague state that victims have reported that 'the police service as a whole [does] not deliver a consistently respectful service to women or handle perpetrators sufficiently assertively'[72] and that, 'in many localities, women continue to report little change in criminal justice responses'.[73] Hanmer and Griffiths identify the basic problem as being 'the low status of domestic violence as police work'.[74] They argue that,

> Good practice issues to be considered in developing new cost effective approaches to domestic violence are improved reporting and increased satisfaction with policing on the part of those experiencing domestic violence, improvements in police organisation, training and management, including information management, audits and statistical reporting, and effective partnership approaches.[75]

Women still feel at risk during the postseparation phase.[76] Connelly and Cavanagh state that 'the attitudes of too many police officers . . . in respect of domestic abuse and the difficulties encountered in enforcing civil protection orders, are based upon stereotypes which have long been associated with domestic abuse and women who are subjected to that abuse'.[77] The responses of individual officers vary, as do the responses of different police stations.[78] There are also reports that the attitudes of police officers outside Domestic Violence Units often contrast greatly with those officers who work within these units.[79] Mullender and Hague comment that, 'This has implications for increased efforts to re-educate the wider and longer-serving police service that times have changed'.[80] Hester and Westmarland state that, essentially, 'the "patchiness" of appropriate police responses to domestic violence still needs to be addressed'.[81] Hague, Mullender, Aris and Dear agree, commenting that, 'the rather mixed outcome in response to police improvements overall . . . supports the premise that, despite transformations in service in some areas, there is still a patchy performance within police services in relation to domestic violence'.[82]

Prosecutorial responses

The negative attitude that prosecutors have traditionally had towards cases of domestic violence has also been well documented. According to the United Nations,

> The decision to prosecute cases of domestic violence rests, in most jurisdictions, with the prosecutors' office which represents the State. These offices have not prosecuted most cases of domestic violence referred to

them. Nor have they treated these cases in the same manner as cases involving violence between strangers.[83]

In relation to the US, Thomas comments that,

> If a domestic violence victim manages to reach the stage in the criminal justice process where she either seeks or requires the assistance or authority of the prosecutor's office, she frequently encounters a lack of enthusiasm or even hostility parallel to that which she found with the police.[84]

As one US prosecutor commented, 'Take a felonious assault case involving a domestic quarrel. Does this deserve to be tried by a 12-man jury? No. We are much better off if they kiss and make up rather than if we put them in jail'.[85] Hopkins, Koss and Bachar highlight another problem with the prosecution of domestic violence cases in the context of the US.[86] In a criminal case, the victim is a witness rather than a party to the case. This means that victims have very little control over prosecution. Indeed Hopkins, Koss and Bachar comment that,

> the traditional criminal justice system, at the urging of battered women's advocates, affirmatively displaces battered women from the centre of prosecutions in a noble effort to take on the primary responsibility of confronting batterers about their violence.[87]

In relation to the UK, the most comprehensive research into the prosecution of domestic violence cases is that carried out by Cretney and Davis. They argue that, 'the difficulty about domestic assault cases lies in the frailty, as prosecutors perceive it, of the woman's commitment to the prosecution enterprise'.[88] There is a very strong belief that women who say that they want to pursue cases against their abusive partners will frequently drop the charges.[89] Also, prosecutors simply do not have the resources to try every case. Therefore, they must make decisions as to which should be pursued and which should be dropped. Cases concerning domestic violence are very likely to be dropped as these do not constitute 'the sort of successful prosecution which brings additional kudos'.[90] Hall comments that,

> The difficulties of prosecuting domestic violence are well known and principally revolve around low reporting rates and the fact that, even when victims do come forward to the authorities, the perception is that complainants in such cases have a tendency to retract their initial police statement at a late stage and become unwilling to give evidence in court.[91]

Edwards states that the Crown Prosecution Service is particularly likely to engage in 'plea-bargaining' in cases of domestic violence.[92] Of the cases that are prosecuted, Cretney and Davis remark that the charges are frequently reduced from assault occasioning actual bodily harm to common assault.[93] Although this is a common occurrence in all assault cases, nevertheless non-domestic cases are much more likely to have an actual bodily harm charge sustained. The Crown Prosecution Service claims that the practice of reducing assault charges is justified as it reduces delay.[94] It seems that it is thought that this is of particular importance in domestic violence cases, as victims are believed to be much more likely to withdraw support for prosecutions. Hester, Hanmer, Coulson, Morahan and Razak interviewed victims of domestic violence who had experienced the criminal justice system in the UK and found that they 'were generally bewildered and shocked by the plea-bargaining and reduction in sentences that tended to take place in court'.[95]

Cretney and Davis argue that the idea that the criminal courts are not the correct forum for domestic violence cases still persists.[96] Domestic violence cases 'are still viewed by police, prosecutors and sentencers through the lens of "the couple" or "the family" '.[97] Hester and Westmarland comment that 'a lack of consistency in criminal justice practice has been found both in relation to individual professionals and in relation to geographical areas'.[98] They also state that 'the criminal justice system often demonstrates little real under-standing of domestic violence and struggles to make appropriate responses to it'.[99] Edwards comments that, 'the likelihood of prosecution remains poor'.[100] She states that, 'all efforts should be directed to improving the likelihood of prosecution of domestic violence cases'[101] as 'Prosecution can reduce domestic violence and is instrumental in intervening in the escalation and repetition of such incidents'.[102]

One much debated issue concerns the question of whether a prosecution should continue even when the victim decides that she does not wish this to happen. Hague and Malos point out that in certain cases where the victim is the only witness, compelling her to give evidence may place her in danger. Nevertheless, policies of dropping prosecutions whenever a police officer or prosecutor thinks that the victim may not wish to proceed are not helpful.[103] In the report of a Home Office Research Study on domestic violence it was commented that,

> On the one hand, prosecution can be seen as likely to aggravate conflict between the partners in a relationship, perhaps leading to an escalation in violence. On the other hand, it can be argued that no violence, whether between family members or strangers, should be tolerated and that it is the responsibility of the whole of the criminal justice system, not just the police, to ensure this. Moreover, it can also be argued that the very nature of domestic violence – its recurrent nature, increasing frequency of attacks and escalating severity of each assault – makes prosecution even more appropriate.[104]

The report also stated that it is unlikely that a general practice of arrests without subsequent prosecutions would be a strong deterrent.[105]

Edwards comments that, 'There is some evidence . . . that the CPS has not lived up to its own promise to always explore all possibilities before abandoning a prosecution'.[106] Hester, Hanmer, Coulson, Morahan and Razak found that in cases in which the parties were back together, 'the victim-witness was deemed less reliable and cases were more likely to be discontinued'.[107] Miles states that, 'the opportunity to admit written evidence in lieu is . . . seldom taken by the prosecution, though some victims may be absent through a desire for reconciliation rather than fear'.[108] Under section 23(3)(b) of the Criminal Justice Act 1988, a written statement can be submitted in place of oral testimony when the witness is in fear.[109] This may only take place if it is in the interests of justice to admit the statement and if admitting the statement would not be unfair to the defendant. Edwards comments that, 'Despite the fact that witnesses are fearful of giving evidence in court . . ., the little use of [section 23(3)(b)] could suggest that prosecutors . . . are reluctant to find alternate ways of supporting these vulnerable prosecutions'.[110]

Judicial responses

Another problem for the victims of domestic violence is the failure of judges to react positively to such cases. As Thomas remarks, 'Judges from every region demonstrate a dangerous unwillingness to understand the causes and consequences of domestic violence and to enforce the laws against it'.[111] Again the problem occurs of violence against women in the home being seen as much less serious than violence between strangers. In many countries judges have a wide discretion in sentencing and normally they adopt a lenient approach when dealing with domestic violence. In relation to the US, Thomas comments that 'judges see penalising a batterer as an assault on the family as an institution'.[112] Nevertheless, Berry states that, 'judges who are committed to giving domestic violence priority as a serious crime can have a tremendous effect on both criminal justice and public attitudes'.[113] For example, if a judge hands down stiff sentences to perpetrators of domestic violence, a clear statement is made that such behaviour will not be tolerated. Also, the opinions of judges tend to be accorded respect in their local communities.[114]

Diduck and Kaganas comment that in the UK charges in domestic violence cases are often reduced and bind-overs are commonly used. This seems to indicate that violence against women in the home is still not seen as entirely criminal. Reduced sentences tend to be handed down if the perpetrator is not viewed as a danger to the public. Factors such as the victim's infidelity may also be taken into consideration. If the couple have not separated, the perpetrator is less likely to be convicted.[115]

It seems that judges are still not treating domestic violence as being as serious as other types of crime. For example, Miles comments that conditional bail and remand are not always used efficiently by police and courts in order to protect victims from intimidation before trial.[116] Edwards states that 'when defendants are proceeded against and convicted at the sentencing stage magistrates and judges continue to pass derisory sentences'.[117] Mullender, Hague, Aris and Dear found that the courts were one of the organisations least likely to respond appropriately to domestic violence.[118] Hester, Hanmer, Coulson, Morahan and Razak found that victims 'felt particularly let down by the court process and the frequently inadequate outcomes'.[119] Those interviewed said that, 'the fines and bind-overs, or short custodial sentences, did not stop the men continuing their violence and harassment in the longer term'.[120]

It certainly appears that domestic violence advocates regard positive judicial attitudes as important in dealing with this issue. Hester and Westmarland comment that 'attrition may be lower where . . . judges or magistrates have domestic violence training'.[121] Edwards remarks that judges should have particular training regarding the admissibility of written statements in place of oral testimony under section 23(3)(b) of the Criminal Justice Act 1988, in order to ensure that this provision is used to its optimum potential in domestic violence cases.[122]

Civil law measures

The Office of Law Reform in Northern Ireland states that, 'The civil law is not a panacea for domestic violence, but it offers a mechanism that victims can embrace to enable them to escape a situation which has become unbearable'.[123] Civil law measures are rarely perfect. The Office of Law Reform also comments that, 'primary civil legislation is a clumsy tool to use to provide protection against such a serious social problem'.[124] Mullender, while certainly accepting the necessity for adequate civil law protection for victims of domestic violence, also lists the obstacles that victims may face when attempting to obtain injunctions and other court orders. She states that,

> These obstacles include unsympathetic solicitors . . ., tight definitions, the need to furnish evidence, unsympathetic courts, and the substitution for action by the court of undertakings by the parties which are easily broken and leave the onus on the woman to take further action. Even where the court does make an order men regularly ignore injunctions and they are rarely enforced. Powers of arrest and orders excluding the man from the home are particularly difficult to obtain . . . Yet legal proceedings are stressful and can lead to reprisals from the man. Not all women know about entitlement to Legal Aid so some never get to court.[125]

Hester and Westmarland also comment that 'continued concern has . . . been expressed about the lack of enforcement of civil orders'.[126]

Edwards states that it is possible to argue that 'the continued provision of injunctive relief under the civil law may undermine the principle that violence against women is a criminal matter'.[127] The continued view of domestic violence as being a 'family matter' may undermine the application of criminal law sanctions.[128] However, Edwards also comments that 'there are powerful arguments in support of the civil law'.[129] For example, some victims of domestic violence may not want to support a criminal prosecution of their partner. In these circumstances the civil law can provide a very necessary measure of protection for victims while they consider their options.[130] Connelly and Cavanagh state that, 'engaging with the civil law enables women to actively respond to current abuse and seek to stop future abuse without reliance on the criminal law and its agents'.[131]

Providing social support measures to victims

It has been accepted by many commentators that legal responses to domestic violence are inadequate in themselves. As Schneider comments, 'Legal intervention may provide women certain protection from battering, but it does not provide women housing, support, child care, employment, community acceptance, or love. It also does not deal with the economic realities of life'.[132] Randall argues that legal responses can only be part of a comprehensive strategy to deal with such a complex problem as domestic violence.[133]

Schneider comments that far more important than criminalisation,

> is the need for provision of state and state-supported resources to deal with the real problems that battered women face – child care, shelters, welfare, work . . . – and thus make it possible for women to have the economic and social independence that is a prerequisite to women's freedom from abuse.[134]

Balos explains that in the drive to put in place criminal law measures to target perpetrators of domestic violence, the need for support services for victims can be largely forgotten. However, one of the major problems facing a woman leaving an abusive relationship is the prospect of homelessness. The woman may well be financially dependent on her partner and may have nowhere else to go. This difficulty is exacerbated by the fact that women suffering from domestic violence tend to be isolated from their friends and family, as quite often abusers will prevent their victims from having contact with third parties. This means that a woman who has been the victim of violence cannot even find refuge with friends or relatives. Indeed it has been found that in the US domestic violence is a primary cause of homelessness.[135] Mullender and Hague comment that,

> According to survivors' testimonies and to research evidence, one of the principal needs of women and children escaping violence in the home is for access to safe and secure temporary and permanent housing options – in other words, for somewhere safe to go.[136]

In the UK, refuges rely on funding from various sources. The Department of the Environment, Transport and the Regions provides funding for costs of housing provision in some circumstances. Other income is obtained from charities, fund raising, trusts, donations and local authorities. However, Hague comments that there is simply not enough money being spent on providing adequate refuge accommodation for victims of domestic violence. Many refuges cannot accommodate half of the women and children who approach them.[137] Refuges specifically for black women and children are even less well funded. A large percentage of refuges depend on volunteers, and paid employees almost invariably receive low salaries.[138]

Mullender states that another problem is making sure that all victims of domestic violence know of the existence of refuges.[139] Smith comments that refuges do not only provide vital emergency accommodation, but that they also provide emotional support to victims of domestic violence. Within a refuge a victim finds other women who have had similar experiences. Simply talking with other victims can assist a woman in rebuilding her self-confidence.[140] As Dobash and Dobash comment, 'Contact with other women helps overcome isolation and a sense of being the only one with a violent partner'.[141] Mullender and Hague state that,

> Refuge staff are generally the only professionals to whom women feel able to tell the full details of their experiences because, in most other contexts, they fear disbelief, revulsion, blame and possible consequences in terms of child protection intervention.[142]

Nevertheless refuges and shelters are not ideal. In the context of the US, Becker remarks that, 'Shelters are not adequate housing. They are crowded, noisy places where few people would be willing to spend even one night. Even so, there is not enough shelter space'.[143] Also, many US shelters will not accept women who have drug or alcohol problems and some do not admit boys over the age of thirteen, so a woman with older children may be unable to utilise such shelters. Becker argues that, if a woman is addicted to alcohol or drugs, she needs a facility with treatment programmes. If she has children she needs a house or apartment.[144] Smith comments that if a woman is not provided with such adequate accommodation she may be forced to return to the abusive relationship.[145]

Levison and Harwin state that the problems for domestic violence victims of living in temporary accommodation may include disruption to employment; disruption to children's schooling; the inability to plan ahead; a lack of support; poor living conditions; and poor security. If the accommodation is not self-contained, additional difficulties may include overcrowding; a lack of privacy; a lack of space for children to play; problems with preparing food; and a lack of amenities.[146] Therefore, 'Housing is of vital importance when considering the safety of people experiencing domestic violence'.[147]

Mullender comments that, although the legal rights of women to housing have been strengthened, nevertheless they often have to return home due to lack of accommodation.[148] Finding a permanent home 'can be one of the most crucial struggles for freedom from violence faced by women'.[149] Indeed, 'Housing can be a crucial determinant of what happens to abused women'.[150] However, Hague states that, government housing throughout the 1980s and early 1990s [was] deliberately designed to reduce the provision of council housing in favour of owner-occupation, housing associations and private rented accommodation . . . These policies have led to a substantial shortage of public-sector housing in the UK . . ., which has led in turn to a huge increase in homelessness, with direct and often tragic effects on the lives of women and children homeless due to violence.[151]

Hague argues that successive governments seem to have been oblivious to the crucial need for housing for victims of domestic violence. For example, the Housing Act 1996 removed the right of those defined as 'statutorily homeless' to be permanently rehoused. They were now only entitled to temporary housing. Hague comments that the legislation 'encourage[d], for both temporary and permanent rehousing, the use of insecure private provision, a housing tenure which is often unsuitable for abused women and children'.[152] The Homelessness Act 2002 did improve the situation by granting new powers to secure accommodation for the homeless;[153] nevertheless, problems still remain. For example, local councils differ greatly as to how they interpret the homelessness legislation. Also, some housing departments ask victims of domestic violence very few questions about the violence they have suffered, while others subject women to close questioning on this issue. The latter approach can be very distressing for the women involved.[154] Essentially, 'there are still resource shortages and a severe lack of social housing'.[155]

Smith argues that economic assistance may well be necessary in order to help a victim of domestic violence to regain her independence. Frequently a woman may need educational or vocational programmes to allow her to gain the necessary qualifications to obtain employment. She may also need child-care facilities while finding a job, and subsequently during her working hours.[156] However, Hague comments that social security benefits have been cut substantially. She remarks that, 'When viewed against lack of benefits, underfunded services, and cuts in health and social services, government policies on domestic violence presently look somewhat fragile and inadequate'.[157]

Sullivan states that some women believe that their partners would actually cease being violent if they knew that the women had access to resources and that accommodation was available.[158] Randall argues that essentially there need to be economic policies in place that would make leaving a viable option for all women suffering from violence in the home.[159] Domestic violence advocates certainly argue convincingly that adequate measures of social support are vital for victims.

Changing attitudes

Blaming the victim

Stanko states that blaming the victim, as opposed to the abuser, is an insidious attitudinal problem in relation to domestic violence. She argues that women are blamed for their own lack of power and are seen as passive or even desirous of their own harm. On the other hand, men's abusive behaviour is tacitly dismissed as 'typical'.[160] Mullender similarly comments that women are viewed as having invited the violence in some way, such as by acting in an unreasonable manner. This can actually lead to sympathy being felt for the abuser.[161]

As Mullender remarks, victims tend to get blamed for failings on the part of their social superiors. This may be seen in the fact that solutions are formulated as if it is individual victims that are to blame. For example, the focus is placed on the women suffering domestic violence rather than on abusive men and the social context that creates the conditions that allow violence in the home to occur.[162] Dobash and Dobash comment that the 'blaming the victim' approach is often accepted by legal, social and medical institutions, thus making it even more difficult for women to report the abuse they are suffering.[163]

Stanko argues that outsiders' blaming of the victim often turns into the victim blaming herself. Many women believe the traditional idea that the home is a haven of peace and security. When this does not turn out to be true, they find it difficult to understand why this should be the case and begin to believe that the violence is in some way their fault.[164] The British Crime Survey report of 1999 stated that 28 per cent of the chronic female victims (those who had been assaulted three or more times) and 51 per cent of the intermittent female victims thought they had to take some responsibility for their last attack.[165] The 2004 British Crime Survey found that only 51 per cent of women who had experienced domestic violence thought their worst incident was a crime, 33 per cent thought that it was wrong, but not a crime, and 13 per cent believed that it was just something that happens.[166] The fact that so many victims of domestic violence did not perceive what had happened to them as a crime may be evidence of victims reducing the seriousness of the incidents, perhaps due to a measure of self-blame. Indeed, Kelly and Radford comment that, 'women . . . tend, and indeed are systematically encouraged, to minimise the violence that [they] experience from men'.[167] Mullender emphasises that any person or organisation seeking to assist a woman suffering from abuse must stress that the violence is not her fault and that the abuser has committed a criminal offence.[168]

One question that is often asked is: why does the victim not leave the abusive relationship? Generally it takes victims of domestic violence a long time to leave their partners, and a significant number never do so. The British Crime Survey found that most victims were living with their assailant at the time of the most recent assault, and a half of these were still doing so when interviewed.[169] However, Schneider remarks that focusing on why a woman stays in an abusive relationship is problematic, as it places the responsibility on the woman and expects her to take control.[170]

Bennett and Williams make the point that men who batter their partners usually show no sign of doing so to the outside world.[171] On the other hand, a victim may find it very difficult to hide her injuries; therefore victims tend to be more conspicuous than abusers. This may be one reason for the fact that, 'the public has had a far greater fascination with "why she stays" than with "why he abuses"'.[172] Many people are of the opinion that victims only remain in violent relationships because of their own pathology.[173]

Much has been written by commentators attempting to analyse the 'psychology' of victims of domestic violence. Walker's concept of 'learned helplessness' is perhaps the best known in its field. This concept sees the victim as passive and helpless. Walker argues that repeated violence diminishes the victim's motivation to respond, and makes her submissive to further abuse. As the violence continues, the victim becomes entirely immobilised[174] and unable to act to improve her situation. On this analysis, victims stay in violent relationships because they become helpless to do anything else.

Nevertheless, there are other commentators who argue that the image of a victim suffering from 'learned helplessness' is merely a stereotype. Mullender and Morley argue that, contrary to being passive recipients of abuse, women suffering from domestic violence usually engage in numerous strategies to cope with the abuse and to attempt to resist. For example, they try to discuss the violence with their partner and to dissuade him from such behaviour. They may refuse to do what their abuser wants, or attempt to protect any children in the household. Victims talk to friends and family, and may call for police assistance or seek legal advice. Many women are extremely concerned about the impact the violence may have on their children, and they go to great lengths to ensure that children do not witness the abuse.[175] A large number of women go through an active process of leaving, returning and leaving again. Dobash and Dobash make the point that this is 'a dynamic, evolving process'.[176] They argue that the fact that these women keep returning to the relationship should not be viewed as a sign of weakness, but as a strategy to end the violence. Leaving for a short period of time is a signal to the abuser that the victim is unwilling to live with abuse, but that she wants to remain in the relationship. Women return to violent relationships for a wide variety of reasons – their partners may agree to change, they may be concerned about their children, they may have few economic resources of their own, or they may fear the violence of their partners if they do not return.[177] Essentially Dobash and Dobash argue that,

> In contrast to therapeutically oriented conceptions of women bound to men in 'symbiotic relationships' in which they suffer 'psychological paralysis' making it unlikely or extremely improbable that they will seek help, evidence on help-seeking shows that women actively seek support and assistance.[178]

Stanko states that women often stay in violent relationships for practical reasons.[179] Victims may be entirely economically dependent on their abusers. If they leave the relationship, they may have no shelter, no financial support and no opportunity of becoming self-sufficient. Essentially, 'Getting out is almost as bad as staying in the relationship'.[180] Diduck and Kaganas comment that many women are caught in a 'no-win' situation, wherein the better course of action appears to be remaining in the relationship.[181]

Domestic violence advocates have thus argued convincingly that the 'blaming the victim' ideology is a major problem in dealing with this issue. It is very easy to ask the question 'why didn't she leave?' and thus place the responsibility for the violence on the victim rather than on the abuser. Nevertheless, commentators such as Mullender and Morley assert that it must be recognised that victims of domestic violence often feel unable to leave, not due to any psychological incapacity, but because of practical considerations. Therefore, attention must be paid to providing women with the resources that they need in order to leave the violent relationship. Also, very often, blame by outsiders can turn into self-blame by the victims themselves. This can make them less likely to seek help. Mullender argues that any agency involved in the assistance of women suffering from domestic violence must therefore make it a clear priority to reassure women that the abuse is not their fault.[182]

Raising awareness of domestic violence within society

Domestic violence advocates have argued that in order to address the problem of domestic violence, it is necessary to raise awareness of the issue within society as a whole. For example, Berry comments that there is still a view among certain elements of the community that violence against women in the home is acceptable in some circumstances, or at least that it is not as serious as violence between strangers.[183] In the context of the US, Garvey remarks that to some extent society is conscious of domestic violence; for example, the issue is frequently dealt with in television programmes, such as police dramas. Newspapers often contain articles concerning violence in the home.[184] However, Garvey comments that,

> The sensationalism has normalised violence. As a media savvy society, we see it but do not feel it. We talk in generalities about individual instances but do not try to understand how they happened and what could be done to stop it. Public consciousness is now blind in a different way.[185]

Hester and Westmarland comment that publicity campaigns, 'should use a wide range of media such as radio, television, posters and stickers. They should aim to educate local residents and staff across agencies that domestic violence is a public crime, and indicate local sources of support'.[186] Outreach workers should regularly visit community groups and agencies to discuss domestic violence and publicise local domestic violence projects.[187] Connelly and Cavanagh remark that if legislative initiatives 'are not paralleled by education programs, which challenge the common myths and misconceptions around domestic abuse, operating and enforcing legislative provisions will be difficult'.[188]

Schneider states that education about domestic violence 'must take place in every elementary school and high school, every court, welfare office, hospital, and law school around the country'.[189] Hester and Westmarland comment that domestic violence prevention programmes should be implemented in both primary and secondary schools, and that domestic violence should at least be included in the Personal, Social, Health and Citizenship Education curriculum. A cross-curricular approach should be adopted and all teachers involved should be trained in using the project materials. Teachers should also feel supported to deal with issues raised through such programmes via the local education authority and other links.[190]

Educating professionals

Hague and Malos state that the work of agencies such as social and healthcare services is extremely important for victims of domestic violence. The attitudes of these agencies to domestic violence can greatly affect whether or not victims make use of them.[191] However, Mullender and Morley argue that professionals such as social workers, doctors and housing officials have a history of being unsympathetic and unhelpful to women suffering from domestic violence. Indeed, 'these professionals and their agencies have been centrally implicated in the very construction and perpetuation of violent relationships'.[192] Another difficulty is that agencies may have no clear policy concerning domestic violence and so may be unsure as to how to act.[193] Dobash and Dobash comment that women have been blamed for the abuse, been told to change their own behaviour and had their concerns discounted.[194] Particular attention has been drawn to the need to educate lawyers about domestic violence. Burman, a US commentator, remarks that, 'Without proper training, lawyers may actually harm, rather than help, their clients who are victims of domestic violence, a clear violation of their ethical and legal obligations to help clients'.[195] In the UK context, Mullender and Hague state that, 'all the public sector agencies tend to suffer from internal inconsistency so that different members of staff might be helpful, indifferent or hostile'.[196] Indeed, 'Women's experience of all the public sector services has traditionally been that they are patchy and inadequate, with practitioners often assuming judgmental or woman-blaming attitudes'.[197]

There have been some attempts in recent years to raise awareness of domestic violence issues in institutions such as the probation service and social services. The Association of Chief Officers of Probation has produced statements on domestic violence and probation officers are becoming involved with programmes for perpetrators of violence in the home.[198] As regards social services, community care plans now often feature domestic violence, and some departments have policies in place for working with victims of violence in the home. Awareness among healthcare professionals is also rising, with a number of accident and emergency departments developing policies on domestic violence. Nevertheless, Hague comments that it is still the case that many health services fail to take violence in the home seriously.[199] The standard of help given to a woman is still 'the luck of the draw', depending on which health services she encounters.[200] Hague, Mullender, Aris and Dear note that victims have expressed particular dissatisfaction with the response of healthcare professionals.[201] Davidson, King, Garcia and Marchant state that, 'Educational interventions for health professionals and health service staff need to be designed to address local circumstances, and to be based on research that has explored women's views about the service and staff attitudes and needs'.[202] Essentially, victims of domestic violence want healthcare professionals to listen; to provide enough time and privacy; to ask about abuse; to respond sympathetically; and to take care about safety issues.[203]

Similarly, Mullender and Hague point out that victims want housing officials to display a believing approach; to provide a non-judgmental service; and to ensure confidentiality.[204] Essentially, 'there is a need for housing and homelessness staff and housing associations to develop further knowledge and expertise concerning domestic violence and its impact upon victims'.[205] Levison and Harwin comment that training of housing staff should be part of a rolling programme, so that it is available to new staff and that existing staff can have their knowledge updated.[206]

Mullender argues convincingly that, 'helping agencies need to develop sensitivity, consistency and a believing and non-blaming approach to the women who approach them'.[207] Smith states that training courses must be organised for all agencies that are concerned with domestic violence, including healthcare professionals, social workers and lawyers. Indeed, interdisciplinary courses could be utilised. Victims of violence in the home and refuge workers could be involved in such initiatives. The overall aim would be to sensitise agencies to the difficulties involved in domestic violence, and to ensure an accurate understanding of the issues.[208]

Ensuring inter-agency cooperation

Berry states that,

> Ideally, all of the entities and agencies that are involved in domestic violence issues within a given community or region should meet and interact on a regular basis to share ideas, plan strategies, develop protocols, and promote an ongoing dialogue with one another and with the public.[209]

The need for inter-agency cooperation between all those concerned with domestic violence is well recognised. The issue of domestic violence encompasses a complex mass of problems which requires the involvement of a variety of services. It is thus essential that there is cooperation between these service providers. Smith comments that it is only with the development of such an approach that victims will be ensured the best possible assistance.[210]

The Crime and Disorder Act 1998 places a duty on the police and local authorities to develop local partnerships to reduce crime and disorder. These partnerships bring together all the relevant agencies, including those concerned with domestic violence.[211] However, Hague is of the opinion that government does not give sufficient funding to inter-agency work, and that this lack of resources is preventing such initiatives from fulfilling their true potential.[212] As Hague remarks,

> official encouragement of unfunded inter-agency coordination is an example of central and local government giving with one hand and taking away with the other by encouraging the approach but not then providing the tools and resources to do the job effectively.[213]

Indeed, Hague claims that government support for inter-agency work is 'a cheap option'.[214] Any funds that are provided may be spent on meetings and conferences, instead of on improving services.[215] Hague says that, 'adequate resourcing for inter-agency domestic violence work is essential if the approach is to be successful'.[216]

Tackling risk factors

US commentators in particular have highlighted the need to tackle certain risk factors associated with domestic violence. For example, Burman comments that,

> Although domestic violence occurs in all socio-economic, educational, cultural, and racial groups, it does not occur at the same rates. Some research shows, for example, that domestic violence is more prevalent among women who are unmarried but cohabitating, are pregnant, . . . have less education, and/or are minorities.[217]

Carter states that it has been recognised that many perpetrators of domestic violence were abused as children; therefore a history of child abuse constitutes another risk factor in the occurrence of domestic violence.[218] Nevertheless, Mullender makes the point that an abuser can never use the fact that he comes from a violent home as an excuse for his behaviour.[219]

The US commentators Banks and Randolph claim that the connection between substance abuse and family violence is extremely complex.[220] It has been found that substance abuse in both men and women often coexists with domestic violence. However, Banks and Randolph comment that it is doubtful whether alcohol or other substances play a direct part in most violent episodes.[221] In the UK, the 1999 British Crime Survey found that a third of attacks took place while the assailant was under the influence of alcohol. However, it was not possible to ascertain whether alcohol caused the violence or contributed to its occurrence.[222] Mullender comments that it is likely that some men drink 'to give themselves dutch courage or permission to be violent, or to provide an excuse to call on after the event'.[223] The survey also found that 8 per cent of female chronic victims said their last assault had taken place while their assailant was under the influence of drugs.[224] It was found that victims of domestic assault had far higher levels of alcohol consumption than non-victims. However, this could be a consequence of the abuse. Victims were also far more likely to say they had recently used illegal drugs.[225] Research carried out in 2009 into perpetrators of domestic violence found that the majority of the perpetrators in the sample appeared to abuse alcohol to some degree.[226]

The 2004 British Crime Survey found that risks of domestic violence among women do not differ greatly by ethnic origin.[227] However, Kelly and Radford state that, 'for black women the reality of racism can create a tension between their experience of abuse, and a felt need to protect the community from intervention by white institutions, especially the police'.[228] It seems therefore that attention should be paid to the question of how to ensure that victims of domestic violence from ethnic minority communities have access to support services.

Battery treatment programmes

Some attention has been given, mostly by US commentators, to the question of whether the establishing of battery treatment programmes constitutes a beneficial response to domestic violence. During such programmes, perpetrators of domestic violence are taught anger management and stress reduction skills. The overall objective is to demonstrate to the batterer that violence is not the best way to deal with difficult situations. Batterer intervention programmes almost invariably involve the discussion of issues in group settings. Usually attendance is the main criterion for successfully completing such a programme; however, it is also possible to base completion on indicators of changed behaviour, such as reports from the victim.[229]

Bennett and Williams argue that battery treatment programmes do possess certain advantages, especially if the view is taken that perpetrators of domestic violence are also in need of assistance. Such programmes have the potential to be successful in teaching batterers to control their anger and desist from violence. Interpersonal skills can be improved and changed behaviour strongly encouraged.[230] Also, some women may prefer their partners to undergo such a programme, as opposed to them receiving a custodial sentence.[231]

However, Bennett and Williams also point out that there are problems associated with battery treatment programmes. Allowing a group of batterers to interact may have the result of promoting misogyny and negative attitudes towards women. A batterer may actually be encouraged to continue engaging in violence by coming into contact with other men who also do so. This can increase the risk to his victim.[232] Also, perpetrator programmes could be viewed as being a 'soft' option, which may not emphasise sufficiently that the abuser's behaviour will not be tolerated. It is possible that the development of such programmes may reduce the possibility of legal changes which could result in abusers being dealt with more severely by the courts than they are at present.[233]

In addition, Becker comments that there is little evidence that batterer intervention programmes are successful, especially when they are mandatory. It is usually the case that abusers are required only to attend, and no assessment is made of any change brought about in the batterer.[234] Mullender and Burton state that 'there has been insufficient and insufficiently rigorous monitoring of perpetrators' programmes in all countries in which they have begun to develop'[235] and that 'much of the practice-based literature makes over-stated, impressionistic claims for success'.[236]

Conclusion

According to commentators in this field, there are many measures that could be beneficially adopted in relation to domestic violence. However, it seems that there are three main categories of measures that are most strongly highlighted by commentators in the UK. First, the criminal justice system should be improved to ensure that police, prosecutors and judges treat cases of domestic violence as on a par with those involving other types of crime. Second, measures of social support, such as refuge accommodation and housing, should be provided. Third, it is necessary that efforts be made to increase awareness of domestic violence. Particular attention should be paid to making professionals who may frequently come into contact with victims of domestic violence, such as doctors, social workers and judges, aware of the issues involved. In assessing whether human rights law may be effective in relation to the issue of domestic violence, this book will focus primarily on the question of whether human rights law can assist in attaining these three types of measures.

Therefore, to what extent can international human rights law contribute to the achievement of the measures discussed? In investigating this issue, two strategies will be examined – the use of a litigation approach and the use of the statements made by international human rights bodies in relation to domestic violence.

3 The jurisprudence of the European Court of Human Rights

In the previous chapter a number of measures that may prove beneficial in contributing to the fight against domestic violence was outlined. It appears that three main categories of measures are most strongly highlighted by commentators in the UK. The first of these categories may be entitled improving the criminal justice system. This encompasses improving police and prosecutorial responses to domestic violence and ensuring that judges hand down appropriate sentences to perpetrators. A second category may be labelled the provision of social support measures to victims. This includes the provision of resources, refuge accommodation, housing and childcare facilities. A third category encompasses measures to raise awareness of the issue of domestic violence, both within society as a whole and also within particular professions that come into contact with victims of domestic violence on a regular basis. It seems that an informative way of assessing the effectiveness of international human rights law in relation to domestic violence is to investigate the potential held by the discourse of rights to achieve the realisation of these measures.

One way in which international human rights law could be used to realise these measures is through a litigation approach. However, could such a strategy be successful in the United Kingdom? The European Convention on Human Rights has been incorporated into UK law. In order to examine the potential held by the use of human rights law through a litigation strategy in the area of domestic violence in this jurisdiction, it is necessary to assess how the case law of the European Court of Human Rights could be used in relation to domestic violence. The European Court has on many occasions placed positive duties on states to intervene in situations where the human rights of an individual are being breached by another private entity. In this manner the European Court has broken through the public/private dichotomy that has been an obstacle to the full effectiveness of human rights law for so long. There is no doubt that the European Court has produced a more comprehensive and advanced jurisprudence in this sphere, than has any other human rights enforcement body in the world. Cases such as *Osman v United Kingdom*[1] illustrate the dynamic approach that the Court has taken in this area. Governments have been repeatedly reminded that not only must they refrain from violating human rights standards, they also have duties to take positive steps to ensure that the rights of individuals are protected effectively. However, does the case law of the European Court of Human Rights hold any potential to contribute towards the achievement of the three categories of measures that are most strongly highlighted by commentators in the UK as being necessary – improving the criminal justice system, providing social support measures for victims and raising awareness of the issue of domestic violence?

Positive obligations under the European Convention on Human Rights

Domestic violence takes place between private individuals; therefore, in order for the European Convention on Human Rights to be used in relation to this issue, the doctrine of positive obligations must be engaged. As Schriver points out, 'The express provisions of the Convention do not require the European Court to impose affirmative duties'.[2] In fact, most of the rights contained in the Convention are couched in very negative terms. For example, article 8 prevents an interference with the exercise of the right to private and family life. It does not actually state that everyone is guaranteed their right to privacy. A similar analysis could be carried out regarding the majority of the Convention rights. As discussed in Chapter 1, 'The concept of human rights developed largely from Western political theory of the rights of the individual to autonomy and freedom'.[3] Nevertheless, the European Court has produced a comprehensive jurisprudence in the sphere of positive obligations. This certainly appears paradoxical. How has a treaty instrument that is rooted definitively in the traditional negative rights approach been used to create such informative and progressive case law in this area?

Starmer explains that there are a number of positive duties on the state that are explicitly imposed by the Convention. For example, under article 3 of the First Protocol, the state has an obligation to hold elections in connection with the right to vote. However, more interestingly and controversially, positive obligations can arise in a more indirect manner. In certain instances, positive duties can be placed on states to protect the rights of individuals from threats posed by other private entities. The European Court has derived this principle from three propositions. First, under article 1 of the Convention, states must secure the rights to everyone within their jurisdictions. This seems to indicate that states must take positive steps to ensure that private individuals can freely enjoy their fundamental rights. Second, it is assumed that rights must be effective, and not merely theoretical.[4] As Clapham comments, 'an "effective" implementation of the Convention means that the changing social context within which it operates has to be considered'.[5] It is increasingly being recognised that breaches of fundamental rights emanate from the private sphere just as easily, or perhaps even more easily, than they can be perpetrated by the state itself. States are now subject to international human rights law, and to vehement public disapproval if they violate its terms. However, individuals are not subjected to such controls. Therefore, it is likely that a far greater percentage of human rights abuses take place in the private arena than in the public sphere. In order to reflect this social reality, the European Court realises that obligations must be placed on states to protect the human rights of individuals from threats posed by other individuals. As Mowbray comments, 'Passive non-interference by governmental authorities with persons' Convention rights is not sufficient to ensure that many of those rights are fully and effectively respected'.[6] Third, under article 13, states must provide effective remedies for violations of rights.[7] Again this provision serves to impose positive duties on states.

Nevertheless, it could be argued that the European Court has built, and is continuing to build, an extremely important body of jurisprudence that has immense ramifications for the Contracting Parties, on a somewhat unstable foundation. An examination of the actual text of the Convention reveals the fact that it contains very few provisions that can be construed as encompassing the doctrine of positive obligations. The reference in article 1 to securing rights, and the article 13 right to a remedy are more than balanced out by the generally negative framework of rights which forms the remainder of the Convention. The principle of effectiveness is a judge-made assumption. Therefore, it seems that by developing the case law in the way that it has, the European Court may be leaving itself open to the charge of reaching beyond its mandate and attempting to force states to comply with obligations to which they never agreed. The Court has certainly taken a very courageous course of action in this field.

However, it is clear that the correct course has been adopted. The European Court generally takes a teleological approach to the interpretation of the Convention, wherein it looks beyond the actual wording of the text to the purpose for which the Convention was created. As Schriver remarks, 'By adopting this dynamic system of interpretation, the European Court has expanded on the broad language of Convention rights and ensured full protection to the individual in the face of changes in European political and social attitudes'.[8] The Court goes beyond the original intentions of those who drafted the Convention and takes account of contemporary standards.[9] It could certainly be argued that the original signatories to the Convention did not just desire to protect against the human rights violations that were taking place at that time, and that they also would have wished to protect against any breaches that may arise in the future. At present, the rights of individuals are threatened greatly by other private entities. Therefore, it may well be that the initial drafters of the Convention would have wanted it to encompass human rights abuses taking place solely in the private sphere. What is certain is that the Court's 'forward-looking and contextual'[10] approach to the interpretation of the European Convention, 'effectively moves all the Member States toward human rights reforms'.[11] This can only be a praiseworthy development in the jurisprudence of the Court.

Nevertheless, it should be remembered that states generally have a degree of discretion as to the method by which they protect the rights of an individual from threats posed by another individual. The Court commented in *Powell and Rayner v United Kingdom* that 'the State enjoys a certain margin of appreciation in determining the steps to be taken to ensure compliance with the Convention'.[12] Therefore, the state still retains a degree of authority in relation to the question of how best to implement the positive obligations to which it is subject. This approach respects the principle of state sovereignty and may make for more cooperative states, and thus more effective human rights protection. It seems that it is necessary for the Court to allow Member States a margin of appreciation in order to secure their continued support. The European Court therefore appears to be adopting a practical as well as a principled approach in the area of positive obligations. However, it is also possible to criticise the margin of appreciation doctrine. It may be argued that allowing states a certain leeway in this field dilutes the strong stance taken by the Court on the effective protection of rights. This margin should therefore be kept as narrow as possible.

One of the seminal cases in the European Court's development of the doctrine of positive obligations is *Osman v United Kingdom*.[13] This involved a teacher who had formed an unhealthy attachment to a pupil. A series of incidents resulted and eventually he shot the pupil's father dead and injured the pupil. The pupil and his mother brought a case to the European Court, arguing that the police had been notified that the lives of the pupil and his father were at risk but had failed to take sufficient measures to prevent breaches of their right to life under article 2 of the Convention, and of their right to private and family life under article 8.

The Court's judgment in this case is pivotal to a discussion of positive obligations and thus it is worth quoting at some length. As regards the right to life it was stated that,

> The Court notes that the first sentence of article 2(1) enjoins the State not only to refrain from the intentional and unlawful taking of life, but also to take appropriate steps to safeguard the lives of those within its jurisdiction . . . It is common ground that the State's obligation in this respect extends beyond its primary duty to secure the right to life by putting in place effective criminal-law provisions to deter the commission of offences against the person backed up by law-enforcement machinery for the prevention, suppression and sanctioning of breaches of such provisions . . . Article 2 of the Convention may also imply in certain well-defined circumstances a positive obligation on the authorities to take preventive operational measures to protect an individual whose life is at risk from the criminal acts of another individual.[14]

Therefore, not only does the state have a duty to implement effective criminal law measures to protect the right to life, it may also have a positive obligation to prevent the right of an individual from being breached by another individual. It can be seen that the European Court has used the concept of state responsibility to transcend the traditional public/private dichotomy, in order to ensure the effectiveness of the Convention rights.

However, the Court also held that not every claimed risk to life would require operational measures to be taken to prevent the risk from coming to fruition. It commented that,

> bearing in mind the difficulties involved in policing modern societies, the unpredictability of human conduct and the operational choices which must be made in terms of priorities and resources, such an obligation must be interpreted in a way which does not impose an impossible or dispropor-tionate burden on the authorities.[15]

It should be emphasised that the authorities must either know or ought to know 'of the existence of a real and immediate risk to the life of an identified individual' for the duty to come into effect.[16]

The positive obligations that may be placed on states are wide ranging. Notably, Starmer claims that the European Court has recognised five main cate-gories of duties that can be imposed on states – an obligation to establish a legal framework providing effective rights protection, a duty to prevent breaches of Convention rights, an obligation to provide information relevant to the breach of Convention rights, a duty to respond to violations and an obligation to provide resources to individuals to prevent breaches of their rights.[17]

In what ways is domestic violence a violation of the European Convention on Human Rights?

Domestic violence seems to violate several of the rights enshrined in the European Convention. There have been many instances in which women suffering domestic violence are eventually killed by their partners. It is thus clear that the practice of domestic violence breaches the right to life as contained in article 2 of the Convention. In *Osman v United Kingdom* it was stated that article 2 'enjoins the state not only to refrain from the intentional and unlawful taking of life, but also to take appropriate steps to safeguard the lives of those within its jurisdiction'.[18] The Court also commented that,

> the State's obligation in this respect extends beyond its primary duty to secure the right to life by putting in place effective criminal-law provisions to deter the commission of offences against the person backed up by law-enforcement machinery for the prevention, suppression and sanctioning of breaches of such provisions.[19]

It seems therefore that the state may be in breach of article 2 if it fails to take adequate steps to protect the right to life of victims of domestic violence.

Article 3 of the European Convention states that everyone has the right to be free from torture and inhuman or degrading treatment or punishment. Choudhry and Herring remark that, 'domestic violence will often be suffi-ciently intense to engage article 3'.[20] Particular attention has been paid to the question of whether domestic violence can be defined as torture. Nguyen comments that,

> Traditionally, the word 'torture' conjures up gruesome visions of dark, dank medieval chambers where unspeakable acts of . . . suffering are inflicted . . . Today, these chambers could easily be found within the confines of a family's home where the husband becomes the torturer and the wife becomes the helpless victim.[21]

The similarities between official torture and domestic violence are striking. If violence against women in the home were to be generally accepted as torture, it would certainly dispose of the aura of sexism and sentimentalism that presently surrounds the issue.[22]

Grdinic claims that the criteria laid down in the case law of the European Court for a practice to constitute torture under article 3 of the Convention are in fact satisfied by incidents of domestic violence.[23] In the case of *Ireland v United Kingdom*,[24] all the judgments seemed to agree on the fact that for a practice to constitute torture, it must first be inhuman. Second, it must be deliberately inflicted; and third, it must cause physical or mental suffering that is very serious and cruel.[25] Does domestic violence truly fulfil these requirements?

Domestic violence certainly constitutes inhuman treatment that is deliberately inflicted. A common argument is that men who abuse their partners act impulsively, and not purposively.[26] However, in most instances of domestic violence, one partner does act intentionally to coerce the other.[27] Therefore it appears that the first two elements of torture are fulfilled.

The third element of torture is that the treatment in question must cause very serious and cruel suffering. This can be either physical or mental. Both official torture and domestic violence usually involve physical brutality.[28] As Selden points out, the weapons used in each are 'frighteningly similar'.[29] However, there is also a psychological component in both situations. Torture involves anguish and fear. Stress and sleep deprivation are often used to break the will of the victim. Threats are made both to the victim and to their family, and intermittent kindness is also commonly used. With domestic violence, threats are often made regarding both the lives of the victims and those of their loved ones. Again there are usually intermittent periods of kindness. Sleeplessness is produced, as in some cases are the symptoms of post-traumatic stress disorder, which is often suffered by torture victims.[30]

It appears therefore that the elements of torture are satisfied by instances of domestic violence. Generally for torture to be recognised as such, it must be inflicted to achieve certain aims, for example obtaining information.[31] However, in *Ireland v United Kingdom* it was stated that, 'Torture is torture whatever its object may be'.[32] Also, torture usually requires an official element. Nevertheless it seems that such official acquiescence may be found when the state has failed to protect the victim of domestic violence.[33] It appears that

violence against women in the home could be accepted by the Court as consti-
tuting torture.[34] If this development were to occur it would serve to draw
attention to the true nature of domestic violence. As Hopkins remarks, 'Inclu-
sion of domestic violence in norms against torture may well help change the
perception of domestic violence on both international and domestic levels'.[35]

Aydin v Turkey[36] involved an applicant who was detained for three days,
during which she was tortured. She was kicked in the arms, legs and eyes,
punched and raped. The European Court held that 'the accumulation of acts
of physical and mental violence inflicted on the applicant and the especially
cruel act of rape to which she was subjected amounted to torture in breach of
Article 3 of the Convention'.[37] The treatment of the applicant in *Aydin* was
remarkably similar to that suffered by victims of domestic violence.[38] The
Court commented that 'Rape of a detainee by an official of the state must be
considered to be an especially grave and abhorrent form of ill-treatment given
the ease with which an offender can exploit the vulnerability and weakened
resistance of his victim'.[39] It seems that a perpetrator of domestic violence has
a similar degree of power over his victim to that which an official of the state
has over one held in his custody. Many cases of domestic violence involve rape,
and in *Aydin* the Court stated that, 'rape leaves deep psychological scars on the
victim which do not respond to the passage of time as quickly as other forms
of physical and mental violence'.[40] In *Aydin* the treatment suffered by the
applicant was held to amount to torture. It could well be argued therefore that
the similar treatment suffered by victims of domestic violence should also be
regarded as torture. Nevertheless, even if the European Court did not take the
major step of deeming domestic violence to be torture, violence against
women in the home certainly constitutes inhuman or degrading treatment in
violation of article 3.

Another provision of the Convention that is very relevant to a case involving
domestic violence is article 8. Article 8(1) states that, 'Everyone has the right
to respect for his private and family life, his home and his correspondence'. It
has been established in the Court's jurisprudence that this right encompasses
bodily integrity. As was stated in *Y.F. v Turkey*, 'A person's body concerns the
most intimate aspect of one's private life'.[41]

It seems therefore that domestic violence clearly breaches articles 2, 3 and
8 of the European Convention on Human Rights. It may also be argued that
article 14, the right to enjoy one's rights free from discrimination, is also
violated as it has been found that domestic violence is largely carried out
against women.[42]

How has the European Court of Human Rights addressed the issue of domestic violence?

Domestic violence is a very widespread problem throughout Europe. It also
seems be a clear violation of four articles of the European Convention on
Human Rights. It is thus somewhat surprising, to say the least, that until

2007 domestic violence had not been directly addressed substantively by the European Court. Up until that point there had only been one admissibility decision of the Court that dealt with the issue. *Myszk v Poland*[43] involved an applicant who had attempted to commit suicide. After she left hospital she moved in with her mother. Her two children remained with her husband in the family home, and she sought access to them. Access was granted by the domestic courts. However, her husband consistently refused to abide by the various orders made. The applicant argued that the state's response to her predicament was insufficient to protect her rights. One of her submissions was that her husband was violent and that her family needed regular therapy. She argued that the state did not provide any effective prevention programmes as regards domestic violence, and that this constituted a breach of her article 8 right to private and family life. The applicant also claimed that the national courts did not treat domestic violence as seriously as they should.

The response of the European Commission to this argument was to reiterate the point made by the Court in *X and Y v the Netherlands* that,

> athough the object of Article 8 is essentially to protect the individual against arbitrary interference by the public authorities, it may also impose positive obligations on the State inherent in an effective respect for family life. These obligations may involve the adoption of measures designed to secure respect for family life even in the sphere of the relations of individuals between themselves.[44]

However, the Commission proceeded to state that,

> the notion of 'respect' enshrined in Article 8 is not clear-cut. Especially where the positive obligations implicit in that concept are concerned, its requirements will vary considerably from case to case according to the practices followed and the situations obtaining in the Contracting States.

The Commission noted that the applicant complained that the state did not provide a sufficient framework for families experiencing difficulties in obtaining family counselling. However, the applicant had failed to specify the exact nature of the difficulties in question, except for the fact that her husband tended to be violent. She had not stated whether she had made efforts to obtain counselling. The Commission commented that 'the positive obligations of the State inherent in an effective "respect" for family life within the meaning of Article 8 of the Convention do not encompass an obligation to provide ex officio effective family counselling to families with problems'. The Commission thus decided that this part of the application was manifestly ill-founded.

In *Myszk v Poland* the application was held to be inadmissible due to the lack of information provided by the applicant on this issue. However, since 2007 the Court has directly addressed the issue of domestic violence in a series of cases – *Kontrova v Slovakia*;[45] *Bevacqua and S v Bulgaria*;[46] *Opuz v Turkey*;[47] and *E.S. and Others v Slovakia*;[48] *A v Croatia*;[49] and *Hajduova v Slovakia*.[50]

In *Kontrova v Slovakia* the applicant had been subjected to domestic violence by her husband. She alleged that the police had failed to take appropriate action to protect her children's lives under article 2 and her private and family life under article 8 of the Convention, despite knowing of her husband's abusive behaviour. He had threatened to kill himself and their two children and he had in fact carried out this threat. Under domestic law in Slovakia, the police had various specific obligations, such as accepting and registering the applicant's complaint; launching a criminal investigation; and immediately commencing proceedings against the applicant's husband. However, they had failed to comply with any of these obligations.

In holding that there had been a breach of the children's right to life, the Court reiterated the frequently cited principle that article 2,

> enjoins the State not only to refrain from the intentional and unlawful taking of life, but also to take appropriate steps to safeguard the lives of those within its jurisdiction . . . It also extends in appropriate circumstances to a positive obligation on the authorities to take preventive operational measures to protect an individual whose life is at risk from the criminal acts of another individual.[51]

In addition, the applicant alleged that the violation of article 2 constituted a violation of her own private and family life under article 8; however, the Court held that in the light of the finding of a violation of article 2, it was not necessary to examine the case under article 8 also.

In this case therefore, the Court found a violation of the Convention in a situation involving domestic violence. However, it should be noted that the breach was found in relation to the right to life of the children. The abuse suffered by the applicant herself was not directly addressed.

The next case in this area was *Bevacqua and S v Bulgaria*. In this instance the applicants were a victim of domestic violence and her young son. It was argued that there had been violations of articles 3 and 8 of the Convention, as the authorities had failed to protect the first applicant against the violent behaviour of her former husband and had failed to take the necessary measures to secure respect for the family life of both applicants.

The Court examined the complaints under article 8, but not under article 3. In holding that there had been a violation of article 8, the Court stated that,

> At the relevant time Bulgarian law did not provide for specific administrative and policing measures (in relation to domestic violence) and the measures taken by the police and prosecuting authorities on the basis of their general powers did not prove effective . . . In the Court's view, the authorities' failure to impose sanctions or otherwise enforce Mr N'.s obligation to refrain from unlawful acts was critical in the circumstances of this case,

as it amounted to a refusal to provide the immediate assistance the applicants needed. The authorities' view that no such assistance was due as the dispute concerned a 'private matter' was incompatible with their positive obligations to secure the enjoyment of the applicants' Article 8 rights.[52]

This case, therefore, was very significant in that the Court held that there was a breach of article 8 in respect of the actual abuse suffered by a victim of domestic violence.

In *Opuz v Turkey* the applicant alleged that the authorities had failed to protect herself and her mother from domestic violence, which had resulted in the death of her mother and her own ill-treatment. She complained that the authorities had failed to safeguard the right to life of her mother, who had been killed by her husband, in violation of article 2 of the Convention. The Court concluded that 'the criminal law system, as applied in the instant case, did not have an adequate deterrent effect capable of ensuring the effective prevention of the unlawful acts committed by [the applicant's husband]'.[53] There had thus been a breach of article 2.

The applicant also alleged that she had been subjected to violence, injury and death threats but that the authorities were negligent towards her situation, which caused her pain and fear in violation of article 3 of the Convention. She argued that the injuries she had suffered amounted to torture within the meaning of article 3. The Court held that the violence suffered was sufficiently serious to amount to ill-treatment within the meaning of article 3, although it did not specify whether it amounted to torture, as opposed to inhuman or degrading treatment. The Court concluded that there had been a violation of article 3 'as a result of the State authorities' failure to take protective measures in the form of effective deterrence against serious breaches of the applicant's personal integrity by her husband'.[54] This case, therefore, represented another very important step in the Court's jurisprudence in this area, in that it had now held that domestic violence can constitute a violation of article 3.

In addition, the applicant claimed that there had been a breach of article 14 of the Convention, an argument which was also upheld by the Court. The applicant demonstrated through statistical data that domestic violence affected mainly women, and established that judicial passivity in Turkey created a climate conducive to domestic violence. It was stated that, 'Bearing in mind . . . that the general and discriminatory judicial passivity in Turkey, albeit unintentional, mainly affected women, the Court considers that the violence suffered by the applicant and her mother may be regarded as gender-based violence which is a form of discrimination against women'.[55] Generally, breaches of article 14 involve direct discrimination. It is usually very difficult for an applicant to argue that indirect discrimination violates article 14.[56] The fact that the Court was willing to find such a violation in the context of a case involving domestic violence is therefore very significant.

In *E.S. and Others v Slovakia* the applicants were a mother and her three children. All four applicants had suffered abuse from the first applicant's husband. The Court held that the article 3 and article 8 rights of all four applicants had been violated due to the failure of the authorities to protect them in an appropriate manner from the treatment to which they had been subjected.[57]

Overall, it can be seen from these cases that states clearly have positive obligations to ensure that their criminal justice systems are of a certain standard in dealing with domestic violence. In this jurisprudence, particular attention was paid to the response of police forces to the issue. These cases undoubtedly constitute an extremely important development in the response of human rights law to domestic violence. Nevertheless, problems still remain.

Limitations on the obligation to take operational measures

As the *Osman* case demonstrates, in order to impose a positive obligation to take operational measures to protect the right of an individual, several criteria must be satisfied. In *Osman* the Court stated that,

> it must be established . . . that the authorities knew or ought to have known at the time of the existence of a real and immediate risk to the life of an identified individual or individuals from the criminal acts of a third party and that they failed to take measures within the scope of their powers which, judged reasonably, might have been expected to avoid that risk.[58]

However, the failure in question does not need to reach the standard of gross negligence in order to constitute a violation of article 2. It is enough to demonstrate that 'the authorities did not do all that could reasonably be expected of them to avoid a real and immediate risk to life of which they have or ought to have knowledge'.[59] Therefore, the authorities will only have a positive obligation to protect an individual's right to life from other individuals in a limited number of cases.

Indeed when the criteria were applied to the facts of the *Osman* case itself, the Court held that no breach of article 2 had been established. It stated that,

> In the view of the Court the applicants have failed to point to any decisive stage in the sequence of events leading up to the tragic shooting when it could be said that the police knew or ought to have known that the lives of the Osman family were at real and immediate risk.[60]

The police could not have acted in a manner contrary to the presumption of innocence, and neither could they have used the powers of arrest and search if they lacked the necessary standard of suspicion. Likewise, although the Court held that article 8 could also give rise to positive duties on the police to take effective preventive measures, there was no breach of article 8 in the present case, as the police had taken all reasonable steps.

The *Osman* case thus illustrates that the doctrine of positive obligations has limitations. It was emphasised that the authorities must actually have notice of an immediate risk to a particular individual, and the state can only be held liable if the authorities fail to take measures that they could reasonably be expected to take. Even though the police in *Osman* had been aware of the teacher's behaviour, they had not kept watch on the Osmans' home, or informed them of what was occurring. They had also allowed the teacher to abscond. Yet it was still held by the European Court that all reasonable steps had been taken and that the state was not in breach of its positive obligations under articles 2 and 8 of the Convention.

Applying this principle to cases of domestic violence, it appears that public authorities could only be held liable for failing to protect a victim if the authorities were already cognisant of the situation. Nevertheless, this would still mean that the state could be held to be in breach of human rights standards if the police omitted to take steps to protect known victims, or failed to respond adequately when called to the scene of an incident of domestic abuse. Another difficulty that arises in this context is that domestic violence takes place behind closed doors. It is an 'unseen' crime which victims are often too frightened or too ashamed to report. The British Crime Survey found that the police come to know of less than one in four of the worst cases of domestic violence.[61] Therefore, many incidents of violence against women in the home remain undetected. This casts doubts on the effectiveness of the duty on the police to take operational measures in relation to the issue of domestic violence. If the police are not alerted, then this duty cannot come into play.[62]

The responses of states to the judgments of the Court

It is also worth noting that the effectiveness of court judgments depends to a substantial degree on the receptiveness of the legislature, and indeed public opinion generally, to change. A case that illustrates this point is *A v United Kingdom*.[63] In this case the applicant was a nine-year-old boy who had been severely beaten by his stepfather with a garden cane. The stepfather was charged with assault occasioning actual bodily harm; however, his defence of reasonable chastisement was successful and he was acquitted by a jury. The applicant took a case to the European Court claiming that his right to be free from torture and inhuman or degrading treatment or punishment under article 3 of the Convention had been violated.

The Court held that a beating of the severity that had been inflicted upon the applicant constituted treatment that was prohibited by article 3. It was then considered whether the state could be held responsible for the violation. The Court stated that,

> the obligation on the High Contracting Parties under article 1 of the Convention to secure to everyone within their jurisdiction the rights and freedoms defined in the Convention, taken together with article 3, requires

States to take measures designed to ensure that individuals within their jurisdiction are not subjected to torture or inhuman or degrading treatment or punishment, including such ill-treatment administered by private individuals.[64]

The Court commented that,

despite the fact that the applicant had been subjected to treatment of sufficient severity to fall within the scope of Article 3, the jury acquitted his stepfather . . . In the Court's view, the law did not provide adequate protection to the applicant against the treatment or punishment contrary to Article 3.[65]

However, the response of the UK to *A v UK* was to enact section 58 of the Children Act 2004, which states that reasonable punishment is no longer a defence in relation to certain offences, such as assault occasioning actual bodily harm or grievous bodily harm. Nevertheless, it still constitutes a defence to lesser offences. It thus seems that although the UK is abiding by the strict letter of the judgment of the European Court, it is not in compliance with the sentiment behind the judgment, which appears to have been to protect children. The use of human rights law through a litigation strategy will not be fully effective, even if the court makes a positive judgment, if the legislature and public opinion generally are not receptive to change.

The provision of resources to victims of domestic violence

It has been argued that the most important needs of victims of domestic violence are for social support measures, such as monetary resources, refuge accommodation and housing.[66] In a small number of cases the European Court has established that in certain circumstances the state has a duty to provide resources to individuals to prevent violations of their rights. The seminal case in this area is *Airey v Ireland*.[67] In this instance the applicant alleged that her husband had frequently threatened her with, and occasionally subjected her to, physical violence. In 1972 he was convicted of assaulting the applicant. He then left the matrimonial home. In Ireland, divorce was not possible in 1979, the date *Airey* came before the European Court. However, spouses could be relieved from the duty of cohabiting by the High Court issuing a decree of judicial separation. The parties to such proceedings could conduct their case in person. However, in the vast majority of cases they had legal representation. The issue in *Airey* revolved around the fact that legal aid was not available in Ireland for the purpose of seeking a judicial separation. The applicant argued that this breached her right of access to a court under article 6 of the Convention, and also her right to private life under article 8. It was accepted by all parties that the applicant could not afford to pay for legal representation.

The Court stated that it was not realistic to expect the applicant to conduct her own case. It was pointed out that witnesses may have to be called and examined, and expert testimony may have to be put forward. Also, the emotional involvement of the applicant in a case of this nature would make the ordeal even more difficult. The Court thus held that a person in the applicant's position could not present her own case in an effective manner.

The Court pointed out that,

> fulfilment of a duty under the Convention on occasion necessitates some positive action on the part of the State; in such circumstances the State cannot simply remain passive and there is no room to distinguish between acts and omissions. The obligation to secure an effective right of access to the courts falls into this category of duty.[68]

By not making the decree of judicial separation effectively accessible the state had breached the applicant's right of access to a court. There had thus been a violation of article 6.

As regards the article 8 claim, the European Court commented that,

> although the object of article 8 is essentially that of protecting the individual against arbitrary interference by the public authorities, it does not merely compel the State to abstain from such interference; in addition to this primary negative undertaking, there may be positive obligations inherent in effective respect for private or family life.[69]

It was pointed out that in Ireland spouses were entitled, in certain instances, to petition for a decree of judicial separation, in recognition of the fact that protection of private life may necessitate being relieved from the duty to live together. In order to ensure effective respect for private life, the state had a positive obligation to ensure that the applicant had effective access to this means of protection. The applicant was unable to seek legal recognition of her separation from her abusive husband. There was thus a breach of article 8.

The *Airey* case is a clear example of the Court's application of the positive obligations doctrine, as regards both article 6 and article 8. The case was a rather dynamic judgment, especially as it took place around 30 years ago. The Court essentially held that states may have to ensure effective access to particular means of protection and that in certain instances this may entail the expenditure of monetary resources. It is unlikely that the original drafters of the Convention intended that this be the case.

It is notable that the decision in *Airey* was not unanimous. It was held by five votes to two that there had been a violation of article 6, and by four votes to three that there had been a breach of article 8. It is somewhat unsurprising that the Irish judge dissented. He pointed out that there was no absolute bar on the applicant's access to the High Court. Another dissenting judge commented that there was, no obligation for the Contracting States to grant free legal aid in civil cases . . . An individual's ability or inability to claim his or her rights under the Convention may stem from several reasons, one of them being his or her financial position. It is, of course, deplorable that this should be so. To correct this situation, the States which have ratified the Convention have taken and are taking countless measures, thus promoting economic and social development in our part of the globe. The ideas underlying the Convention, as well as its wording, make it clear that it is concerned with problems other than the one facing us in this case. The war on poverty cannot be won through broad interpretation of the Convention for the Protection of Human Rights and Fundamental Freedoms.[70]

He went on to opine that such a broad interpretation of the Convention, 'would open up problems whose range and complexity cannot be foreseen but which would doubtless prove to be beyond the power of the Convention and the institutions set up by it'.[71] The judge also stated that the duty to respect the applicant's private and family life did not include a duty to provide her with financial support in order to assist her to obtain a judicial separation.

These views highlight the difficulties surrounding the enforcement of socio-economic rights that were discussed in Chapter 1. Oloka-Onyango comments that,

The marginalization of [socio-economic rights] can be discerned not only from the level of international attention paid to them, but also with respect to the approach of governments, judges, non-governmental actors, and even academics to the subject.[72]

In *Airey*, Judge Thor Vilhjalmsson was of the opinion that, 'The war on poverty cannot be won through broad interpretation of the Convention for the Protection of Human Rights and Fundamental Freedoms'.[73] He argued that the provision of social support measures simply does not fall within the ambit of human rights law. The Court in *Airey* did hold that ensuring effective access to particular means of protection may in certain situations entail the expenditure of monetary resources; however, it must be remembered that the Court did not hold that civil legal aid must be granted in such situations as that which arose in *Airey*. The Court merely stated that there must be effective access to the protective measure of a decree of judicial separation. This obligation could have been fulfilled by, for example, simplifying the procedures.

It seems therefore that one cannot argue on the basis of *Airey* that the state has an obligation to provide victims of domestic violence with social support measures such as financial resources, refuge accommodation and permanent housing. As was discussed in Chapter 1, there generally are limits on what courts can achieve. As Chayes comments, it is much more difficult for courts to order that affirmative programmes be put in place than it is for them to hold that a certain practice be halted.[74] Nevertheless, it is not impossible for courts to make such affirmative orders. It is unlikely that the European Court would specifically hold that refuges should be built. However, it is not inconceivable that it could order that steps should be taken to re-house victims of abuse. In *Dulas v Turkey*[75] the applicant had been forcibly evicted from her home by security forces. Her possessions were completely destroyed and she was forced to leave her village. The European Court held that the applicant's right to be free from inhuman and degrading treatment under article 3 had been breached. Paglione comments that,

> women forced to abandon their homes by their violent partners and individuals forced to leave their homes by state agents are victims of the same process; they are coercively removed from their homes, chased away, and left without their possessions and with no alternative place to go.[76]

It is not impossible that the Court could hold that the rights of victims of domestic violence are similarly violated if the state does not take sufficient steps to provide victims with accommodation.

The Court does seem to be prepared to move with the times and there is a growing consensus that important counters to domestic violence are the provision of social assistance and the promotion of awareness of the problem. The European Court has repeatedly stated that the Convention is a 'living instrument which . . . must be interpreted in the light of present-day conditions'.[77] As Mowbray comments, the Court has sought to apply the Convention rights 'in ways that provide genuine benefits to the 800 million persons falling within its jurisdiction'.[78]

The margin of appreciation

Another potential difficulty for the development of the jurisprudence of the European Court on domestic violence arises due to the margin of appreciation. This doctrine is illustrated by *Stubbings and Others v United Kingdom*.[79] The case involved a number of women who alleged they had been subjected to abuse as children. It was only as adults that they recognised the connection between the abuse they had suffered and their subsequent mental health problems. However, under the terms of the Limitation Act 1980, civil proceedings could only be commenced either within six years of the assault, or within six years of the victim's eighteenth birthday. The applicants in *Stubbings* were all time-barred from taking proceedings. They brought a case to the European Court, claiming that their rights under articles 6, 8 and 14 of the Convention had been violated.

However, the Court held that there had been no breaches of the rights of the applicants. It commented that the right to a court contained in article 6 was 'not absolute, but may be subject to limitations; these are permitted by implication since the right of access by its very nature calls for regulation by the State'.[80] It was held that the limitations applied in this instance were proportionate to the aims to be achieved, and thus there had been no violation of article 6.

As regards the alleged breach of article 8, the Court acknowledged that the concept of 'private life' covered the physical and moral integrity of the person. It was reiterated that there may 'be positive obligations inherent in an effective respect for private or family life', and that these 'may involve the adoption of measures designed to secure respect for private life even in the sphere of the relations of individuals between themselves'.[81] However, the Court emphasised that states had a margin of appreciation as to the means by which they chose to fulfil their obligations. In this case, the state had not exceeded its margin of appreciation, and thus there had been no violation of article 8. The Court commented that, 'article 8 does not necessarily require that States fulfil their positive obligation to secure respect for private life by the provision of unlimited civil remedies in circumstances where criminal law sanctions are in operation'.[82]

Nevertheless, as the two dissenting judges in the case pointed out, it seems that the state was allowed a very wide margin of appreciation in this case. Judge MacDonald commented that the statutory time limit was 'disproportionate in that it unreasonably deprives the applicants of a right to access to court and thus lies beyond the margin of appreciation enjoyed by States in establishing time limits for the introduction of proceedings'.[83] Judge Foighel stated that he found, 'the margin of appreciation recognised by the majority far too wide, since the English legislation denies the very essence of the right of access to court, in a situation where applicants had no realistic opportunity to go to court at any earlier stage'.[84]

The *Stubbings* case again illustrates the fact that the European Court may allow a relatively wide margin of appreciation when dealing with the issue of positive obligations, although this could, of course, change. The Court has used the concept of state responsibility to transcend the public/private dichotomy to some extent. However, it seems that the public/private divide may still be problematic in that the European Court appears to grant a wider margin of appreciation in cases involving only private individuals than it does in 'traditional' human rights cases, where it is the state that is carrying out the human rights abuse directly. Therefore if, for example, a case concerning the state's positive obligations in relation to the provision of social support measures to victims of domestic violence came before the Court, it is probable that a similarly wide margin of appreciation may be afforded.

Conclusion

The European Court of Human Rights has certainly taken an activist approach in interpreting the fundamentally negative provisions of the European Convention in such a way as to impose positive obligations on states to protect the rights of individuals from threats posed by other private individuals, in certain circumstances. Cases such as *Osman v United Kingdom*[85] illustrate the dynamic nature of the Court's jurisprudence in this area. As Mowbray comments, 'The Court's case law regarding positive obligations has contributed to the partial erosion of the generational gap between convention rights and later generations of international human rights'.[86] Domestic violence constitutes a clear violation of articles 2, 3, 8 and 14 of the Convention, as has now been recognised by the Court in its recent jurisprudence. It has now been firmly established that states have positive obligations to ensure that their criminal justice systems are of a sufficient standard to deal with domestic violence. Particular attention has been paid to the response of the police to the issue, although it should be remembered that there are limitations on the obligation to take operational measures to protect the rights of an individual.

The European Court has certainly used the concept of state responsibility to transcend the public/private dichotomy. The Court has shown itself to be willing to enter the private sphere and deal with cases in which the rights of one individual have been breached by another. However, it is possible that the public/private divide may still cause difficulties for the effectiveness of human rights law. It appears from the *Stubbings*[87] case that states may be granted a wider margin of appreciation in cases involving their positive obligations to protect the rights of individuals from being violated by the actions of other private entities, although this could, of course, change.

The case of *A v United Kingdom*[88] illustrates a further difficulty with the effectiveness of a litigation strategy. If a court makes a dynamic judgment upholding human rights standards, such a judgment may not be fully effective if bodies such as the legislature do not also have a commitment to human rights norms. The result of *A v UK* also illustrates the point that states may adhere to the strict letter of the law without acting in the spirit of human rights standards. Such an attitude will decrease the effectiveness of human rights law.

There are limits on what courts can achieve, particularly in the area of socio-economic rights. Generally courts must adhere to the particular issue in the actual cases before them. They cannot make sweeping statements on societal issues. The European Court in *Airey*[89] did envisage cases in which the state may be obliged to expend monetary resources in order to ensure access to particular forms of protection. Nevertheless, one cannot argue on the basis of this case that there is a general obligation on states to provide refuge accommodation for all victims of domestic violence. However, courts can set general standards and one should not discount the possibility that the European Court may in the future place an obligation on states to take steps to re-house victims.

4 The Human Rights Act 1998

Could the United Kingdom courts rise to the challenge?

The previous chapter outlined the potential held by the case law of the European Court of Human Rights on positive obligations to contribute to the fight against domestic violence. Although there are limitations on this potential, nevertheless the European Court has developed jurisprudence that could be used beneficially in this area. Governments have been repeatedly reminded that not only must they refrain from violating human rights standards, they also have duties to take positive steps to ensure that the rights of individuals are protected effectively. The European Convention has been incorporated into UK law by the Human Rights Act 1998.[1] However, could the UK courts rise to the challenge and use Convention rights to assist victims of domestic violence?

This chapter will refer to the issues raised in Chapter 1 of the book. The issue of the public/private divide will be examined through a discussion of the horizontal effect of the Human Rights Act. The problem of conflicting rights is brought into focus by the difficulty of alleged perpetrators relying on human rights law. Problems surrounding the implementation of rights are highlighted by the issue of deference; the limits on what courts can achieve and difficulties surrounding socio-economic rights; and questions relating to the ability of law to deal with an 'unseen' crime. Essentially, the chapter will examine whether the UK courts could use the Human Rights Act to achieve the three categories of measures that are most highlighted by commentators in the UK as being necessary in the area of domestic violence – improvements in the criminal justice system, the provision of social support measures for victims, such as refuge accommodation, and the implementation of awareness raising programmes (see Chapter 2).

The horizontal effect of the Human Rights Act 1998

The issue of whether the Human Rights Act would have horizontal effect certainly provoked a great deal of speculation. A somewhat heated debate developed on the question of whether the Act would have any effect between private individuals.[2] As discussed in Chapter 1, the public/private dichotomy has caused great difficulties concerning the effectiveness of human rights law.

However, it was also noted that human rights law has developed in such a manner as to create a range of ways in which it may now enter into the private sphere. Horizontal effect can arise either directly or indirectly. In jurisdictions such as South Africa, human rights obligations are placed directly on individuals. However, the European Court of Human Rights takes a more indirect approach whereby duties can be placed on the state to ensure that the rights of individuals are protected from violation by other private parties. Horizontal effect also arises in an indirect manner under the Human Rights Act. This was shown in cases such as *Douglas, Zeta-Jones and Northern and Shell plc v Hello! Ltd.*,[3] *Venables and another v News Group Newspapers Ltd and others*[4] and *Campbell v MGN Ltd.*[5]

The first case concerned an injunction that had been granted preventing *Hello!* magazine from publishing unauthorised photographs of the wedding of two celebrities. The question arose of whether the Human Rights Act had horizontal effect, thus requiring the court to protect the right to privacy of the claimants. It was noted that, under section 6 of the Act, the courts, as public authorities, must act in a way that is compatible with Convention rights. Therefore, this could mean that courts had a duty to protect individuals from interference with their article 8 rights even where the threat was from a private body, as was the case in this instance. Although somewhat ambivalent,[6] *Douglas v Hello!* could thus be used to argue that the courts have a duty to protect the article 8 rights of victims of domestic violence from the threats posed by their abusers.

In the *Venables* case, the killers of James Bulger were seeking to have an injunction granted preventing the publication of details of their new identities. They claimed that there was a risk to their article 2 right to life and article 3 right to be free from inhuman or degrading treatment. Butler-Sloss LJ held that the court had a positive obligation to protect the rights of the claimants. She stated that the information in question could be protected by the law of confidence. The injunction was granted. In relation to domestic violence it could be argued that the courts likewise have positive obligations to protect the article 2 and article 3 rights of victims from violation through the actions of perpetrators.

In *Campbell v MGN Ltd* the defendant newspaper had published various articles concerning the claimant. These articles stated that she was a drug addict and that she was attending Narcotics Anonymous. Details of her treatment were published, as were photographs of the claimant leaving the meetings. The claimant brought proceedings for breach of confidence and compensation under the Data Protection Act 1998. The judge upheld the claim. The Court of Appeal discharged the judge's order and the claimant appealed to the House of Lords. The primary issue in this case was the question of how a balance was to be struck between the claimant's right to respect for private and family life under article 8 of the European Convention on Human Rights and the right of the newspaper to freedom of expression under article 10 of the Convention.

The House of Lords held that the right to privacy had to be balanced against the right of the media to impart information to the public. The court had to decide whether a legitimate aim was pursued by the publication of the material and whether the benefits that would be achieved by publication were proportionate to the interference with the right to privacy. It was held that the interference with the claimant's right to privacy was unjustifiable. There was no pressing social need to disclose the information and no democratic or political values were at stake. The private nature of meetings such as those of Narcotics Anonymous encouraged people to attend, and disclosure of the information in question had potential to cause considerable harm. The House of Lords stated that in order to assess whether disclosure would be objectionable, it was necessary to put oneself into the shoes of a reasonable person who was in need of the treatment in question. Taking the article as a whole along with the photographs, a drug addict undergoing treatment would be expected to find the disclosure very distressing and offensive. The orders of the trial judge should therefore be restored.[7]

This case constitutes a clear example of the horizontal effect of the Human Rights Act. The right of the claimant to private and family life was upheld by the House of Lords against encroachment by another private party. It could likewise be argued that the Human Rights Act could be used to uphold the article 8 rights of victims of domestic violence.

It can now be stated with certainty that those who predicted that the Human Rights Act would have at least some degree of horizontal effect have been vindicated. By acknowledging the horizontal effects of the Human Rights Act, the courts have laid the doctrinal foundations for using the Act to provide assistance to victims of domestic violence. The fact that the Act does have horizontal effect demonstrates that the UK judges are willing to transcend the public/private dichotomy in cases involving human rights. This finding seems to indicate that the public/private divide may not now pose as great a problem for the effectiveness of human rights law as once was the case. Those involved in the original drafting of the main human rights treaties would certainly not have envisaged that the discourse of rights would be used in cases such as those discussed in this section.

Has domestic violence been recognised as a human rights issue in the United Kingdom?

In *McPherson v Secretary of State for the Home Department*[8] the appellant came to the United Kingdom from Jamaica. Two of her children also came to the UK. However, the appellant was convicted of supplying a Class A controlled drug and a deportation order was signed by the Home Secretary. The two children were also served with notices of intention to deport. The appellant claimed that deporting her to Jamaica would breach her rights under article 3 and article 8 of the European Convention. The article 8 claim related to her relationship with the two children. The article 3 claim related to her fear of violence on the part of her former partner.

It was held by the Court of Appeal that the appellant's claims should be remitted to another adjudicator, as the previous adjudicator had made no decision on the article 8 point. However, Arden LJ commented that,

> If the appellant were able to show to the requisite standard of proof that the remedies provided under the law of Jamaica against domestic violence are unlikely to be an effective deterrent, in my judgment she would have shown that her removal from the United Kingdom to Jamaica would violate her rights under art 3 of the European Convention on Human Rights.[9]

Arden LJ cited the judgment of the European Court in *Osman v United Kingdom*,[10] in which the Court stated that 'The State's obligation . . . extends beyond its primary duty to secure the right to life by putting in place effective criminal law provisions to deter the commission of offences against the person'. Arden LJ commented that, in her judgment, the requirement that the provisions of the law safeguarding the right to life must be 'effective' applied equally to the right to be free from torture and inhuman and degrading treatment under article 3, as both articles 2 and 3 are non-derogable rights. She also cited *X and Y v the Netherlands*[11] as establishing the need for 'effective deterrence', and stated that 'to be "effective", measures for the purpose of art 3 must be those which attain an adequate degree of efficacy in practice as well as exist in theory'.[12]

The *McPherson* case clearly illustrates the fact that the UK courts have recognised domestic violence as a human rights issue. This development in itself is welcome, given the fact that for many years domestic violence was not seen as a human rights issue, even by the international human rights community. At first glance it appears that *McPherson* displays a willingness to use the Human Rights Act in an effective manner, and this case does accord some hope in relation to how the courts might apply the Act in a case of domestic violence, in that it is acknowledged that domestic violence constitutes a violation of article 3 of the European Convention. It is also stated that, not only must states take measures to prevent violations of article 3, but these measures must have 'an adequate degree of efficacy in practice'. It could therefore be argued, for example, that not only must it be possible for a victim to have her abuser prosecuted, it must also be ensured that police, prosecutors and judges act in such a manner as to make the system effective and efficient. However, it must be remembered that in *McPherson*, it was the Jamaican system for dealing with domestic violence that was at issue. It would not be such a radical step for a UK court to criticise the Jamaican system as it would be for it to hold that the UK system were inadequate. It seems that domestic violence is an even greater problem in Jamaica than it is in the UK.

Another fairly encouraging case is *R v Immigration Appeal Tribunal and another, ex parte Shah; Islam and others v Secretary of State for the Home Department*.[13] In this case the appellants were two Pakistani women who had been forced by their husbands to leave their homes. They sought asylum in the UK, arguing that they were refugees as they had a fear of persecution due to 'membership of a particular social group' within the meaning of article 1 A(2) of the Convention relating to the Status of Refugees. Both women had suffered domestic violence. The House of Lords found that this constituted persecution in Pakistan as the state was unwilling or unable to offer the women any protection. It would be useless for them to complain to the police or the courts.

Lord Hoffmann stated that the Convention was concerned not with all cases of persecution, but with persecution which was based on discrimination.[14] However, he also proceeded to comment that the meaning of the term 'social group' could not be confined to the groups that the framers of the Convention may have had in mind.[15] The House of Lords held that the appellants certainly feared persecution within the meaning of the Convention. As Lord Hoffmann commented,

> What is the reason for the persecution which the appellants fear? Here it is important to notice that it is made up of two elements. First, there is the threat of violence to Mrs Islam by her husband and his political friends and to Mrs Shah by her husband. This is a personal affair, directed against them as individuals. Second, there is the inability or unwillingness of the state to do anything to protect them. There is nothing personal about this. The evidence was that the state would not assist them because they were women. It denied them a protection against violence which it would have given to men. These two elements have to be combined to constitute persecution within the meaning of the convention.[16]

The House of Lords also ruled that this fear of persecution was due to 'membership of a particular social group'. Lord Hoffmann stated that,

> In the case of Mrs Islam, the legal and social conditions which . . . existed in Pakistan and which left her unprotected against violence by men were discriminatory against women. This means that she feared persecution because she was a woman. There was no need to construct a more restricted social group simply for the purpose of satisfying the causal connection which the convention requires.[17]

This important case meant that women who had suffered domestic violence in their own countries and who were not protected by the public authorities there, could claim the status of refugees. However, again, this case involved women who suffered domestic violence in other countries. In no way did the case involve any criticism of the UK system for dealing with domestic violence.

The deference shown by judges

It can be seen therefore that the courts have recognised some degree of horizontal effect under the Human Rights Act. They have also recognised that domestic violence is a human rights issue. These are certainly positive developments. However, a number of problems remain. In Chapter 1 of this book it was emphasised that the effectiveness of the courts depends on the attitudes of individual judges. As Palmer comments, 'Rights are capable of being given a wide range of interpretations'.[18] If judges are unwilling to use human rights instruments in a dynamic way, this will create difficulties for the effectiveness of human rights law. The judiciary displays a deferential attitude when dealing with certain types of cases under the Human Rights Act.[19]

For example, in many cases the courts appear to be willing to accord a wide degree of discretion to public authorities in relation to planning decisions. In the *Alconbury* case[20] it was stated that,

> A degree of central control is essential to the orderly . . . development of town and country. Parliament has entrusted the requisite degree of control to the Secretary of State . . . To substitute for the Secretary of State an independent . . . body with no central electoral accountability . . . would be profoundly undemocratic.

A similar approach was taken in a number of immigration cases. For example, in *Isiko*[21] it was held that,

> In cases involving immigration policies . . . it will be appropriate for the courts to recognise that there is an area of judgment within which the judiciary will defer, on democratic grounds, to the considered opinion of the elected body or person whose decision is said to be incompatible.

It seems that the judiciary displays a deferential attitude when dealing with certain areas that are relevant to domestic violence. For example, the courts tend to adopt a particularly deferential approach in relation to questions surrounding the allocation of resources. The argument is put forward that judges do not have the expertise to assess sufficiently the issues involved in such cases.[22] In *R (on the application of Douglas) v North Tyneside Metropolitan Borough Council and another*[23] it was stated that,

> It is not for the courts to interfere with the Secretary of State's funding arrangements provided they are lawfully made and applied . . . The courts in my judgment have to be careful when considering an issue of justification . . . not to trespass into the discretionary area of resource allocation. That is an area that is not justiciable.[24]

Such an approach may be problematic as regards the issue of domestic violence as it has been commented that it is social support measures that are most needed by victims.[25]

It also seems that policing is an area in which the courts will allow a wide margin of discretion. In *Osman v United Kingdom* the European Court of Human

Rights stated that it was necessary to bear in mind 'the difficulties involved in policing modern societies'.[26] *Re E*[27] involved an application for judicial review by the mother of one of the children affected by 'the Holy Cross dispute', in which loyalist protesters in Belfast tried to prevent pupils at a Roman Catholic primary school and their parents from walking to the school along their usual route. The applicant sought a declaration that the Chief Constable of the Royal Ulster Constabulary and the Secretary of State for Northern Ireland failed to ensure safe passage for her and her daughter to the Holy Cross Primary School. It was claimed that the rights of the children and parents under articles 2, 3 and 14 of the European Convention on Human Rights and article 2 of the First Protocol had been violated. The application for judicial review was dismissed and the applicant's subsequent appeals were unsuccessful. The court commented that,

> policing options and decisions do not readily permit . . . uncomplicated solutions, . . . It is precisely because the Police Service is better equipped to appreciate and evaluate the dangers of such secondary protests and disturbances that an area of discretionary judgment must be allowed them, particularly in the realm of operational decisions.[28]

As policing is a crucial issue in relation to domestic violence, a wide margin of discretion in this area may prove problematic.

The limits on what courts can achieve and difficulties surrounding socio-economic rights

Oxfordshire County Council v R (on the application of Khan) and another[29] involved an applicant who was a national of Pakistan. She was granted leave to enter the United Kingdom to join her husband, and she went to live with him in Oxford. However, she suffered severe domestic violence. She left the matrimonial home, but was subsequently kidnapped by her husband and his family. She escaped, but was captured again by her husband's family. The police then intervened and she took a place in a refuge. The Oxfordshire County Council undertook an assessment of her needs, pursuant to section 47 of the National Health Service and Community Care Act 1990. It was decided that Mrs Khan needed safe and secure accommodation, legal advice and finances. Her solicitors requested accommodation under section 21 of the National Assistance Act 1948 and the provision of financial support under section 2 of the Local Government Act 2000. However, the Council replied that Mrs Khan did not meet the criteria for such social support, as she was not suffering from a physical disability, learning disability or mental health condition. In reply to the argument that she was at risk of physical harm from her husband, the Council stated that Mrs Khan could take steps to prevent such violence by going to the police or taking out an injunction.

Arguments were made under articles 3 and 8 of the European Convention and it was considered whether section 3 of the Human Rights Act required the relevant legislation to be interpreted in such a way as to avoid violations of the Convention rights. The Court of Appeal emphasised 'the extremely limited scope for the operation of arts 3 and 8 in this area'.[30] It was stated that the European Court has not yet given a decision that a state has violated articles 3 or 8 due to a failure to provide welfare support. Nevertheless, it was acknowledged that the European Court has recognised the possibility of such a breach. The Court of Appeal concluded that, 'while Strasbourg has recognised the possibility that art 8 may oblige a State to provide positive welfare support in special circumstances, it has made it plain that neither art 3 nor art 8 imposes such a requirement as a matter of course'.[31] It was decided that section 3 of the Human Rights Act did not require the relevant legislation to be interpreted in any special manner.

This case indicates that the UK courts may be reluctant to hold that the state has a duty under the Convention rights to provide accommodation, financial resources or childcare facilities to victims of domestic violence. The Court of Appeal in *Khan* appeared to be strongly opposed to the view that the state may be under an obligation to provide such social support measures.

Indeed there are other cases in which the courts have demonstrated their reluctance to hold that the state has a duty to provide financial resources. *R (on the application of Douglas) v North Tyneside Metropolitan Borough Council and another*[32] concerned a claimant who had been refused a student loan for a part-time higher education course. He argued that he had been discriminated against on grounds of age and therefore his rights under article 14 of the European Convention, taken together with article 2 of the First Protocol, had been violated. In dismissing his claim, the court stated that,

> It is not for the courts to interfere with the Secretary of State's funding arrangements provided they are lawfully made and applied. Funding arrangements for further education fall within the general area where social and economic judgments are required that involve the allocation of finite resources and the balancing of competing claims. The courts in my judgment have to be careful when considering an issue of justification such as would arise in the present case were art 2 to be engaged not to trespass into the discretionary area of resource allocation. That is an area that is not justiciable.[33]

In *Anufrijeva*[34] the claimants argued that the local authority had failed to discharge their duty to provide them with accommodation that met the special needs of one family member, resulting in the quality of family life being impaired. The court concluded that,

> Art 8 is capable of imposing on a state a positive obligation to provide support. We find it hard to conceive, however, of a situation in which the

predicament of an individual will be such that Art 8 requires him to be provided with welfare support, where his predicament is not sufficiently severe to engage Art 3. Article 8 may more readily be engaged where a family unit is involved. Where the welfare of children is at stake, Art 8 may require the provision of welfare support in a manner which enables family life to continue.[35]

Again the overall tenor of the judgment indicates the reluctance of the courts to place duties on the state to provide social support measures. Nevertheless, it could be argued that domestic violence does violate the article 3 rights of the victim. It could also be claimed that in many cases of violence against women in the home, the welfare of children is at stake.

In *R (on the application of Limbuela) v Secretary of State for the Home Department; R (on the application of Tesema) v Secretary of State for the Home Department; R (on the application of Adam) v Secretary of State for the Home Department*[36] the House of Lords held that the state had a duty to provide accommodation and support to asylum seekers in a state of destitution, if their circumstances fell within the category of inhuman or degrading treatment under article 3 of the European Convention on Human Rights. This case does give some hope that the House of Lords (now the Supreme Court) could potentially hold that the state has a duty to provide support to victims of domestic violence. Nevertheless, it must be remembered that the respondents in this case were each suffering or facing 'a life of extreme deprivation, sleeping rough on the streets of London, not permitted to work and denied all support'.[37] They had no reliable access to food or to washing facilities. The House of Lords was making its decision based on these very extreme circumstances and it seems that the case does not therefore automatically indicate that the courts would be willing to place obligations on the state to provide social support measures to victims of domestic violence.

As was discussed in Chapter 1, in the UK at least, courts cannot make sweeping statements on societal issues. In addition, imposing positive obligations on states to provide monetary resources, accommodation and childcare facilities to victims of domestic violence gives rise to the same criticisms with which socio-economic rights have always been met. For example, it is argued that states should not be obliged to take costly steps to ensure an individual's rights. Steiner and Alston highlight the arguments that treating socio-economic entitlements as rights 'undermines the enjoyment of individual freedom, distorts the functioning of free markets by justifying large-scale state intervention in the economy, and provides an excuse to downgrade the importance of civil and political rights'.[38] Beetham remarks that, while states may be reasonably required to refrain from torturing their citizens, it is not clear that they can equally be required to guarantee them a livelihood.[39] However, what is at stake in domestic violence cases is not simply 'livelihood', but often life itself. In *Re Limbuela*[40] the House of Lords held that the state has a duty to provide support and accommodation for asylum seekers in a state of destitution. It is not entirely inconceivable that it may be held that the state has a duty to provide support for victims of domestic violence.

Another criticism of socio-economic rights is that judges are not equipped to take decisions about the allocation of resources, and that such a task should be left to politicians. Palmer comments that constitutional fears about the extension of the powers of the judiciary through the Human Rights Act have focused particularly on the potential for judicial activism in relation to such matters.[41] Chayes states that 'the court has little basis for evaluating competing claims on the public purse'.[42] It could equally be argued that judges should not be in a position to require states to provide resources for victims of domestic violence. Nevertheless, in *Airey v Ireland*[43] it was commented that there is no 'water-tight division' separating the sphere of socio-economic rights from the field covered by the European Convention.[44] Similarly, Fredman argues that it is too simplistic to view socio-economic rights as being completely distinct from civil and political rights.[45]

The problem of alleged perpetrators relying on human rights law

As was discussed in Chapter 1, the fact that rights will conflict with each other is an unavoidable problem in human rights law. For example, the rights of victims of domestic violence may conflict with the rights of alleged perpetrators. In carrying out the necessary balancing exercise, the courts may be inclined to uphold the rights of alleged perpetrators at the expense of the rights of victims. Certainly the right to a fair trial, enshrined in article 6 of the European Convention, is very necessary. It is essential that the rights of defendants are protected. However, it is possible for arguments to be made under article 6 that are unfavourable to the interests of women. Indeed, Temkin comments that 'the European Convention on Human Rights, with its emphasis on the rights of defendants, poses a possible threat to women'.[46] It seems that judges in the UK are predisposed to protecting fair trial rights, as these rights fall particularly within their area of interest.

One example of the Human Rights Act being used to assist defendants at the expense of the interests of complainants is found in the case of *R v A*,[47] which was a rape trial in which the defendant wished to cross-examine the complainant regarding her previous sexual relationship with him. In the past this question would have been decided by reference to the Sexual Offences (Amendment) Act 1976. This Act allowed sexual history evidence to be admitted only when it would have been permitted at common law and the judge ruled that it would be unfair to the defendant to exclude the evidence. However, the judiciary interpreted the Act very widely to allow evidence to be admitted that would not have been allowed at common law.[48] As McColgan comments, 'The promiscuous admission of sexual history evidence in rape trials contributed to the high acquittal rates therein and, at least as significantly, deterred many women from prosecuting'.[49]

However, the provisions of the 1976 Act were replaced by the Youth Justice and Criminal Evidence Act 1999.[50] Section 41 of the Act provides that, where a person is charged with a sexual offence, no evidence may be adduced or question asked in cross-examination by or on behalf of the accused about any sexual behaviour of the complainant, except with leave of the court. Leave must not be given unless one of the stated conditions in section 41(3) is satisfied and a refusal of leave might have the result of rendering a conclusion unsafe. The conditions are that:

> The evidence or question relates to a relevant issue in the case and:
>
> (a) the issue is not one of consent;
> (b) or it is an issue of consent and the sexual behaviour is alleged to have taken place at or about the same time as the event in question;
> (c) or it is an issue of consent and the sexual behaviour is so similar to behaviour that took place as part of the event in question, or to any other sexual behaviour which took place at or about the same time as the event, that the similarity cannot reasonably be explained as a coincidence.

Also, under section 41(4), no evidence or question shall be regarded as relating to a relevant issue if it appears reasonable to assume that the purpose for which it would be adduced or asked is to establish or elicit material for impugning the credibility of the complainant as a witness.

The judicial response to this reform was generally negative. Indeed, the judges were viewed as one of the problems that the legislation was created to tackle.[51] As Lord Williams in the House of Lords Committee Stage of the Bill commented,

> Unless we start we shall get nowhere. Of course there will be some difficulties. Of course, the inertia of the judicial machine will continue. Apparently, to the outside observer, it regards itself as fundamentally more important than those concerned with it; namely the complainants, the public and the defendants.[52]

There were no judges on the Bill's Working Group.[53]

As McColgan comments,

> The reaction of the judicial element of the House of Lords to this reform points to the wisdom of having refrained from handing over to them the power to strike down primary legislation, as distinct from simply declaring it incompatible with the ECnHR.[54]

The Law Lords firmly believed that the safeguards under the 1976 Act were completely adequate. Essentially the judiciary was generally of the view that evidence of sexual history could properly be admitted as being relevant to the issue of consent, while the legislature believed that the sexual behaviour of a complainant on previous occasions would only be relevant to the question of whether she consented in this instance in very rare cases.[55] The Lord Chief Justice reported that there was 'outrage and disbelief' among the judiciary regarding accusations of the 1976 Act being improperly applied.[56] In response Lord Williams commented,

> The proposition that six men falsely accused of terrorist offences in Birmingham had been wrongly accused was met year upon year by the judiciary ... with outrage and disbelief. Indeed that was not the only occasion when our system determined that outrage and disbelief were not necessarily the safest guides to the most just outcome.[57]

The judicial response to the 1999 legislation, a reform designed to protect women bringing cases of rape from being subjected to a humiliating cross-examination on their sexual history, certainly does not indicate that the judiciary would rise to the challenge of using the Human Rights Act to protect victims of domestic violence in an effective manner.

R v A[58] was a rape trial in which the defendant's counsel wanted to cross-examine the complainant about an alleged sexual relationship between her and the defendant during the three weeks prior to the alleged rape. The trial judge held that, under the terms of the Youth Justice and Criminal Evidence Act, such cross-examination could not take place. The defendant claimed that the exclusion of this evidence would be a breach of his article 6 right to a fair trial, and that the provision should thus be read in such a way as to allow the cross-examination to take place. Interestingly, instead of declaring the legislation incompatible with the European Convention, the House of Lords held that the legislation must be interpreted in such a way as to comply with article 6. It was stated that,

> due regard always being paid to the importance of seeking to protect the complainant from indignity and from humiliating questions, the test of admissibility is whether the evidence (and questioning in relation to it) is nevertheless so relevant to the issue of consent that to exclude it would endanger the fairness of the trial under article 6 of the Convention. If this test is satisfied the evidence should not be excluded.[59]

It is very interesting to note that the House of Lords took a rather wide approach to the interpretative obligation under section 3 of the Human Rights Act in this case. Indeed, Lord Steyn claimed that the interpretative obligation authorised the reading of section 41 of the Youth Justice and Criminal Evidence Act 'as subject to the implied provision that evidence of questioning which is required to ensure a fair trial under Article 6 ... should not be treated as inadmissible'.[60] Sandy argues that, if this interpretative method were to be followed, 'it would revolutionise the interpretation of statutes'.[61] The intention of Parliament would be entirely overruled.[62] Lord Steyn stated that a declaration of incompatibility should only be made if a 'clear limitation on Convention rights is stated'.[63] However, it seems very unlikely that such a situation would occur. It is noteworthy that the House of Lords appeared to take quite an activist approach to protecting the rights of defendants in this case, at the expense of the interests of complainants. The approach of the House of Lords seems to entail actually reading additional words into the statute in a manner that may be contrary to the intentions of Parliament. This appears to be stretching the interpretative obligation too far. Ekins comments that 'it is illegitimate for the courts to frustrate the will of Parliament in the guise of interpretation'.[64] In *Ghaidan v Godin-Mendoza*[65] it was stated that although section 3 of the Human Rights Act does allow courts to 'read in', the words must be 'consistent with the fundamental features of the legislative scheme'.[66] Also, 'The meaning imported by application of s3 must be compatible with the underlying thrust of the legislation being construed'.[67] If the House of Lords was truly of the opinion that section 41 of the 1999 Act as it stood violated article 6 of the Convention, then as Clare comments, 'The proper route would surely have been to declare the statute incompatible with Article 6. The result of this ruling is that s.41 remains intact in terms that are now on their face misleading'.[68] The judgment in *R v A* has caused a great deal of confusion as regards the dividing line between compatible interpretation under section 3 of the Human Rights Act and the issuing of a declaration of incompatibility under section 4.[69]

If the House of Lords had issued a declaration of incompatibility under section 4 of the Human Rights Act, the onus would then fall on Parliament to decide whether or not to amend the 1999 legislation. At the time the legislation was enacted, the government believed that its provisions were entirely compatible with the Convention rights. It thus seems unlikely that the government would be in favour of amending the legislation. If Parliament decided not to alter the legislation in any way, the courts would simply have to apply it as it stood. However, as the House of Lords decided to use the interpretative obligation, the courts now have greater leeway as to when evidence of the sexual history of the complainant may be admitted in a rape trial. Kavanagh comments that, 'It would be naïve to think that considerations about whether Parliament is already prepared to change the law would not influence the judicial decision about whether to adopt an interpretation under s.3, or a declaration of incompatibility under s.4'.[70] The attitude of the House of Lords in *R v A* does not lead one to believe that the judiciary could rise to the challenge of using the Human Rights Act to secure the rights of victims of domestic violence.

Nevertheless, judges do not always uphold the rights of alleged perpetrators against those of victims. For example, in *Chief Constable of Cleveland Police v McGrogan*[71] the claimant was arrested on a Saturday, on suspicion of assault occasioning actual bodily harm after attacking his partner. The police officers were aware of many previous such incidents between the couple. The victim did not wish to press charges, although she was very frightened that the claimant would return. The police believed that it was very probable that the claimant, who was being held in a cell as he had become violent in the police holding room, would return to the victim's home on his release and that a breach of the peace would result. The police therefore detained the claimant until he could be brought before a court on Monday, reviewing the detention at intervals. The claimant brought an action against the police for wrongful arrest and false imprisonment. The judge concluded that by Sunday the detention could no longer be justified. The police appealed.

One of the issues considered by the Court of Appeal was whether a violation of article 5(1) of the European Convention, which states that 'Everyone has the right to liberty and security of person', had occurred. The Court cited *Steel and Others v United Kingdom*[72] which comprised a number of cases relating to the arrest and detention of protesters for breaches of the peace. In one of these cases the applicant was detained for 44 hours before being brought before a magistrate. It was held that there was no violation of article 5(1). Likewise the Court of Appeal held there had been no breach of article 5(1) in the instant case. It was decided that the detention of the claimant was still justified on the Sunday, due to factors such as the fear of the victim, and therefore the appeal was allowed.

Although in *Chief Constable of Cleveland Police v McGrogan* the claimant's case was eventually unsuccessful, this case nevertheless emphasises the fact that human rights arguments can be made to strengthen the case of an alleged perpetrator of domestic violence, at the expense of his alleged victim. In this case the police took an entirely appropriate course of action in removing the alleged perpetrator and detaining him until he could be brought before a court. The police were aware of a history of such incidences of domestic violence and they justifiably believed that the victim might be endangered if the claimant were to be released. It is to be hoped that the Human Rights Act does not serve to make police officers reluctant to take appropriate measures to protect victims of domestic violence in the short term.

Re B (Disclosure to Other Parties)[73] concerned four children who were in the care of the local authority under interim care orders. Their mother had been married to the father of the eldest two, had never married the father of the third child and was currently married to the father of the fourth child. The father of the third child was joined as a party to the care proceedings and demanded access to all the filed documents. The mother claimed she had suffered severe domestic violence at his hands and argued that the ambit of disclosure should be limited in order to protect both her privacy and that of her children. Essentially there was a conflict between the litigant's right to a fair trial under article 6 of the European Convention and the mother's and her children's right to private life under article 8.

The court authorised the non-disclosure of certain documents. It was stated that,

> a limited qualification of [the litigant's] right to see the documents may be acceptable if it is reasonably *directed* towards a clear and proper objective – in other words, if directed to the pursuit of the legitimate aim of respecting some other person's rights under Art. 8 – and if it represents no greater a qualification of [the litigant's] rights than the situation calls for.[74]

It was held that, 'showing a proper respect for the other parties' Art 8 rights requires that there should not be disclosed to [the litigant] the documents . . . identified . . . and . . . that his Art 6 rights will not be impaired if he does not see these documents'.[75] It seems therefore that in this case the court upheld the rights of a victim of domestic violence against the claims of the alleged perpetrator. Nevertheless, the court in this case may well have been motivated by a belief that judges have a discretion as to evidence and it is for them to decide whether it should be disclosed.

It is an inherent problem in human rights law that rights will often conflict and it may frequently be the case that alleged perpetrators of domestic violence may argue that their own rights have been violated. Therefore a balancing exercise will have to be carried out. The *R v A* case seems to indicate that judges in the UK may be predisposed to protecting the fair trial rights of defendants. In *McGrogan* the court did decide against the alleged perpetrator of domestic violence; however, it should be noted that it was the right to liberty, as opposed to the right to a fair trial that was at stake. Also, the decision in *Re B* may have been based more on the court's desire to uphold the judge's discretion as to the disclosure of evidence, than on any particular desire to uphold the rights of a victim of domestic violence.

Interesting parallels may be drawn between the attitude of the judiciary in the UK and that of the Canadian judiciary. Particularly strong parallels can be drawn between the decision of the House of Lords in *R v A* and that of the Canadian Supreme Court in *Seaboyer*.[76] In this well-known case the question for the Canadian Supreme Court was whether the 'rape-shield' provisions of the Criminal Code infringed the principles of fundamental justice or the right to a fair trial as contained in sections 7 and 11(d) of the Canadian Charter of Rights and Freedoms. Section 276 of the Criminal Code stated that in rape trials,

> no evidence shall be adduced by or on behalf of the accused concerning the sexual activity of the complainant with any person other than the accused unless,
>
> (a) it is evidence that rebuts evidence of the complainant's sexual activity or absence thereof that was previously adduced by the prosecution;
> (b) it is evidence of specific instances of the complainant's sexual activity tending to establish the identity of the person who had sexual contact with the complainant on the occasion set out in the charge; or
> (c) it is evidence of sexual activity that took place on the same occasion as the sexual activity that forms the subject-matter of the charge,

where that evidence relates to the consent that the accused alleges
he believed was given by the complainant.

The Supreme Court held that section 276 of the Criminal Code was inconsistent with sections 7 and 11(d) of the Charter. The Court commented that
in achieving its purpose – the abolition of the outmoded and inappropriate
use of evidence of past sexual history – section 276 went too far and rendered
inadmissible evidence that may be essential to ensure a fair trial for the
defendant. Therefore section 276 was struck down.

The Canadian Supreme Court has a reputation for being much more activist
than the House of Lords; however, when confronted with a situation in which
the rights of an alleged perpetrator of violence against women clashed with
those of his alleged victim, both bodies took a remarkably similar approach.
Both acted in such a manner as to limit the protection afforded to the victim
by the legislature – the Supreme Court by striking down the provisions and
the House of Lords by using the interpretative obligation to limit their
impact.

However, it must be emphasised that the right to a fair trial is extremely
important. This book does not argue that limitations should be placed on this
right. It seems that it is simply the case that it is an unavoidable problem with
human rights law that rights conflict, and the fact that the rights of alleged
perpetrators of domestic violence may conflict with the rights of victims is
a difficulty with the use of human rights law in relation to this issue.
Nevertheless, it must be ensured that the courts balance the rights of victims
against those of alleged perpetrators in a manner that is fair and logical. It
should not be the case that courts are automatically predisposed to prioritising
the rights of alleged perpetrators. Also, as discussed in Chapter 2, the rights
of victims can be better protected in the criminal justice system if they are
kept informed of developments and are treated in a manner that is sensitive to
their needs by actors in the criminal justice system, such as police officers.

The ability of law to deal with an 'unseen' crime

The fact that there are so few domestic violence cases that incorporate human
rights arguments before the UK courts is indicative of another inherent difficulty with the effectiveness of a litigation approach in relation to domestic
violence. As discussed in Chapter 1, violence against women taking place in
the home constitutes an 'unseen' crime, which victims are often too frightened
or ashamed to report. It is widely recognised that only a minority of cases of
domestic violence ever come to the attention of the police. Many incidents are
never reported. In an ongoing cycle of domestic abuse, it is unlikely that the
police will be called to every violent incident. If they are called and prove to
be unhelpful, it is improbable that the victim will contact them again.[77] The
British Crime Survey found that the police come to know of less than one
in four of the worst cases of domestic violence.[78] Even if victims do report

incidents of domestic violence, they may not wish to take matters further. Frequently victims simply do not want to become involved in litigation.

The question of whether prosecutors should proceed with cases even if this is contrary to the wishes of the victim is an issue that has raised much debate. In 2001 the CPS issued its 'Policy On Prosecuting Cases of Domestic Violence'.[79] This document states that if a victim withdraws a complaint, this does not necessarily mean that the case will be dropped. The policy states that, 'In some cases the violence is so serious, or the previous history shows such a real and continuing danger to the victim or the children or other person, that the public interest in going ahead with a prosecution has to outweigh the victim's wishes'.[80] A similar approach was again taken by the CPS in its 2005 policy document.[81] In 2009 the CPS issued another policy document, which stated that, 'The views and interests of the victim are important, but they cannot be the final word on the subject of a CPS prosecution. Any future risks to the victim, their children or any other potential victim have to be taken into consideration'.[82]

Under the Human Rights Act the test of standing is very narrow. The person wishing to bring a case under the Act must be a victim.[83] For human rights law to be used effectively to protect victims of domestic violence through a litigation approach, victims themselves must be willing to take cases to court. For this reason, it is unlikely that the effectiveness of human rights law will be optimised as regards an 'unseen' crime such as domestic violence if a litigation strategy alone is adopted.

Conclusion

There are three main categories of measures that are most strongly highlighted by commentators in the UK as being beneficial in relation to domestic violence. These are, first, improving the criminal justice system; second, providing social support measures to victims; and, third, raising awareness of the issue of domestic violence. Could the use of human rights law through a litigation strategy contribute to the achievement of these objectives in the UK?

It seems that the case law of the European Court of Human Rights does have potential to be used effectively in relation to domestic violence. However, at present it appears that this potential may be restricted to improving the criminal justice system. The European Court has not taken the step of placing on states a duty to provide social support measures for victims or an obligation to take measures to raise awareness of the issue of domestic violence.

The UK courts have recognised a certain degree of horizontal effect under the Human Rights Act. It seems therefore that the public/private dichotomy is being transcended, at least to some extent. The courts have also recognised that domestic violence constitutes a human rights issue. However, problems still remain. Courts are applying a doctrine of deference that calls for deferring to the judgment of political authorities in precisely those areas most likely to be of use to victims of domestic violence.

There are limits on what courts can achieve. In particular, the *Khan* case indicated that the UK courts may be unlikely to place duties on the state to provide resources for victims of domestic violence. This is a major drawback to the effectiveness of a litigation strategy as it has been argued that the most pressing needs of victims of domestic violence are for adequate measures of social support.[84] Also, the rights of victims of domestic violence may frequently come into conflict with those of alleged perpetrators. In carrying out the necessary balancing exercise, it appears that judges in the UK may be predisposed to protecting the fair trial rights of alleged perpetrators. In addition, the effectiveness of a litigation approach depends largely on the willingness of victims to bring cases before the courts. This is problematic in relation to the issue of domestic violence, which is largely an 'unseen' crime. Overall, it certainly seems that a litigation strategy has limited potential in seeking to use human rights law to contribute to the fight against domestic violence.

Nevertheless, the *Re Limbuela* case[85] may give some cause for hope. Also, it seems that the House of Lords (now the Supreme Court) may be becoming more willing to use international law. In *Re McKerr*[86] Lord Steyn cited the rule that an unincorporated treaty cannot create rights or obligations in domestic law. However, he commented that there was an increasing body of support for the opinion that human rights treaties have a special status. Lord Steyn proceeded to state that,

> The rationale of the dualist theory . . . is that any inroad on it would risk abuses by the executive to the detriment of citizens. It is, however, difficult to see what relevance this has to international human rights treaties which create fundamental rights for individuals against the state and its agencies. A critical re-examination of this branch of the law may become necessary in the future.[87]

In *A and others v Secretary of State for the Home Department*[88] the House of Lords certainly seemed to display an increasing willingness to use international law. This case concerned the issue of whether the Special Immigration Appeals Commission could receive evidence that had or might have been obtained by torture. It was held that evidence which might have been obtained under torture cannot be used in legal hearings. During the judgment the Convention Against Torture and Other Cruel, Inhuman or Degrading Treatment or Punishment was discussed and detailed references were made to resolutions of the UN General Assembly, resolutions of the Security Council, a General Comment of the UN Human Rights Committee, and statements and recommendations made by the Committee against Torture. As discussed in detail in the next chapter, the UN human rights bodies have made detailed statements on the issue of domestic violence.[89] It is possible that there may come a time when the Supreme Court will be willing to use these statements in such a manner as to be beneficial in a case involving domestic violence. It is therefore submitted that the apparent increasing willingness on the part of the Supreme Court to make use of international standards should be encouraged to continue.

5 The approach of the international human rights bodies to domestic violence

It seems that there are difficulties involved in using human rights law through a litigation strategy in the area of domestic violence. Could international human rights law be used more effectively outside of a litigation approach, by influencing policy and administration?

None of the United Nations human rights treaties specifically refer to domestic violence. Nevertheless, the UN human rights bodies have brought the issue of domestic violence within their ambit by relying on provisions such as the right to life; the right to equality; the right to liberty and security of person; the right to equal protection under the law; the right to be free from all forms of discrimination; the right to the highest standard attainable of physical and mental health; and the right not to be subjected to torture, or other cruel, inhuman or degrading treatment or punishment.[1] Instruments that are relevant to the issue of domestic violence include the Convention on the Elimination of All Forms of Discrimination Against Women, General Recommendation No.19 of the CEDAW Committee,[2] reports of the Second, Third and Fourth World Conferences on Women, resolutions of the General Assembly, the UN Declaration on the Elimination of Violence against Women,[3] reports of the Special Rapporteur on Violence against Women and resolutions of the Commission on Human Rights. Of these instruments, in strict theoretical terms, only CEDAW is binding on states. This Convention was adopted by the UN General Assembly in 1979 and came into force in 1981. It prohibits any,

> distinction, exclusion or restriction made on the basis of sex which has the effect or purpose of impairing or nullifying the recognition, enjoyment or exercise by women, irrespective of marital status, on the basis of equality between men and women, of human rights or fundamental freedoms in the political, economic, social, cultural, civil, or any other field.[4]

As of 2010 there are 186 states that are party to CEDAW. This means that of the UN treaties it has one of the largest numbers of signatories. As many issues concerning domestic violence are covered by multiple documents produced by the UN, in order to avoid repetition this chapter will focus mainly on the statements produced by the CEDAW Committee and the Special Rapporteur on Violence against Women. Some reference will however be made to the other instruments outlined above.

It should be noted that regional organisations such as the African Union and the Organisation of American States have adopted treaty provisions on violence against women. For example, the Organisation of American States created the Inter-American Convention on the Prevention, Punishment and Eradication of Violence Against Women. Similarly, in July 2003 the African Union adopted the Protocol on the Rights of Women, which requires African governments to eliminate violence against women. However, as this book focuses on how international human rights law could be used in the United Kingdom in relation to domestic violence, these instruments will not be analysed.

Various categories of recommendations have been made to states. These include improving their criminal justice systems, improving measures of civil protection, providing measures of social support for victims, improving societal awareness, improving the awareness of professionals, developing inter-agency approaches, tackling risk factors associated with domestic violence, developing programmes for perpetrators and undertaking research into domestic violence.

Improving the criminal justice system

In 1992 the Committee on the Elimination of All Forms of Discrimination Against Women produced General Recommendation 19. This was an extremely important document as it officially interpreted CEDAW as prohibiting violence against women, in both the public and private contexts. Domestic violence is not explicitly mentioned in CEDAW; however, the General Recommendation stated that, 'The full implementation of the Convention required States to take positive measures to eliminate all forms of violence against women'.[5] It was commented that,

> The definition of discrimination includes gender-based violence, that is, violence that is directed against a woman because she is a woman or that affects women disproportionately. It includes acts that inflict physical, mental or sexual harm or suffering, threats of such acts, coercion and other deprivations of liberty. Gender-based violence may breach specific provisions of the Convention, regardless of whether those provisions expressly mention violence.[6]

The document stated that gender-based violence may breach *inter alia* the right to life; the right not to be subject to torture or to cruel, inhuman or degrading treatment or punishment; and the right to liberty and security of person.[7] It was emphasised, that discrimination under the Convention is not restricted to action by or on behalf of Governments ... Under general international law and specific human rights covenants, States may be responsible for private acts if they fail to act with due diligence to prevent violations of rights or to investigate and punish acts of violence, and for providing compensation.[8]

In this way the concept of state responsibility was used to great effect to transcend the public/private divide that has posed substantial difficulties for the effectiveness of human rights law in relation to issues such as domestic violence.

The General Recommendation recognised that,

Family violence is one of the most insidious forms of violence against women. It is prevalent in all societies. Within family relationships women of all ages are subjected to violence of all kinds, including battering, rape, other forms of sexual assault, mental and other forms of violence, which are perpetuated by traditional attitudes.[9]

General Recommendation 19 was an extremely important document in that it interpreted CEDAW in such a manner as to prohibit violence against women, both in the public context and in the private sphere. However, in relation to the measures that states should take to improve the responses of their criminal justice systems to cases of domestic violence, the Recommendation was somewhat brief. It was stated that measures necessary to overcome family violence included 'criminal penalties where necessary'[10] and that 'states parties should ensure that laws against family violence and abuse ... give adequate protection to all women, and respect their integrity and dignity'.[11] There was no indication as to how states should ensure that laws against domestic violence should respect the 'integrity and dignity' of all women.

Following the Vienna Conference of 1993, a Special Rapporteur on Violence against Women was appointed by the UN Commission on Human Rights. The Special Rapporteur's mandate is to,

seek and receive information on violence against women, its causes and consequences, from Governments, treaty bodies, specialized agencies, other special rapporteurs ... [and] recommend measures, ways and means, at the national, regional and international level to eliminate violence against women and its causes, and to remedy its consequences.[12]

It has been commented that the Special Rapporteur on Violence against Women has 'brought international consciousness to a new level'.[13] Radhika Coomaraswamy was appointed to the post in 1994 and in 1996 she produced a framework for model legislation on domestic violence.

The framework for model legislation dealt in a relatively detailed manner with how a state's criminal justice system should respond to cases of domestic violence. For example, in relation to complaint mechanisms it was stated that,

> The law shall provide for victims, witnesses of domestic violence, family members and close associates of victims, State and private medical service providers and domestic violence assistance centres to complain of incidents of domestic violence to the police or file action in court.[14]

The duties of police officers in domestic violence cases were laid down in detail. For example, the law should provide that police officers should respond to every request for assistance in cases of alleged domestic violence.[15] Also, police officers should not regard calls concerning alleged domestic abuse as being of a lower priority than calls alleging violence by strangers.[16] The police should respond promptly even where the person reporting the incident was not the victim, but was a witness of the violence, a friend of the victim or a professional working at a domestic violence assistance centre.[17] Police officers should interview the parties in separate rooms,[18] record the details of the complaint,[19] advise the victim of her rights[20] and arrange transport for the victim to a medical facility if necessary.[21] The police should also arrange transport for the victim and her children to a shelter, if it is required.[22] The offender should be removed from the home or, if this is not possible and the victim remains in danger, the offender should be arrested.[23]

In addition, the police officer must provide the victim with a written statement outlining all the legal procedures available to her.[24] Essentially the police must take all reasonable measures to ensure that the victim is safe.[25] The Special Rapporteur also laid down the particulars that should be included in a report of an incident involving domestic violence.[26] The police commissioner should compile annually the data collected from the domestic violence reports and submit a summary report to Parliament.[27]

The Special Rapporteur laid down proper practice for prosecutors and courts in cases involving violence against women in the home. For example, if a court dismisses criminal charges, the specific reasons for dismissal should be recorded.[28] During the course of the trial, the defendant should have no unsupervised contact with the plaintiff.[29] Clear sentencing guidelines should be established[30] and an order for counselling should not be made in place of a sentence in cases involving aggravated assault.[31]

It can be seen; therefore; that recommendations have clearly been made to states to improve the responses of their criminal justice systems to cases involving violence against women in the private sphere.[32] If greater efforts were made by states to comply with these recommendations, it seems that a positive outcome would emerge. In particular, it appears that the measures regarding the responses of police, prosecutors and courts to domestic violence set out in the report of the Special Rapporteur on Violence against Women, outlining a framework for model legislation on domestic violence, would lead to beneficial results if implemented.

Improving the civil law

The international human rights bodies have also made statements on the need for states to provide adequate measures of civil protection for victims of domestic violence.

For example, in its General Recommendation 19, the CEDAW Committee recognised that 'effective legal measures, including . . . civil remedies'[33] were necessary to protect women from violence occurring in the private sphere. Likewise, the report of the Special Rapporteur on Violence against Women, containing the framework for model legislation on domestic violence, went into great detail concerning the restraining orders and protection orders that states should make available.[34] Such orders should have the capacity *inter alia* to compel the offender to vacate the family home, regulate the offender's access to dependent children, restrain the offender from contacting the victim and compel the offender to pay the victim's medical bills. It certainly seems that the Special Rapporteur fully understood the necessity for adequate measures of civil protection to be available to victims of domestic violence. This report, together with General Recommendation 19 of the CEDAW Committee, makes it clear that states should implement effective civil law protection for victims of domestic violence.[35]

It is also worth noting that in another report issued in 1996, the Special Rapporteur gave detailed consideration to the issue of child contact in cases of domestic violence. It was stated that,

> In cases of domestic violence, women should be granted full custody of the children. In cases of woman-battering, the batterer should not be granted visitation . . . In cases in which visitation rights are granted, visitation should be supervised and arranged in a way so as not to cause the woman any contact with the batterer. Details such as transportation, the site of the visitations, financial support for the visits and the persons authorized to supervise the visits should all be included in the court decree.[36]

Providing measures of social support for victims

It could be argued that the provision of social support measures for victims of domestic violence is perhaps the state response that is most needed by victims.[37] It seems that the necessity for such provision has been recognised by the international human rights institutions. For example, in its General Recommendation 19, the CEDAW Committee placed an obligation on states to provide 'protective measures, including refuges, counselling, rehabilitation and support services for women who are the victims of violence or who are at risk of violence'.[38]

Again the report of the Special Rapporteur on Violence against Women containing the framework for model legislation detailed the precise services that states should provide for victims of domestic violence. For example, the state must provide emergency services including immediate transport from the victim's home to a medical centre, shelter or other place of safety, emergency legal counselling and crisis counselling.[39] In addition, states should provide services to assist in the rehabilitation of victims through counselling and job training[40] and also programmes for domestic violence to be administered independently of welfare assistance programmes.[41] In another report issued by the Special Rapporteur in 1996, it was stated that, 'recognizing the nexus between domestic violence and homelessness, priority should be given to victim-survivors of domestic violence in State-sponsored housing'.[42]

It can thus be observed that the international human rights bodies have certainly made comprehensive recommendations to states to provide social support measures, such as refuge accommodation, counselling and job training for victims of domestic violence.[43] In 2008 the Committee of Ministers of the Council of Europe established an ad hoc committee to prepare a legally binding instrument on violence against women. It is noteworthy that this committee reported that such an instrument 'should set up comprehensive measures enabling victims to benefit from support, advice and services, according to their needs'.[44]

Improving societal awareness

In its General Recommendation 19, the CEDAW Committee recommended that states provide public education programmes to change attitudes concerning the status of men and women.[45] The approach of the Special Rapporteur's framework for model legislation on domestic violence regarding the issue of increasing societal awareness is interesting. In the Declaration of Purpose it is stated that one of the purposes of the legislation is to provide 'programmes to assist in the prevention and elimination of domestic violence which include raising public awareness and public education on the subject'.[46] However, nowhere in the substantive parts of the document is it recommended that states adopt measures to raise public awareness. This omission is somewhat surprising, given the fact that this report is generally so comprehensive in its approach. Nevertheless, the Special Rapporteur has made it clear in other documents that states should take steps to raise societal awareness of violence against women. For example, in 1996 the need for 'demystifying domestic violence'[47] was highlighted, and in 2003 'the adoption of a societal project to delink masculinity from an association with oppressive uses of power'[48] was recommended.

The Fourth World Conference on Women was held in 1995 in Beijing. It is noteworthy that the Beijing Platform for Action was particularly emphatic concerning the need for measures to be taken to increase societal awareness of domestic violence. It was stated that governments should support initiatives of women's organisations to raise awareness of the issue of violence against women[49] and that they should organise and fund community-based campaigns to raise awareness about violence against women as a human rights violation.[50] In addition they should 'organize and fund information campaigns and educational and training programmes in order to sensitize girls and boys and women and men to the personal and social detrimental effects of violence in the family, community and society'.[51]

The Platform for Action even pointed out that governments should,

> raise awareness of the responsibility of the media in promoting non-stereotyped images of women and men, as well as in eliminating patterns of media presentation that generate violence, and encourage those responsible for media content to establish professional guidelines and codes of conduct; also raise awareness of the important role of the media in informing and educating people about the causes and effects of violence against women and in stimulating public debate on the topic.[52]

The Beijing Platform for Action clearly demonstrates an awareness of the need to tackle the root causes of domestic violence by addressing attitudes within society. Indeed this appears to be the issue that was most developed within the Platform for Action. The document certainly made clear and detailed recommendations to states to take action to raise societal awareness of the true nature of domestic violence.[53] Similarly the Committee of Ministers of the Council of Europe has emphasised that states should,

> mobilise public opinion by organising or supporting conferences and information campaigns so that society is aware of the problem and its devastating effects on victims and society in general and can therefore discuss the subject of violence towards women openly, without prejudice or preconceived ideas.[54]

The ad hoc committee referred to above has also stated that a legally binding instrument on violence against women should include an obligation to implement awareness-raising programmes and campaigns.[55]

Improving the awareness of professionals

In addition to raising the awareness of society generally concerning the issues involved in domestic violence, it has been commented that it is also necessary to provide particular educational programmes for those who may regularly come into contact with victims in a professional capacity, such as doctors and other healthcare professionals, lawyers, judges and social workers.[56] In its General Recommendation 19 the CEDAW Committee emphasised that gender-sensitive training of judicial and law enforcement officers and other public officials was essential for the effective implementation of the Convention.[57]

In the report of the Special Rapporteur containing a framework for model legislation on domestic violence it was stated that one of the aims of the draft legislation was to,

> Train judges to be aware of the issues relating to child custody, economic support and security for the victims in cases of domestic violence by establishing guidelines for protection orders and sentencing guidelines which do not trivialize domestic violence.[58]

The details of what should be included in such training were laid out.[59] Judicial officers should be given guidance on the issuing of protection orders and sentencing guidelines. There should be an initial course and then an annual review.

The report also laid out details for the training of police officers in dealing with cases involving domestic violence. Police should be educated in 'The nature, extent, causes and consequences of domestic violence'[60] and the legal rights, services and facilities available to victims.[61] In addition, police officers should be taught techniques for handling incidents of domestic violence that promote the safety of the victim.[62] Educators, psychologists and victims should all be involved in the training of police officers.[63]

The report of the Special Rapporteur is very important as it outlined the details of what education courses for police and judicial officers should actually contain. However, there appears to be one crucial omission from the Special Rapporteur's consideration of the recommendation to states to put into place education programmes for particular professionals. The report focuses solely on the need to educate police and judicial officers. It does not mention the equally pressing need to educate other professionals, such as doctors and social workers, who may also come into contact with victims of domestic violence on a regular basis. This is an important issue as very often a victim may turn to a healthcare professional or social worker for assistance, rather than turning to the police and the criminal justice system. Nevertheless, the need to educate other professionals has been recognised by the Special Rapporteur in other documents. For example, in 2002 it was commented that 'States should train all public officials in the administration of justice, education and health sectors to be sensitive and energetic with regard to issues relating to violence against women'.[64]

The statements of the UN human rights bodies have clearly recommended that states provide specific educational programmes on domestic violence for those who may come into contact with victims of domestic violence on a regular basis in a professional capacity, such as police officers, judges, healthcare professionals and social workers.[65] Nevertheless, it seems that the recommendation to educate police and judicial officers is more developed than is the recommendation to educate other professionals. The report of the Special

Rapporteur containing a framework for model legislation on domestic violence dealt in detail with the elements that should be included in education programmes on domestic violence for actors in the criminal justice system; however, somewhat surprisingly, it did not mention the need to train other professionals at all. This is a rather important omission as the Special Rapporteur's report is generally much more detailed concerning the duties that states should fulfil than are any of the other human rights documents dealing with domestic violence. It appears that it would be beneficial to detail the elements that should be included in educational programmes for medical personnel and social workers, as these will clearly differ greatly from the elements that should constitute programmes for police and judicial officers. Nevertheless, it must be remembered that the UN incorporates a huge number of states, with a wide variety of cultures. Therefore it may be somewhat difficult to make detailed recommendations in this area. It may be felt that it is preferable to leave the question of how to educate professionals such as medical personnel on domestic violence up to individual Member States and simply recommend that states ensure that such educational campaigns are effective. It is perhaps easier to lay down exact universal criteria as to how police officers should be instructed to deal with domestic violence, than to produce universal criteria as to how doctors should respond to this issue. It seems that cultural considerations do need to be taken into account to ensure that the response of medical personnel and social workers reaches the optimal level of effectiveness.

Developing inter-agency approaches

It appears that the international human rights bodies recognise that in order for an effective strategy to deal with domestic violence to be implemented, it is necessary for an inter-agency approach to be adopted. Although this issue is not dealt with in General Recommendation 19 of the CEDAW Committee or in the reports of the Special Rapporteur on Violence against Women discussed in this chapter, nevertheless in 1985 the General Assembly urged Member States to ensure coordination of social welfare and criminal justice measures.[66] The General Assembly expanded on this recommendation in 1990 by urging Member States,

> to begin or continue to explore, develop and implement multidisciplinary policies, measures and strategies, within and outside of the criminal justice system, with respect to domestic violence in all its facets, including legal, law enforcement, judicial, societal, educational, psychological, economic, health-related and correctional aspects.[67]

Again in 1993 the General Assembly urged states to, 'consider the possibility of developing national plans of action to promote the protection of women against any form of violence . . . taking into account . . . such cooperation as can be provided by non-governmental organizations'.[68] On a similar note, in 2001 the Commission on Human Rights called upon states 'to establish and/ or strengthen, at the national level, collaborative relationships with relevant non-governmental and community-based organizations'.[69] This statement was reiterated by the Commission in 2004.[70]

It can thus be seen that states have been urged to develop an inter-agency approach to tackling the issue of domestic violence. States should pay particular attention to the need to work together with non-governmental organisations. The valuable work of such bodies has been clearly recognised by the UN human rights institutions. Notably the Council of Europe Ad Hoc Committee stated that,

> eliminating violence against women requires evidence-based, comprehensive and coordinated policies involving all decision-making levels of the state (governments, parliaments and local and regional authorities), various sectors, agencies and institutions, including the civil society at large and women's NGOs. These policies should focus on the needs of the victims and cover all aspects relevant to the prevention of violence and protection of victims as well as the improvement of multi-agency co-operation between the different areas and actors and the promotion of networking at national and international level.[71]

Tackling risk factors

It has been commented that certain categories of women may be more at risk from suffering domestic violence than others. For example, it appears that violence against women is more prevalent in situations in which either one or both partners is involved in substance abuse.[72] In addition, women from ethnic minorities[73] or rural communities may not have sufficient access to support services. The international human rights community has recognised the need to pay particular attention to tackling risk factors associated with domestic violence.

For example, even in 1985 the General Assembly expressed concern that the abuse of alcohol and drugs may be an exacerbating factor in domestic violence and that further research should be carried out on this question.[74] In 1990 the General Assembly recognised the need to consider specialised approaches concerning the elderly and those especially vulnerable due to disability. It also showed an awareness that many perpetrators and victims of domestic violence were abused as children.[75]

The CEDAW Committee in its General Recommendation 19 commented that, 'Rural women are at risk of gender-based violence because of traditional attitudes regarding the subordinate role of women that persist in many rural communities'.[76] It was thus commented that states should ensure that rural women have access to services for victims of violence.[77] In 1993 the General Assembly stated that it was,

> concerned that some groups of women, such as women belonging to minority groups, indigenous women, refugee women, migrant women, women living in rural or remote communities, destitute women, . . . women with disabilities [and] elderly women . . . are especially vulnerable to violence.[78]

However, it did not proceed to make specific recommendations to states to take particular measures to protect such groups. The report of the Special Rapporteur containing a framework for model legislation on domestic violence made no mention whatsoever of the need to pay particular attention to risk factors involved in domestic violence. Nevertheless, in another report issued in 1996, the Special Rapporteur commented that there should be outreach efforts in marginalised communities where there were problems of domestic violence.[79]

The Beijing Platform for Action recommended that states, 'take special measures to eliminate violence against women, particularly those in vulnerable situations, such as young women, refugee, displaced and internally displaced women, women with disabilities and women migrant workers'.[80] In particular, states should 'ensure that women with disabilities have access to information and services in the field of violence against women'[81] and 'establish linguistically and culturally accessible services for migrant women and girls, including women migrant workers, who are victims of gender-based violence'.[82]

In 2001 the Resolution of the Commission on Human Rights reiterated the concern of the General Assembly that certain groups of women are particularly vulnerable to violence.[83] However, like the General Assembly, it did not then address the question of the measures that should be taken to protect such women from domestic violence. The same approach was taken by the Commission in its 2004 Resolution.

The approach of the UN human rights bodies towards the tackling of risk factors associated with domestic violence seems to be somewhat poorly developed. Certain documents, such as the resolutions of the General Assembly in 1993 and the Commission on Human Rights in 2001 and 2004 expressed concern that certain groups are more vulnerable to domestic violence; however, they did not then proceed to address the question of the specific measures that should be taken to protect such groups. The report of the Special Rapporteur containing a framework for model legislation on domestic violence, generally so detailed, made no mention whatsoever of the need to tackle risk factors.

If the documents do attempt to address risk factors in any depth, they tend only to deal with one or two relevant factors. For example, the 1985 Resolution of the General Assembly addressed only the issue of substance abuse. The General Assembly's 1990 Resolution mentioned the elderly and those vulnerable due to disability, and displayed an awareness that many perpetrators and victims were abused as children. General Recommendation 19 of the CEDAW Committee highlighted the vulnerability of rural women. The

Beijing Platform for Action dealt in the greatest depth with the risk factors surrounding domestic violence, recommending that states take special measures to eliminate violence against women in vulnerable situations. It certainly seems that it would be more beneficial if the UN human rights bodies were to develop this recommendation in a more detailed manner.

Developing programmes for perpetrators

In certain circumstances it may be more beneficial to develop treatment programmes for perpetrators of violence against women than to apply classic criminal justice measures such as imprisonment. In many cases the victim of domestic violence wants the relationship to continue and attendance by the perpetrator at a battery treatment programme can facilitate this goal. The UN human rights bodies have paid some attention to the issue of educating perpetrators of violence against women.

For example, General Recommendation 19 of the CEDAW Committee recommended that states provide rehabilitation programmes for perpetrators.[84] The report of the Special Rapporteur outlining a framework for model legislation recommended that states deliver services to assist in the rehabilitation of abusers.[85] It was stated that, 'The law shall mandate counselling programmes for perpetrators as a supplement to and not as an alternative to the criminal justice system'.[86] The report also gave some detail as to what such programmes should include. They should be designed to assist the perpetrator in taking responsibility for his violence and making a commitment not to inflict further violence[87] and they should educate him on the illegality of violence.[88] However, the report emphasised that funding for perpetrator programmes should not be taken from resources that are assigned to assist victims.[89]

It can thus be seen that states have been urged to develop rehabilitation programmes for perpetrators of domestic violence.[90] Some detail was included in the report of the Special Rapporteur as to the elements that should be included in such programmes. Nevertheless, these guidelines are still somewhat broad. However, it seems that the exact content of battery treatment programmes is best left to the Member States, as individual nations can then adapt such programmes so as to be most effective within their own particular cultural circumstances.

It should also be noted that recommending that states provide treatment programmes for perpetrators of domestic violence may be somewhat controversial. There is little evidence for the proposition that such programmes are effective.[91] Battery treatment programmes tend to involve perpetrators interacting in group situations. This may actually encourage batterers to continue engaging in domestic violence.[92] It seems that if battery treatment programmes are used, they should be only one of a wide range of measures utilised in the fight to combat domestic violence. However, this argument seems to be recognised by the UN bodies. For example, the report of the

Special Rapporteur stressed that resources should not be taken from the provision of services for victims in order to establish treatment programmes for perpetrators.

Undertaking research

The UN human rights bodies have also recommended that states implement further research into issues surrounding domestic violence. For example, General Recommendation 19 of the CEDAW Committee stated that the Member States 'should encourage the compilation of statistics and research on the extent, causes and effects of violence, and on the effectiveness of measures to prevent and deal with violence'.[93]

It is noteworthy that the Beijing Platform for Action displayed a particular awareness of the need to implement research on domestic violence. It was stated that,

> The absence of adequate gender-disaggregated data and statistics on the incidence of violence makes the elaboration of programmes and monitoring of changes difficult. Lack of or inadequate documentation and research on domestic violence . . . impede efforts to design specific intervention strategies.[94]

The need for research was felt so strongly that one of the strategic objectives of the Platform for Action was to 'study the causes and consequences of violence against women and the effectiveness of preventive measures'.[95] The findings of such research should be widely disseminated.[96]

Amending CEDAW?

The international human rights bodies have thus made a fairly comprehensive set of recommendations to states in relation to domestic violence. States have been urged to improve their criminal justice systems, improve measures of civil protection, provide measures of social support for victims, improve societal awareness, improve the awareness of professionals, develop inter-agency approaches, tackle risk factors associated with domestic violence, develop programmes for perpetrators and undertake research into domestic violence.

However, there is perhaps one fundamental omission. CEDAW itself does not expressly mention the issue of domestic violence. It seems that as General Recommendation 19 is an official interpretation of CEDAW, this Recommendation has the effect of ensuring that the issue of domestic violence is encompassed by the treaty. Nevertheless, it could be argued that amending CEDAW to include domestic violence expressly would add more force to the obligations laid down in this area. Interestingly, both the African Union and the Organisation of American States have adopted treaty provisions on violence against women.[97]

At present it seems that one almost has to twist CEDAW in such a manner as to encompass the issue of domestic violence. Of course, it should be remembered that such stretching of human rights instruments is common. For example, the European Convention on Human Rights was originally designed for use by adults in resisting state power. However, the European Convention is now frequently applied in cases in which the rights of one individual have been violated by another private entity. The original drafters of the Convention would certainly not have regarded a case such as *A v United Kingdom*,[98] which involved a child being beaten by his stepfather, as falling within the scope of the treaty.

The Optional Protocol to CEDAW

The Optional Protocol to CEDAW came into force in December 2000. This Protocol allows individuals or groups to submit claims of breaches of the Convention to the CEDAW Committee. Essentially the Protocol gives to every woman in states that have ratified it, an opportunity to go to the CEDAW Committee and say that the state is failing to protect her rights under the Convention. The Preamble to the Optional Protocol states that it is a reaffirmation of states' 'determination to ensure the full and equal enjoyment by women of all human rights and fundamental freedoms and to take effective action to prevent violations of these rights and freedoms'. Angela King, the Special Adviser on Gender Issues and Advancement of Women to the UN Secretary-General, commented that,

> The adoption of this Optional Protocol is one of the commitments made by states at both the Vienna Conference on Human Rights and the Fourth World Conference on Women in Beijing in 1995. It thus represents one of the major accomplishments in the realisation of the objectives set out in the Platform for Action.[99]

In December 1999, Kofi Annan, the Secretary-General of the UN, stated,

> In the course of the twentieth century, we have made great strides in defining universal norms of gender equality. As we enter the twenty-first century, it is time to implement those norms. The Optional Protocol we have opened for signature today will be an invaluable tool for doing that. In States that have ratified it, women whose rights have been violated will henceforth be able, once they have exhausted national remedies, to seek redress from an international body – the Committee on the Elimination of Discrimination Against Women.[100]

The Optional Protocol was certainly a major step forward in the strengthening of CEDAW. Complaints procedures already existed under such treaties as the International Covenant on Civil and Political Rights; the Convention against Torture and Other Cruel, Inhuman or Degrading Treatment or Punishment; and the International Convention on the Elimination of All Forms of Racial Discrimination. Therefore, it was appropriate that CEDAW should also be given its own complaints procedure. Byrnes comments that,

> In general, it is true to say that where decisions are rendered against a state under [a complaints procedure], the state will take steps to bring its domestic law and practice into conformity with the international law position as determined or opined by the relevant supervisory body. However, this is not to say that there are not exceptions or that the steps taken by a state party to rectify inconsistencies will adopt a generous approach to remedying the defects identified by the international body.[101]

Article 2 of the Optional Protocol allows individuals or groups of individuals who are victims of any breaches of CEDAW to submit complaints to the Committee. Crucially, communications may also be submitted on behalf of individuals with their consent, unless acting on their behalf without their consent may be justified. This is a much wider test of standing than that which is contained in the European Convention of Human Rights or the Human Rights Act 1998. Under both these instruments the person bringing the case must be the actual victim. However, under the Optional Protocol a communication may be made on behalf of an individual or a group of individuals. For example, a domestic violence group could make a communication alleging that the state has failed to fulfil its positive duties under CEDAW in the area of violence against women in the home.

Article 3 of the Optional Protocol states that communications must be in writing and must not be anonymous. The state concerned must be a party to the Protocol. Under article 4, the CEDAW Committee may only consider a communication if all domestic remedies have been exhausted, or if the application of such remedies would be unnecessarily prolonged or unlikely to bring relief to the complainant. A communication is inadmissible if the same matter has already been examined by the CEDAW Committee or has been considered by another international procedure. It is also inadmissible if it is incompatible with CEDAW, manifestly ill-founded, an abuse of the right to petition, or if the subject of the communication occurred prior to the entry into force of the Optional Protocol for the state in question. Under article 5, the CEDAW Committee may recommend interim measures to the state party at any time between the receipt of a communication and its decision. Under article 7, when a communication is submitted, the Committee should bring it to the attention of the state in question. The state then has six months to submit an explanation to the Committee. Communications are considered by the Committee in closed meetings. The views of the Committee are then transmitted to the parties. The State is required to respond in writing within six months, including a description of any action it has taken on the matter.

The Optional Protocol also establishes an inquiry procedure, whereby if the Committee receives reliable information indicating grave or systematic breaches of CEDAW by a state, the Committee may invite the state to co-operate in the examination of that information by submitting observations. The Committee may then conduct an inquiry. If the state consents, the inquiry may incorporate a visit to the state. The Committee transmits the findings of the inquiry to the state concerned, and the state then has six months to submit its observations to the Committee.[102]

The creation of the Optional Protocol was certainly an advantageous development for the strengthening of CEDAW. In a publication produced by the Inter-Parliamentary Union, in conjunction with the UN Division for the Advancement of Women, it was stated that the communications procedure,

> allows the Committee to develop a new body of jurisprudence on how to guarantee women's rights [and] assists states parties in determining the content of their obligations under the convention and thus assists them in implementing those obligations.[103]

The inquiry procedure,

> enables the Committee to address systematic and widespread violations; allows the Committee to recommend measures to combat the structural causes of discrimination against women; [and] provides the Committee with an opportunity to set out a broad range of recommendations to achieve equality between men and women.[104]

Mary Robinson, the then UN High Commissioner for Human Rights, commented in December 2000 that the Optional Protocol,

> will act as an incentive for Governments to take a fresh look at the means of redress that are currently available to women at the domestic level. This is perhaps the most important contribution of the Optional Protocol. It is action at the national level which will create the environment in which women and girls are able to enjoy all their human rights fully and where their grievances will be addressed with the efficiency and speed they deserve.[105]

The UK acceded to the Optional Protocol on 17 December 2004. This is a hopeful development in relation to the protection of women from violence.

It is to be hoped that the Optional Protocol will contribute to the creation of a greater level of public awareness of human rights standards in relation to discrimination against women. Article 13 of the Protocol requires states to make both CEDAW and the Protocol widely known and to facilitate public access to information concerning the recommendations of the CEDAW Committee. The UK should benefit from such developments, as it seems that

CEDAW is relatively little known in this state. If individuals and women's groups were to gain a better understanding of the obligations placed on the state by CEDAW, this in turn may place further pressure on the state to comply with these obligations.

However, it must be remembered that the Optional Protocol is optional. States that have ratified CEDAW are under no obligation to ratify the Protocol. Also, although the communications procedure allows the CEDAW Committee to make recommendations as to the measures that should be adopted to remedy a breach of the Convention, it has no means of forcing the state concerned to comply with these recommendations. Likewise, a state that ratifies the Optional Protocol may still opt out of the inquiry procedure. Even states that have not chosen to opt out of the inquiry procedure may only be subject to inquiries to which they give their full cooperation. It seems that similar enforcement difficulties arise in relation to the Optional Protocol as arise concerning the main CEDAW provisions. As Ritz comments, 'The Optional Protocol lacks compelling sanctions and penalties for non-compliance.'[106]

Nevertheless, the Optional Protocol procedures may provide an incentive for states to comply more fully with their obligations under CEDAW. If the CEDAW Committee finds that an individual's complaint is justified and recommends that certain measures be taken to remedy the situation, the state involved may be subjected to condemnation if it fails to take the measures in question. Likewise if a state fails to allow the Committee to conduct an inquiry into a human rights abuse, international criticism may result. Perhaps the most valuable aspect of the Optional Protocol is the potential it holds for increasing international pressure on states to comply with their duties under CEDAW.

The Optional Protocol procedure does bear similarities to a litigation process in that making a communication to the CEDAW Committee could be said to be akin to taking a case before a court. However, in crucial respects the procedure under the Optional Protocol may hold more potential in the area of domestic violence than does a traditional litigation approach. For example, the CEDAW Committee has already made recommendations that states should provide social support measures for victims of domestic violence and implement public awareness campaigns. Also, generally, traditional courts must restrict their judgments to the actual case scenario that is before them; however, in dealing with communications the Committee is free to take a broader approach. In addition, the CEDAW Committee would be predisposed to protecting the rights of victims of violence against women, in contrast to the seeming predisposition of the UK judiciary to protect the fair trial rights of alleged perpetrators.

AT v Hungary[107] was the first decision of the CEDAW Committee on the merits of a communication under the Optional Protocol. The views of the Committee were adopted in January 2005. It was stated that Hungary was in violation of CEDAW for failing to take sufficient measures to protect a victim of domestic violence. There were no protection orders or suitable shelters available to the victim and no specific legislation had been enacted to deal with domestic violence. The CEDAW Committee made recommendations concerning the author of the complaint specifically, and also more general recommendations. The Committee commented that the state should take effective and immediate measures to ensure Ms AT's safety and give her a safe home, child support and legal assistance, in addition to reparation for the violation of her rights. In general, the Committee stated that Hungary should, 'assure victims of domestic violence the maximum protection of the law by acting with due diligence to prevent and respond to such violence against women'.[108] The state should also provide regular training on CEDAW to judges, law enforcement officials and lawyers. All allegations of domestic violence should be investigated in a thorough manner and victims provided with sufficient access to justice.

In August 2007 the CEDAW Committee examined two more communications surrounding the issue of domestic violence. *Goecke v Austria*[109] concerned a victim of domestic violence who had eventually been killed by her husband. The communication was brought by the Vienna Intervention Centre against Domestic Violence and the Association for Women's Access to Justice, on behalf of the family members of the deceased. The CEDAW Committee stated that the police and the Public Prosecutor had failed to respond in an adequate manner to protect the victim, despite knowing that she was in serious danger. The victim had called the police several hours before she was killed and the CEDAW Committee stated that, in the light of the long record of domestic violence, by not responding immediately the police had failed to exercise due diligence to protect the victim. The police had requested that the victim's husband be arrested after earlier incidents of domestic violence; however, the public prosecutor had dismissed these requests. The Committee commented that, although it was,

> necessary in each case to determine whether detention would amount to a disproportionate interference in the basic rights and fundamental freedoms of a perpetrator of domestic violence, such as the right to freedom of movement and to a fair trial, . . . the perpetrator's rights cannot supersede women's human rights to life and to physical and mental integrity.[110]

The Committee found that Austria was in violation of the victim's rights to life and to physical and mental integrity under CEDAW and recommended that the state act with due diligence to prevent and respond to violence against women and prosecute perpetrators of domestic violence in a vigilant manner. The state should 'ensure that criminal and civil remedies are utilized in cases where the perpetrator in a domestic violence situation poses a dangerous threat to the victim'.[111] It should also ensure enhanced coordination among law enforcement and judicial officers, and strengthen training programmes on domestic violence for judges, lawyers and law enforcement officials.

Yildirim v Austria[112] also concerned a victim of domestic violence who had eventually been killed by her husband. Again the communication was brought by the Vienna Intervention Centre against Domestic Violence and the Association for Women's Access to Justice, on behalf of the family members of the deceased. The victim had been in ongoing contact with the police and had authorised the prosecution of her husband. The CEDAW Committee stated that the Public Prosecutor's dismissal of the requests of the police to arrest the victim's husband and place him in detention constituted a violation of the state's due diligence obligation to protect the victim. Again the Committee emphasised that 'the perpetrator's rights cannot supersede women's human rights to life and to physical and mental integrity'.[113] The recommendations which had been made to the state in *Goecke v Austria* were then reiterated.

As Byrnes and Bath remark, 'The major substantive contribution thus far of the Committee under the individual complaints procedure is with regard to the due diligence standard in relation to violence, particularly in the family context'.[114] In its consideration of the complaints surrounding the issue of domestic violence, the Committee has clearly emphasised that not only must an adequate legal framework be in place, but that this framework must be implemented in a substantive and meaningful way by the relevant officials, such as police and prosecutors. However, it seems that there remains a general lack of awareness of the Optional Protocol and its potential. As of 2010, only 10 communications have been considered by the Committee. As Murdoch comments, 'The minimal utilisation of the right of communication . . . suggest[s] a widespread lack of awareness or understanding of the Optional Protocol on the part of individuals'.[115]

Transcending the public/private dichotomy

As discussed earlier in the book, the public/private dichotomy has caused immense difficulties for the effectiveness of human rights law. However, the international human rights bodies have made it clear that states must take steps to protect the rights of individuals, such as victims of domestic violence, from being violated by other individuals.

As discussed previously in this chapter, General Recommendation 19 of the CEDAW Committee was crucial as it officially interpreted CEDAW as prohibiting violence against women, in both the public and private spheres. It was stated,

> that discrimination under the Convention is not restricted to action by or on behalf of Governments . . . Under general international law and specific human rights covenants, States may be responsible for private acts if they fail to act with due diligence to prevent violations of rights or to investigate and punish acts of violence, and for providing compensation.[116]

In this way the concept of state responsibility was used to transcend the public/private divide that has posed great problems for the effectiveness of human rights law as regards issues such as domestic violence. Indeed, the ease with which the CEDAW Committee broke through the dichotomy again seems to indicate that the public/private divide does not pose as great an obstacle to the effectiveness of human rights law as once was the case. The clear intention was to bring domestic violence within the ambit of CEDAW, albeit by using some degree of 'creative interpretation'.[117] Nevertheless it seems that the CEDAW Committee was entirely justified in interpreting the Convention to prohibit violence in both the public and private contexts.

Hernandez-Truyol comments that the 1993 Vienna Conference had 'finally pierced the veil of the private closet in which women have suffered harms from time immemorial'.[118] The conference document stressed 'the importance of working towards the elimination of violence against women in the public and private life'.[119] In the wake of this conference, the Declaration on the Elimination of Violence against Women was adopted. Under this Declaration states should 'exercise due diligence to prevent . . . acts of violence against women, whether these acts are perpetrated by the State or by private persons'.[120] Again the concept of state responsibility was used to great effect.

Likewise, the preliminary report of the Special Rapporteur on Violence against Women stated that, 'All States are not only responsible for their own conduct or the conduct of their agents, but are now also responsible for their failure to take necessary steps to prosecute private citizens for their behaviour, in compliance with international standards'.[121] The Beijing Platform for Action emphasised that governments should 'exercise due diligence to prevent, investigate and, in accordance with national legislation, punish acts of violence against women, whether those acts are perpetrated by the State or by private persons'.[122]

Conclusion

In conclusion, therefore, it seems that a fairly comprehensive set of recommendations has been made to states by the international human rights bodies in relation to domestic violence. Indeed, statements have been made on all the types of measures discussed in Chapter 2 of this book. If states were to comply with all of these recommendations it certainly appears that this would contribute greatly to the fight to combat domestic violence.

However, a number of the recommendations may suffer from a lack of precision that could cause difficulties concerning implementation. For example, in relation to improving the criminal justice system, there is no mention of how the state should respond when faced with a case in which the victim does not wish to proceed with a prosecution. In many cases women who have suffered domestic violence do not want to have their assailants prosecuted due to a belief that a prosecution will simply lead to an escalation of violence. The question of whether a prosecution should proceed even without the consent of the victim is an extremely difficult one. Should the wishes of the victim be respected in all cases, or are there some instances in which the violence is simply so horrific that intervention is essential regardless of the victim's views? Are there cases in which a prosecution is necessary in the interest of society?

Nevertheless it must be remembered that the question of how to balance punishing offenders with protecting victims in cases of domestic violence is extremely controversial. There does not appear to be any real consensus among those working in the field of domestic violence as to how to proceed in a case in which a victim of severe domestic violence does not wish her assailant to be prosecuted. It is perhaps too much to expect the international human rights bodies to arrive at definite conclusions on such questions. The fact that the statements of the bodies concerned with how criminal justice systems should respond to domestic violence lack specificity in this respect may well hinder their implementation; however, it is debatable whether any greater level of precision could have been achieved. This seems to highlight one of the difficulties concerning the effectiveness of international human rights law in relation to complex issues such as that of domestic violence. It may not be the function of human rights bodies to make decisions regarding controversial details of policy. International human rights bodies can certainly state that domestic violence constitutes a violation of the rights of the victims and that states should therefore take steps to combat domestic violence. However, it seems more unlikely that such bodies can make decisions as to what precisely should be done in cases in which the victim does not wish her assailant to be prosecuted, especially as such a question is fraught with controversy even among those working in the field of domestic violence.

This lack of precision may well hinder the implementation of the statements of the UN human rights bodies concerning the way in which the criminal justice systems of Member States should respond to cases of domestic violence. Although it has been clearly recommended that states should improve the responses of their criminal justice systems, the monitoring of states' responses would be easier if the recommendation was outlined in greater detail.

Nevertheless, the international human rights bodies have made wide-ranging recommendations to states as regards domestic violence. However, are these recommendations being implemented?

6 Implementation of the statements of the international human rights bodies in the United Kingdom

As discussed in the previous chapter, the international human rights bodies have certainly made wide-ranging recommendations to states concerning the issue of domestic violence. States have been informed that they should improve their criminal justice systems, provide social support measures to victims, take measures to improve societal awareness of the issues involved in domestic violence, adopt education programmes for professionals, develop inter-agency approaches, tackle risk factors involved in domestic violence, develop programmes for perpetrators and implement research. However, what impact have the statements had to date in the United Kingdom?

It appears that the UK is complying with the recommendations to some extent. However, it also seems that, in general, compliance is merely incidental. Although the UK is now acting in a way that correlates with the statements in some areas, nevertheless it appears that changes in policy have not taken place because of the recommendations, but are rather due to pressure emanating from other sources such as academic commentators and domestic violence groups. As was discussed in Chapter 1, enforcement difficulties constitute a major problem for international human rights law. The statements made by the UN human rights bodies on the issue of domestic violence are certainly no exception in this regard. Indeed, it seems that this issue is the overwhelming problem with using international human rights law in this way.

Is the United Kingdom complying with the recommendations?

In order to assess the impact that the statements made by the international human rights bodies in relation to domestic violence have had in the UK, the first question that must be addressed is whether or not the UK is complying with the recommendations.

States should ensure that 'criminal penalties' are in place in relation to domestic violence[1]

The international human rights bodies have made it clear that states need to put in place legislation under which domestic violence is a criminal offence.

As domestic violence constitutes assault, in the UK it is a criminal offence under the Offences Against the Person Act 1861. Although this Act was certainly not passed to deal with domestic violence, nevertheless under the legislation, the perpetrator may be held to have committed common assault,[2] aggravated assault,[3] assault occasioning actual bodily harm[4] or grievous bodily harm,[5] or unlawful wounding.[6] The Protection from Harassment Act 1997 (Protection from Harassment (Northern Ireland) Order 1997) may also be used in cases of domestic violence. The Act contains both criminal law and civil law provisions. Section 1 prohibits any person from engaging in a course of conduct which he knows, or ought reasonably to know, constitutes harassment. Section 7 states that 'harassment' includes alarming or causing distress to a person and may take the form of words or conduct. A 'course of conduct' involves conduct on at least two occasions. Under section 2, it is a summary offence to pursue a course of conduct in breach of the prohibition against harassment in section 1. Under section 4, it is an offence, triable either way, to pursue a course of conduct that puts a person in fear of violence. Both these offences constitute arrestable offences. Section 5 empowers the court to make restraining orders in relation to any person convicted under sections 2 or 4. Under section 5(5) it is an offence for a defendant, without reasonable excuse, to contravene a restraining order. The statute also creates a tort of harassment. The court may award damages and grant an injunction restraining the defendant from pursuing conduct that amounts to harassment. Under section 3(6) it is an arrestable offence to violate such an injunction without reasonable cause.[7]

It seems therefore that in the UK there is certainly legislation in place under which domestic violence constitutes a criminal offence.

States should 'ensure that the re-victimization of women does not occur because of . . . enforcement practices or other interventions'[8]

However, the international human rights bodies have also made it clear that not only must appropriate legislation be in place, it should be implemented in such a way as to ensure that victims of domestic violence are treated fairly and in a manner that is sensitive to their needs. It should therefore be ensured that actors in the criminal justice system, such as police and prosecutors, are sensitive to the particular issues involved in cases of domestic violence.

Substantial efforts have been made to improve the responses of the police to the issue of domestic violence. In 1990 a Home Office circular was distributed which stressed the obligation to protect victims from further attack, the necessity of treating domestic violence seriously, the use of the power of arrest, the dangers of mediating between the perpetrator and the victim and the need to keep full records.[9] A further circular on domestic violence, issued in 2000, emphasised that arrest would usually occur when an offence is committed and that charging should occur in all but exceptional cases.[10] In 2008 the National

Policing Improvement Agency issued guidance on investigating domestic violence which stated that,

> Proactive investigation will always be required in cases of domestic abuse as the victims, children, neighbours and other witnesses may be reluctant to disturb the perceived privacy of family life. They might also fear threats, emotional pressure and violent reprisals from suspects.[11]

Domestic Violence Units have been established, with responsibility for following through cases of domestic violence and for giving support to victims. These units also attempt to ameliorate general police responses to domestic violence through training programmes and by ensuring that police officers attending incidents of domestic violence have relevant background information.[12] Domestic Violence Units can, in addition, refer victims to agencies equipped to deal with their emotional and socio-economic needs.[13] Domestic violence procedures are examined by Her Majesty's Inspectorate of Constabulary and recommendations are made. There is ongoing research into police practice in relation to domestic violence.

Nevertheless, there is concern over whether these policies are actually being put into practice. In a Home Office Research Study entitled 'Policing Domestic Violence in the 1990s', published in 1995,[14] it was suggested that although almost all police forces had adopted policies on domestic violence that adhered to the 1990 Home Office Circular, the translation of this policy into practice was limited. It was found that,

> While there was a general awareness among officers about how domestic violence *should* be policed, this awareness was not always reflected in the way they dealt with such cases. It appeared that managers were overly optimistic about how effective they had been in getting the message across to their operational colleagues and were somewhat out of touch about what was happening at ground level.[15]

Over half of officers said they had not received any new guidelines on domestic violence. As Miles comments, 'There is still evidence of bad practice among some officers, which can make calling the police a lottery for the victim'.[16] Hester and Westmarland comment that, 'The "patchiness" of appropriate police responses to domestic violence still needs to be addressed'.[17] In a consultation carried out by the Home Office in 2009, the 'patchy and inconsistent' nature of police responses was again highlighted.[18] Problems have been identified even with the Specialist Domestic Violence Units. These include concerns regarding the extent to which the needs of victims from ethnic minorities are met and the extent to which victims still feel stereotyped and patronised.[19] As Burton remarks, 'Changing working rules and police culture is not as easy as changing the formal policy and guidance'.[20]

It seems that although the UK has policies in place in this area that comply with the recommendations of the international human rights bodies, nevertheless these policies are not being put into practice uniformly. It appears that it is still part of police culture that domestic violence cases are seen as being a waste of time. Such cases are downgraded due to their familial and emotional aspects.

In relation to the prosecution of cases of domestic violence, again it seems that the UK has policies that correspond with the recommendations of the international human rights bodies. In 2001 the Crown Prosecution Service issued its 'Policy On Prosecuting Cases of Domestic Violence'.[21] This document states that it will not automatically be assumed that calling the victim to give evidence is the only method of proving a case. It should be considered whether other evidence is available. If it is necessary to call the victim, all options should be considered in order to assist victims to give their best evidence in court. If a victim withdraws a complaint, this does not necessarily mean that the case will be dropped. The policy document states that, 'As a general rule we will prosecute all cases where there is sufficient evidence and there are no factors preventing us from doing so'.[22] All options should be fully explored when deciding whether or not to proceed with a prosecution where the victim withdraws her complaint. The safety of the victim, children and any other vulnerable individuals should be a paramount concern. The document states that, 'In some cases the violence is so serious, or the previous history shows such a real and continuing danger to the victim or the children or other person, that the public interest in going ahead with a prosecution has to outweigh the victim's wishes'.[23] It is pointed out that a victim can be required to give evidence against her partner and that in very limited circumstances, if the victim is in fear, her statement may be used as evidence without calling her to give evidence. Generally the document emphasises that, in cases of domestic violence, if the evidential test is passed and the victim is willing to give evidence, a prosecution should almost always be brought. If the victim withdraws her support for a prosecution, factors such as the seriousness of the offence, the victim's injuries, the effect on children, the continuing threat to the victim and the current state of the victim's relationship with the defendant should be taken into account. The CPS states that, 'generally, provided we have sufficient evidence, the more serious the offence or the greater the risk of further offences, the more likely we are to prosecute in the public interest – even if victims say they do not wish us to do so'.[24] A similar approach was adopted by the CPS in its 2005 'Policy for Prosecuting Cases of Domestic Violence'.[25] This document states that,

> We know that domestic violence is likely to become more frequent and more serious the longer it continues and can result in death. Because of this, we will sometimes take proceedings even if a victim asks us not to do so. In these cases, we will make the fullest inquiries through the police, to ensure that our decision to prosecute is made against a background of

all available information and with the safety of the victim and any children at the forefront of our minds.[26]

In 2009 the CPS issued a further policy document in which it states that 'the views and interests of the victim are important, but they cannot be the final word on the subject of a CPS prosecution. Any future risks to the victim, their children or any other potential victim have to be taken into consideration'.[27] However, as Choudhry and Herring comment, 'all too often, policies and rhetoric are not matched on the ground by effective responses and solid investigative practice'.[28]

When producing its 2001 review of the progress made towards the implementation of the Beijing Platform for Action, the UN Division for the Advancement of Women issued a questionnaire to all signatory states concerning their own particular progress in this area. The Women's National Commission, which is the UK Government's independent advisory body on women, compiled its own report in response to the government's submission.[29] The WNC works with a range of organisations, including independent women's NGOs, faith groups, political parties and organisations that provide services to women. The WNC's report describes the changes and problems that have affected the advancement of women in the UK since Beijing.

The report stated that in the UK the criminal law in relation to domestic violence needed to be enforced more rigorously by the police and the courts, with a higher standard of evidence collection and stricter sentences. Women who have been subjected to domestic violence should be given support in bringing charges against the perpetrators.[30] The report also recommended that 'the police make special provision for the protection of refuges and refuge workers in their area'.[31] It is well-documented that women suffering from domestic violence are most at risk at the time they leave the relationship. Therefore it is vital that the safety of both those using refuges and those working in them is a priority for the police.[32]

The Beijing Platform for Action stated that the law should be periodically reviewed and analysed 'to ensure its effectiveness in eliminating violence against women, emphasizing the prevention of violence and the prosecution of offenders'.[33] The WNC commented, however, that measures to review the operation of law, policy and practice in the UK in this area are inadequate and the report recommended that central coordination and monitoring by government is necessary.[34]

It seems therefore that the UK is complying to some extent with the recommendations made by the international human rights bodies in relation to improving the response of the criminal justice system to cases of domestic violence. Policies are certainly in place which correspond with these recommendations. Nevertheless, there is some evidence that the policies are not being put into practice and there is still a substantial amount of dissatisfaction with the operation of the criminal law in relation to domestic violence.[35] As Connelly and Cavanagh comment, 'Although the increased public profile of domestic abuse has led to improvements in policing and prosecutorial decision-making, further improvement is clearly needed'.[36]

States should provide 'civil remedies . . . to protect women against . . . violence and abuse in the family'[37]

The international human rights bodies have also made statements on the necessity for states to provide sufficient measures of civil protection for victims of domestic violence.

In the UK one of the most important pieces of civil legislation in relation to domestic violence is Part IV of the Family Law Act 1996, which applies in England and Wales. Similar provisions for Northern Ireland are found in the Family Homes and Domestic Violence (Northern Ireland) Order 1998. This legislation makes provision for non-molestation orders, which prohibit molestation, and occupation orders, which regulate occupation of the family home.

Part IV of the Family Law Act certainly succeeded in simplifying the law in this area. However, Humphries comments that the courts appear reluctant to grant occupation orders.[38] In *G v G (Occupation Order: Conduct)* it was stated that 'It has been said time and time again that orders of exclusion are Draconian and only to be made in exceptional cases'.[39] Humphries concludes that,

> the decisions upon occupation orders are made in exactly the same way as their predecessors, and are made only in exceptional circumstances because they are so Draconian. However, there is no guidance upon what are exceptional circumstances.[40]

Nevertheless, Edwards comments that 'despite the shortcomings, bringing the remedies under one Act has produced a more effective remedy for dealing with domestic violence'.[41]

The Office of Law Reform carried out a review of the Family Homes and Domestic Violence (Northern Ireland) Order 1998 and the findings were published in October 2003. The report concluded that the legislation is generally working well. It was stated that the Order 'provides a great deal of protection for victims of domestic violence and sends a clear message to perpetrators that domestic violence is unacceptable and will not be tolerated'.[42] Nevertheless it was recognised that several changes should be made. For example, the legislation ought to be amended to state clearly that ex parte orders should be made for a short duration, so as to comply with human rights obligations. Also, it should be considered whether it was necessary to alter the legislation to state clearly that exclusion zones can be attached to non-molestation orders. There was, in addition, an issue as to whether the criminal tariff for breach of a non-molestation order should be increased.[43]

It should also be noted that the Protection from Harassment Act 1997/ Protection from Harassment (Northern Ireland) Order 1997 (as discussed previously in this chapter) contains civil law remedies that may be used in relation to domestic violence. Edwards comments that the use of the civil law injunction under this legislation varies between regions.[44]

In the UK's fifth report to the CEDAW Committee, the government stated that a draft Bill on domestic violence would be published.[45] Such legislation was indeed enacted. The Domestic Violence, Crime and Victims Act 2004 includes provisions criminalising the breaches of non-molestation orders made under the Family Law Act 1996, thus allowing the police always to arrest for breach,[46] and extending protection to couples who have never cohabited.[47] The Act also extended the availability of restraining orders under the Protection from Harassment Act 1997 to cover all offences.[48] In addition, the legislation allows restraining orders to be used where a person is not convicted of a criminal charge but the court considers that it is necessary to make an order to protect the victim.[49] In research carried out in 2008, it was found that professionals were of the opinion that being able to arrest for common assault was a positive move. Advocates also indicated that victims welcomed the provisions criminalising breaches of non-molestation orders.[50]

It can thus be seen that the UK now has fairly comprehensive measures of civil law protection that may be used by victims of domestic violence. It appears that overall these measures are working reasonably well. It therefore seems that the state is fulfilling the recommendations made by the international human rights bodies in this area.

'In cases of domestic violence, women should be granted full custody of the children. In cases of woman-battering, the batterer should not be granted visitation rights'[51]

One area in which it seems that the UK is not complying with the recommendations of the international human rights bodies is in relation to child contact applications in cases of domestic violence. In a report issued in 1996, the Special Rapporteur on Violence against Women gave detailed consideration to this issue. It was stated that,

> In cases of domestic violence, women should be granted full custody of the children. In cases of woman-battering, the batterer should not be granted visitation rights so that they may be protected from abuse and from being used as leverage. In cases in which visitation rights are granted, visitation should be supervised and arranged in a way so as not to cause the woman any contact with the batterer. Details such as transportation, the site of the visitations, financial support for the visits and the persons authorized to supervise the visits should all be included in the court decree.[52]

Contrary to the Special Rapporteur's recommendation that 'the batterer should not be granted visitation rights', in the past the UK courts appear to have adopted the view that contact should usually take place and that this approach should only be departed from if there is strong evidence that contact would have a detrimental effect. The courts have traditionally taken the view that the fact that a man abuses his partner has no relevance to his ability to be a fit father.

However, in *Re L (a child) (contact: domestic violence); Re V (a child) (contact: domestic violence); Re M (a child) (contact: domestic violence); Re H (children) (contact: domestic violence)*[53] it seems that the court was beginning to realise that domestic violence is relevant when assessing parenting ability. This case involved four appeals from fathers who had been refused direct contact with their respective children. All the men involved had been violent or had threatened violence towards their spouses or partners. Dame Elizabeth Butler-Sloss stated that,

> The family judges and magistrates need to have a heightened awareness of the existence of and consequences . . . on children of exposure to domestic violence between their parents . . . In a contact . . . application, where allegations of domestic violence are made which might have an effect on the outcome, those allegations must be adjudicated upon and found proved or not proved . . . In cases of proved domestic violence, . . . the court has the task of weighing in the balance the seriousness of the domestic violence, the risks involved and the impact on the child against the positive factors, if any, of contact between the parent found to have been violent and the child. In this context, the ability of the offending parent to recognise his past conduct, be aware of the need for change and make genuine efforts to do so, will be likely to be an important consideration.[54]

All four appeals were dismissed.

Nevertheless, it is worth noting that the court appeared to adopt a slightly different approach in *Re H* from that in the other three appeals. *Re H* primarily involved threats made to the mother rather than actual violence. The family lived in Germany. However, the mother fled with the children to England. Although admitting that the mother was very frightened of the father, Dame Elizabeth Butler-Sloss nevertheless commented that the removal of the children from Germany to England was 'reprehensible and regrettable'.[55] She also stated that she hoped 'the father will use constructively the opportunity of indirect contact with his children'.[56] Although the appeal was dismissed, it would nonetheless seem from the general tone of the remarks made by the court that contact may be allowed more easily when the case concerns threats as opposed to actual violence.

The Special Rapporteur also stated that, in cases in which contact is allowed, visitation should be supervised and arranged in a way so that the victim has no contact with the batterer. Various details such as transport, the site of the visitations, and the persons authorised to supervise the visits should be included in the court order. It seems that the courts in the UK do not routinely follow these recommendations.

The report of the WNC produced in 2000 commented that judges often fail to give adequate weight to the effect on children of witnessing domestic violence.[57] Thus it was recommended 'that further training and guidance is given to judges to help them give due weight to the risk of granting contact to a violent parent. The law in respect of child contact . . . needs monitoring in more detail'.[58] As Bell comments, 'A previous pattern of coercive control commonly involving regular physical and psychological . . . aggression . . . can have profound implications for children's safety and welfare, despite the parents' relationship having ended'.[59] Burton makes the point that, although contact is supposed to be about the welfare of the child, rather than about a father's rights, 'in some cases the courts seem to lose sight of this principle'.[60]

States should provide 'Protective measures, including refuges, counselling, rehabilitation and support services for women who are the victims of violence or who are at risk of violence'[61]

The UN human rights institutions have certainly made comprehensive recommendations to states to provide social support measures to victims of domestic violence, such as refuge accommodation, counselling and job training. The CEDAW Committee considered the UK's third and fourth periodic reports in 1999. The UK's fourth report noted that the accommodation needs of victims of domestic violence were addressed through both local and national action.[62] However, the CEDAW Committee responded by recommending 'that a unified and multifaceted national strategy to eliminate violence against women be implemented to include legal, educational, financial and social components, in particular support for victims'.[63]

The UK in 1999 published a document entitled 'Living Without Fear: an integrated approach to tackling violence against women'. In this publication the government stated, 'We will deliver on the commitment to tackle violence against women made at the fourth UN World Conference on Women held in Beijing in 1995'. This document outlined good practice in the area of domestic violence and described the government's commitment to introducing an integrated policy and funding framework for support services, as well as to improving the criminal justice system's response to victims, and to increasing awareness of issues surrounding domestic violence. However, sufficient funding has not been provided to allow such practice to be wholly implemented.

The WNC's report of 2000 highlighted 'the chronic under-funding of existing core services for abused women and children'.[64] The primary difficulty highlighted was 'the continuing absence of clear commitment to secure core funding for women's refuge and outreach services providing independent advocacy and support'.[65] The report stated that, 'There is a vital need to develop a co-ordinated national strategy for the provision and funding of refuges, helplines, outreach, counselling and other specialist services for women and children who are survivors of domestic or sexual violence'.[66] According to the report, the government should indicate exactly how much funding is provided for measures to target violence against women and how much is planned. The funding of local refuge support services was described as being 'patchy and inadequate'.[67] Another problem highlighted was that the funding of the Women's Aid Federations is inequitable across the UK. In particular, funding for the Women's Aid Federation of England is disproportionately low compared with the funding given to its counterparts in Scotland, Wales and Northern Ireland.[68] The WNC recommended 'that secure core funding be guaranteed by Government on an equitable basis across the UK, to ensure that refuge services are available to all women who need them regardless of where they live'.[69]

The UK's fifth and sixth reports to the CEDAW Committee were considered in 2008. The sixth report stated that the government had put £32.1 million of capital funding into refuge accommodation between 2003 and 2006, in order to create new refuge places and renovate existing ones, resulting in approximately 511 new or upgraded units. In 2005–2006, £200,000 was provided to develop minimum service standards for the Women's Aid network of domestic violence services.[70] Also, a scheme entitled 'Supporting People' was established in 2003. The report stated that the scheme could help domestic violence survivors to live more independent lives in their own homes in addition to supporting domestic violence refuges for women who had no recourse to public funds.[71] Nevertheless, in its Concluding Observations on the reports, the Committee noted with concern 'the lack of adequate support and services for victims'[72] and the impending closure of a number of domestic violence shelters.[73] It recognised that the difficulty was 'compounded by the funding crisis facing NGOs working in the area of violence against women and the forced closure of a number of such organizations'.[74] Therefore it urged the government to provide increased and sustained funding to civil society groups involved in the area of women's rights.[75] In addition, the Committee recommended 'the establishment of additional counselling and other support services for victims of violence'.[76]

The Women's National Commission's shadow report of 2005 also highlighted the crucial problem of funding for services for victims of domestic violence. Indeed, the shadow report commented that funding was in a 'perilous state'.[77] The report stated that women need services that provide information, support and advocacy and that these services need to be funded. A study of women's groups in London showed that feminist, campaigning and human rights sectors received a mere 1 per cent of the total funding granted to the organisations in the study.[78] Four per cent of the women's groups were found to operate on no funding at all,[79] while 59 per cent had had crises in funding between 1996 and 2000.[80] It is noteworthy that the government withdrew funding from the Rape Crisis Federation in 2003. The WNC's report of 2007 recommended that 'the Government take further measures . . . to provide the support and outreach services necessary to meet the needs of women who have experienced gender-based violence, and that these should be fully accessible'.[81]

Levison and Harwin also highlight the problem of underfunding of refuge services. They point out that refuge services rely on housing benefit as a means of funding and therefore often cannot accommodate women who are unable to meet the full cost of the charges.[82] Barran remarks on the 'lack of specialist support for victims of domestic abuse'.[83] Overall, it seems that the UK is not complying with the recommendations of the international human rights bodies in relation to providing sufficient measures of social support to victims of domestic violence.

States should implement 'public information and education programmes'[84] and 'train all public officials in the administration of justice, education and health sectors to be sensitive and energetic with regard to issues relating to violence against women'[85]

The international human rights bodies have made clear recommendations to states that they should adopt measures both to improve societal awareness of domestic violence and to educate professionals coming into contact with victims of domestic violence concerning the issues involved.

In the UK's fourth periodic report to the CEDAW Committee the state pointed out that since the last report, there had been a number of public awareness campaigns implemented on the issue of domestic violence.[86] In introducing the report the UK's representative stated that the government was now committed to improving women's position in society.[87] However, Hague and Malos point out that this public awareness raising work has so far been short-term and sporadic. They state that there needs to be a sustained campaign to change attitudes within society.[88] Nevertheless, in 2009 the Home Office published a strategy on violence against women which stated that it was committed to 'developing a national communications strategy designed to challenge attitudes towards [violence against women] among all members of the public, and to raise awareness of existing services which support women'.[89]

During the 1990s, domestic violence training became an issue of increasing interest,[90] and by 2009 the government had recognised that 'raising awareness of domestic violence with a wide range of practitioners and providing appropriate training and tools is key to early identification and intervention'.[91] As regards social services, a number of departments now have policies in place on working with victims of domestic violence. However, Hague and Malos state that, 'it is still unusual for very much support from social services to be forthcoming solely to meet abused women's needs, if there is not some other factor (like the existence of children) involved'.[92] Awareness among healthcare professionals is also rising, with various accident and emergency departments developing domestic violence policies. However, Davidson, King, Garcia and Marchant comment that 'systematic attempts to identify and help women experiencing domestic violence are still few and far between in the health services in the UK'.[93] Healthcare workers differ in the degree to which they regard domestic violence as being a health issue. Also, sometimes victims of domestic violence have reported a negative attitude towards them on the part of healthcare professionals.[94] Often such professionals advise victims to leave their partners, without realising how difficult this course of action might be.[95] If the professional is dealing with other members of the family, in addition to the woman experiencing domestic violence, they may feel that their care for the other family members is in some way complicated. Another problem may be that opportunities for speaking to the woman on her own may be limited in particular healthcare settings.[96] Essentially, 'Health care systems may not be best organised to best meet the needs of victims of domestic violence'.[97]

In the UK's sixth report to the CEDAW Committee, it was stated that in 2005 the Crown Prosecution Service had launched a three-year training programme for all prosecutors and caseworkers. By December 2006, over 2,400 CPS staff had been trained in dealing with domestic violence.[98] In 2009 the Home Office stated that it was committed to working with a wide range of professional bodies to explore how training on violence against women could be included in continuing professional development for all frontline staff.[99]

States should 'implement multidisciplinary policies, measures and strategies, within and outside of the criminal justice system, with respect to domestic violence in all its facets, including legal, law enforcement, judicial, societal, educational, psychological, economic, health-related and correctional aspects'[100]

States have been urged by the international human rights bodies to adopt coordinated strategies to deal with domestic violence, whereby all relevant agencies work together to achieve the most effective outcome.

In the UK's fourth report to the CEDAW Committee, it was stated that by 1996 over 200 domestic violence forums had been established across Scotland, England and Wales.[101] The government recognised the need to develop a framework for local action.[102] It is also true that the Crime and Disorder Act 1998 places a duty on the police and local authorities to develop local partnerships to reduce crime and disorder. These partnerships bring together all the relevant agencies, including those concerned with domestic violence. The government's 'Living Without Fear' publication included interdepartmental guidance on a multi-agency approach to violence against women.[103] In 2009 the government stated that the number of Multi-Agency Risk Assessment Conferences, which focus on the safety of high-risk victims of domestic violence, had risen to 200, and that 'a multi-agency approach to dealing with victims of domestic violence is crucial to understanding the dynamics and context of individual cases'.[104] It certainly seems that in this area the UK is implementing the recommendations of the international human rights bodies.

States should 'take special measures to eliminate violence against women, particularly those in vulnerable situations'[105]

The international human rights bodies have recommended that particular measures should be taken to tackle certain risk factors associated with domestic violence, such as alcohol and drug abuse. It should also be ensured that women from ethnic minorities have sufficient access to support services. Nevertheless, as discussed in the previous chapter, the approach of the UN human rights bodies towards the tackling of risk factors does seem somewhat poorly developed.

The UK Government commented in 'Safety and Justice: The Government's Proposals on Domestic Violence' that 'there is a clear link between alcohol misuse and domestic violence'.[106] It was stated that the Prime Minister's Strategy Unit was undertaking a study to develop an alcohol harm reduction strategy for England. This would include issues such as anti-social behaviour and alcohol-related crime.[107] The government also claimed to be committed to educating young people as regards responsible attitudes towards drinking.[108] An Alcohol Reduction Strategy for England was indeed published in March 2004. This strategy aimed to tackle harm caused by the misuse of alcohol.[109]

In addition, it was commented in 'Safety and Justice' that, 'research indicates that drugs are less likely to be an issue in domestic violence than alcohol, but where they are a factor, they are more likely to be related to chronic victimisation'.[110] A ten-year drug strategy (2008–2018) is in place. This strategy aims to restrict the supply of illegal drugs and reduce the demand for them.[111]

The government stated in 2003 that 'whilst there has been considerable research done on domestic violence, little of this has focused on domestic violence among the black and minority (BME) communities'.[112] There was, however, a Development and Practice Report issued by the Home Office in 2005 entitled 'Tackling Domestic Violence: providing advocacy and support to survivors from Black and other ethnic minorities',[113] the purpose of which was to provide guidance for practitioners working with victims of domestic violence from ethnic minority communities. In 2007 a CPS Domestic Violence Equality and Diversity Review was carried out, which included an analysis of domestic violence data by ethnicity. Focus groups were held in 2008 with a range of communities to address diversity issues.[114]

States should provide 'rehabilitation programmes for perpetrators of domestic violence'[115]

The UN human rights bodies have urged states to develop rehabilitation programmes for perpetrators of domestic violence. In the UK, government backing has been given to probation service work with perpetrators and to voluntary sector projects.[116] A number of men's programmes have formed a network called Respect, which issues good practice guidelines for such programmes. The network holds conferences and meetings and any new projects can join.[117] Mullender and Burton comment, however, that provision in this area is 'currently expanding, poorly resourced and inadequately evaluated'.[118] Nevertheless, it must be remembered that battery treatment programmes are a controversial area. There is some doubt about whether such programmes can actually work.[119] The effectiveness of even the best US programmes has not yet been conclusively shown.[120] Indeed, 'perpetrators' programmes are a field of intervention in which it is possible to do harm as well as good'.[121]

States 'should encourage the compilation of statistics and research on the extent, causes and effects of violence, and on the effectiveness of measures to prevent and deal with violence'[122]

The international human rights bodies have recommended that states conduct research into issues surrounding domestic violence. This is one area in which the UK Government is certainly fulfilling the recommendations made. The Home Office has commissioned many pieces of informative research into domestic violence in recent years.[123]

Why is the United Kingdom complying/not complying with the recommendations?

It seems that the UK is complying to a limited degree with the recommendations of the international human rights bodies in relation to the issue of domestic violence. However, it must be remembered that the changes in government policy in this area, although they correlate to some extent with the recommendations, may not necessarily have taken place because of these recommendations. In recent times, the UK Government has come under pressure to act on the issue of domestic violence from a number of sources, of which the international human rights bodies are only one. Other sources include academic commentators and groups such as Women's Aid. All these parties are broadly advising the government to implement the same types of measures and are doing so at the same time. It is thus extremely difficult to ascertain the exact contribution that statements by the international human rights bodies have made to policy on domestic violence. However, in areas in which the UK appears to be implementing the recommendations, it is necessary to examine the extent to which it is likely that this is due to the recommendations themselves. Also, in areas in which the UK is not implementing the recommendations, it is necessary to assess why this is the case.

Improving the criminal justice system

The UK has in place legislation under which domestic violence is a criminal offence. However, it can certainly be stated that this legislation was not enacted because of the recommendations of the international human rights bodies. The Offences Against the Person Act was passed in 1861, long before any of these bodies were established. The Act encompasses all types of assault and was certainly not enacted to deal specifically with domestic violence. As regards the Protection from Harassment Act 1997, this legislation was passed primarily to deal with the issue of stalking, although it can also be used in cases of domestic violence. As was commented in the House of Commons during debates on the Bill,

> Although the Bill is generally perceived to be about stalking, its tentacles are likely to spread far wider. In some ways it is like four Bills rolled into one – an anti-stalking Bill, a feuding neighbours Bill, a domestic violence Bill and a Bill that extends civil injunction remedies in such cases to the criminal courts.[124]

It can certainly be stated that domestic violence was not the main issue in the minds of those who enacted the legislation and that the statements of the international human rights bodies did not play a part in its passing.

Steps have been taken to improve the response of the police to the issue of domestic violence, although problems do remain. It seems, however, that the measures that have been adopted are unlikely to be the result of the statements made by the international human rights bodies. In recent years a large amount of research has been undertaken in relation to the response of the police to cases of domestic violence. For example, in 1989 a very influential and important study, commissioned by the Research and Planning Unit of the Home Office, was carried out by Lorna Smith.[125] This report was very critical of the police. Smith commented that 'the single most common police response is non-intervention, that is, officers state that there is nothing they can do and leave the incident to which they have been called'.[126] Essentially the police were not treating incidents of domestic violence as even being criminal in character. It is noteworthy that in the next year a Home Office circular was distributed which recommended that the police adopt pro-arrest and pro-prosecution policies in relation to domestic violence.[127] The circular stated that domestic violence units and domestic violence liaison officer posts should be established. The necessity of treating domestic violence as a criminal offence was heavily emphasised. It certainly seems that this change in policy was due to the research that had been implemented only one year previously.

During the 1990s a great deal of research was carried out into the response of the police to domestic violence. For example, in 1994 research commissioned by the Home Office Police Department was undertaken by Morley and Mullender.[128] In 1995 another Home Office Research Study examined 'Policing domestic violence in the 1990s'.[129] Two papers in the Police Research Series dealt with domestic violence,[130] while one of the 'Reducing Domestic Violence . . . What Works?' research papers, produced in 2000, focused on 'Policing Domestic Violence'.[131]

In 2000 another Home Office circular was issued on the response of the police to domestic violence.[132] This was a detailed document that outlined good practice in this area. It seems that this circular owes much more to the research papers produced during the previous decade than to the statements of the international human rights bodies. For example, research carried out by Hanmer and Griffiths, which had been produced earlier in the year,[133] had outlined a number of the elements contained in good policing practice in relation to domestic violence. These included 'standardised definitions of domestic violence and repeat victimisation between forces and other agencies'.[134] The circular stated that, 'A shared definition [of domestic violence] is . . . important amongst agencies working together locally, both to ensure effective operations and to ensure meaningful and comparable data for the assessment of progress and use of resources'.[135] The circular also stated that Force Policy should include 'a definition of repeat victimisation'.[136] Hanmer and Griffiths had emphasised the need for 'consistent interventions'.[137] The circular similarly stated that Chief Officers should 'ensure that investigations are carried out and are of a consistent quality'.[138] Hanmer and Griffiths had commented that there should be 'organisation and management based on unequivocal leadership, robust accountability and good management support'.[139] The circular further stated that:

> divisional commanders should establish and document lines of accountability for their domestic violence response. There must be a clear direct line of supervision for domestic violence officers. This area of policing is stressful and mechanisms should be in place to help alleviate as much stress as possible.[140]

Hanmer and Griffiths had commented that good policing practice includes 'training of all police staff in domestic violence awareness, policy, good practice and new initiatives'.[141] The circular stated that 'all personnel who are likely to come into contact with victims of domestic violence . . . should receive training. This should cover awareness issues, policy, good practice, new initiatives and how to investigate such incidents'.[142] Hanmer and Griffiths remarked that there should be 'performance monitoring of officers, divisions and forces, police attendance and the use of resources'.[143] The circular stated that Chief Officers should 'produce meaningful performance indicators to concentrate efforts and ensure that policy is adhered to'.[144]

It would certainly appear from the similarities even of the wording between the circular and the research produced only months earlier that the research had had a substantial impact on the circular. It would also seem that research produced in 1998 by Plotnikoff and Woolfson[145] had a significant impact on the circular. For example, this research had found that, 'Domestic incidents involving police officers, either as victims or offenders, presented problems for [domestic violence officers]. Guidance on dealing with such issues was addressed in only one force'.[146] The circular recommended that Force Policy should include 'guidance for dealing with police officers and civilian staff who may themselves be victims or perpetrators of domestic violence'.[147] The research had found that '[domestic violence officer] records were seldom accessible by other officers, which undermined their general intelligence potential'.[148] The circular stated that Chief Officers should 'ensure the domestic violence records are accessible 24 hours a day'.[149] The research had also found that, 'despite close links between the two areas, domestic violence and child protection indices were rarely integrated'.[150] The circular also stated that Chief Officers should 'link domestic violence information with child protection data, as there is routine cross over of information'.[151]

On the other hand, there is no evidence that the statements of the international human rights bodies have had any impact.[152] The circular does contain a statement drawing attention to the right to life found in article 2 of the European Convention on Human Rights.[153] However, this point is not elaborated upon and it is not clearly stated that domestic violence may constitute a violation of the right to life. It is not recognised in the circular that domestic violence breaches other rights, such as the right to be free from inhuman or degrading treatment. CEDAW is certainly not mentioned and neither are any of the statements made by the international human rights bodies.

Nonetheless, it is noteworthy that the guidance on investigating domestic violence issued by the National Policing Agency in 2008 states that the Human Rights Act 1998 places positive obligations on police officers to take reasonable action to safeguard the rights of victims and children under articles 2, 3 and 8 of the European Convention on Human Rights.[154] It is also stated that failure to make an arrest when there are grounds to do so may leave the police force vulnerable to legal challenge under the Act. The document proceeds to emphasise that the police are required under the Human Rights Act and the 2000 circular to take positive action in all domestic abuse cases. If an arrest is not made in such a case where a power of arrest exists, the reason for this decision should be recorded.[155] Although these statements are fairly brief, they may nevertheless demonstrate that developments in human rights law may have had some degree of impact on the formulation of this guidance.

However, on the whole, it seems that the statements of the human rights bodies had little effect on the development of police policy in relation to domestic violence. This conclusion is perhaps not surprising as it seems likely that pressure emanating from within a state will have a greater impact than pressure emanating from external bodies that can impose no sanctions if their recommendations are ignored.

Providing measures of civil protection

As stated previously, one of the most important pieces of civil legislation in relation to domestic violence is Part IV of the Family Law Act 1996. However, it seems that the statements of the international human rights bodies played very little part, if any, in the enactment of this legislation. By the mid 1990s there were various statutes which could be utilised by victims of domestic violence seeking the protection of the civil law. However, this body of law had developed incrementally and was therefore 'complex, confusing and riddled with anomalies both substantive and jurisdictional'.[156] In addition to statutes such as the Matrimonial Homes Act 1983, the Domestic Violence and Matrimonial Proceedings Act 1976 and the Domestic Proceedings and Magistrates' Courts Act 1978, there was also the 'inherent jurisdiction' which was inherited from the Court of Chancery. The issue was examined by the Law Commission, which issued a Report entitled 'Domestic Violence and Occupation of the Family Home'.[157] The Commission stated that it had three aims in reforming the civil law in this area.[158] The first objective was to remove inconsistencies and to obtain a clear and comprehensive code. The second was to provide sufficient protection, and the third aim was to avoid the exacerbation of hostilities between the adults involved, in so far as this would be compatible with providing protection for both adults and children. The main proposal of the Commission was for a coherent set of civil law remedies in relation to domestic violence to be contained in a single statute. It was recommended that this statute should include non-molestation orders and occupation orders.[159] The Family Homes and Domestic Violence Bill was introduced in 1995. However, this Bill was withdrawn for further consideration due to a campaign by those who believed that it would erode the distinction between the legal rights of married and unmarried couples and thus undermine the institution of marriage. A number of changes were made and the relevant provisions became Part IV of the Family Law Act 1996.

As Lord Mackay of Clashfern, the then Lord Chancellor, stated in December 1996,

> Parliament has taken action in the Family Law Act 1996 to simplify and improve the existing civil law on domestic violence and occupation of the family home in order to offer increased protection to victims of domestic violence. The complexity and inconsistencies of the current law have been the cause of a great deal of justified complaint. Part IV of the Act aims to address that unsatisfactory situation by creating a clear, simple and comprehensive code with a single, consistent set of remedies which will be available in all courts with jurisdiction in family matters.[160]

It seems therefore that Part IV of the Family Law Act was passed in order, as the Law Commission stated, to remove the inconsistencies that had previously existed in this area. There was certainly no mention of a need to implement the recommendations of the international human rights bodies. Rather, it appears that the legislation was the result of what Lord Mackay termed 'a great deal of justified complaint' within the UK itself.

The Domestic Violence, Crime and Victims Bill was introduced on 18 June 2003 by John Bercow, the Member of Parliament for Buckingham. Bercow's main reason for introducing the Bill seems to have been the extremely high levels of domestic violence that are evident in the UK.[161] He commented that the report of a recent British Crime Survey had revealed that in the previous year around 635,000 incidents of domestic violence took place in the UK. He also stated that an assault on a woman takes place on average every 26 seconds and that two women per week die as a result of domestic violence. Bercow commented that according to the World Health Organization, domestic violence contributes to death and disability to a greater extent than cancer, road accidents and war.

Bercow also referred to the major costs to the criminal justice system, the National Health Service, social services and the economy due to domestic violence.[162] There was certainly no mention of the recommendations of the international human rights bodies, either by Bercow in introducing the Bill or by other Members of Parliament in debating the legislation. It seems that the British Crime Survey research into the extent of domestic violence in the UK may well have been a key factor in the introduction of the Bill.

Child contact

The UK does not appear to be complying with the recommendations of the international human rights bodies in relation to child contact applications in cases of domestic violence. The Special Rapporteur on Violence against Women has stated that in such cases 'the batterer should not be granted visitation rights'.[163] The UK courts have traditionally taken the view that the fact that a man abuses his partner has no relevance to his ability to be a fit parent. In the case of *Re L (a child) (contact: domestic violence); Re V (a child) (contact: domestic violence); Re M (a child) (contact; domestic violence); Re H (children) (contact: domestic violence)*[164] the court did seem to recognise that domestic violence is relevant when assessing parental ability. However, it appears that in this case the court was influenced by the evidence given by a number of experts and by 'A Report to the Lord Chancellor on the Question of Parental Contact in Cases where there is Domestic Violence',[165] rather than by any recommendations emanating from the international human rights bodies. It was stated in this Report that there should be more awareness of the impact of domestic violence on children, and also of its impact on resident parents. Arrangements needed to be put in place to protect both the child and the resident parent from harm. The court was also influenced by a report prepared by two child psychiatrists, Dr Sturge and Dr Glaser, that outlined the risks of allowing contact.[166] The *Re L* case was decided in 2000, the year in which both of these reports had been issued. By contrast, the Special Rapporteur had made her recommendations regarding contact in 1996. It would thus seem that the court was influenced in its decision by the two reports and not by the Special Rapporteur's recommendations. This finding serves to emphasise the point that pressure emanating from within a state may well be more likely to achieve results than pressure emanating from international human rights bodies.

Re G (Domestic Violence: Direct Contact)[167] was decided one month after the *Re L* case. *Re G* involved a child whose father had killed her mother after a history of domestic violence. The local authority placed the child with a foster family. The father sought regular contact, but this was refused. The court held that the father was an unsuitable carer and that his lack of remorse or of any effort to recognise the impact of his violence made direct contact problematic. Bridge comments that the views of Dr Sturge and Dr Glaser in *Re L* were very relevant to this case, especially the point that domestic violence exhibits a serious failure in parenting and a failure to protect both the child and the child's carer.[168] It thus seems that although the attitudes of the UK courts towards contact in cases of domestic violence are moving towards the position adopted by the Special Rapporteur, nevertheless this shift appears to be due to factors other than the Special Rapporteur's comments.

Providing measures of social support for victims

The provision of measures of social support to victims of domestic violence is one area in which the UK Government is certainly not fulfilling the recommendations of the international human rights bodies. It is perhaps not surprising that this is the area in which the government seems to be most reluctant to act. Providing measures of social support entails spending larger amounts of financial resources than any other category of measure discussed in this book. The fact that the government chooses not to spend such amounts of money on the provision of social support measures may be indicative of an attitude whereby domestic violence is still seen as a 'women's issue' and therefore not of such pressing importance as other issues. It seems that a basic reluctance on the part of government to spend large sums of money if at all possible may be preventing the adoption of comprehensive measures of social support for victims.

Changing attitudes

In relation to increasing societal awareness of domestic violence, the UK Government is certainly implementing the recommendations of the international human rights bodies, at least to some extent. Various public awareness campaigns have been carried out in recent years. There have also been attempts to increase the awareness of professionals who may be particularly likely to come into contact with victims of domestic violence, such as those working in the health services. This category of recommendations is perhaps the one that has been developed most by the international human rights bodies and it is certainly possible that the statements may have encouraged the government to take steps to increase awareness of domestic violence.

On the other hand, groups such as Women's Aid have also highlighted the need for the government to take steps to increase awareness of the issues involved in domestic violence. Academic researchers have made similar recommendations. For example, in 2000 Davidson, King, Garcia and Marchant stated that,

> Education and training regarding domestic violence should be incorporated into the curricula for all health professionals and into post-graduate education as well. Training should be made available for all NHS staff working with women, particularly in primary care, maternity services, paediatrics, psychiatry and emergency care.[169]

Similarly, in 2004 Taket commented that,

> All health professionals and staff working in health settings should ideally receive training on inquiring about domestic violence. Given the importance of domestic violence as a factor impacting on health, training about enquiry should be part of pre-registration curricula *and* post-registration on-the-job training for *all* health professionals.[170]

It is extremely difficult to assess the role that the statements of the international human rights bodies have had in relation to the measures that have been adopted to raise awareness of domestic violence. Nevertheless, the possibility that the statements have had an impact in this area cannot be ruled out.

Ensuring inter-agency cooperation

In its Concluding Observations on the third and fourth periodic reports of the UK, the CEDAW Committee recommended that 'a unified and multifaceted strategy to eliminate violence against women be implemented to include legal, educational, financial and social components, in particular support for victims'.[171] The UK's fifth report seems to indicate that the government acted on the criticisms it had received. In the fifth report the government recognised that 'preventing and eliminating this crime requires a unified and multifaceted national approach, including active joined-up working across all Government departments to deliver co-ordinated policy action on this important issue'.[172] It appears that the government put its rhetoric into practice by producing multi-agency guidance for addressing domestic violence in March 2000[173] and by establishing a Ministerial Working Group in 2001, in order to ensure a coordinated approach. The fifth report stated that,

> The group is . . . working to strengthen the Government's multifaceted and integrated approach to tackling violence against women, in particular domestic violence, including legal, educational, financial and social components, in particular support for victims.[174]

This group brought together Ministers from the main departments to focus on 'developing joined up policy' on various areas of action, including increasing safe accommodation choices for women and children; awareness raising and education; and ensuring appropriate and consistent responses from the police and Crown Prosecution Service.[175] The UK's sixth report stated that the group 'provides high-level leadership and accountability across Government bringing together Departments central to tackling domestic violence . . . together with colleagues from the Devolved Administrations'.[176] In addition, the Women and Equality Unit was working in partnership with the Home Office 'to ensure effective joined up working in Government on this issue'.[177] It certainly appears that the government acted on the recommendation of the CEDAW Committee to implement 'a unified and multifaceted national approach'.

It seems therefore that the statements of the international human rights bodies have had a significant impact on government policy on inter-agency cooperation. However, it appears that other factors have also played a part in developments in this area. Academic researchers have pointed out the advantages of adopting an inter-agency approach. For example, in 2000 Hague commented that among the potential benefits of such strategies are 'clear and transparent communication mechanisms; better targeted resources; common approaches to service delivery based on women's needs and preferences [and] more effective pooling of resources'.[178] Hague also points out that the first multi-agency projects were established in the 1980s, as a result of pressure from the refuge movement and changes in public attitudes.[179] It seems therefore that the statements of the international human rights bodies were not responsible for the initial adoption of an inter-agency approach. Nevertheless, it appears from the dialogue that took place between the UK and the CEDAW Committee that the statements did play a role in the development of this approach. It is however noteworthy that in its Concluding Observations on the fifth and sixth reports of the UK, the CEDAW Committee expressed the view that the national strategy was still not sufficiently comprehensive.[180]

Tackling risk factors

The UK certainly has strategies in place to deal with drug and alcohol related crime. However, these are general rather than specific strategies to domestic violence. It seems therefore that the statements of the international human rights bodies relating to these issues are very unlikely to have had an impact in the UK.

As regards the recommendation that states should ensure that women from ethnic minorities have access to support services, the Home Office did issue a Development and Practice Report in 2005 that was intended to provide guidance to practitioners working with victims of domestic violence from ethnic minority communities.[181] However, it was stated in the report that its purpose was to 'draw out from research the messages for practice development, implementation and operation'.[182] The report was based on various pieces of research in this field[183] and the statements of the international human rights bodies certainly had no part to play in its compilation.

Battery treatment programmes

The UK Government has given backing to work with perpetrators carried out by the voluntary sector and by the probation service. However, as was pointed out by Mullender and Burton, perpetrator programmes are controversial as there is no conclusive evidence for the proposition that they are effective.[184] Battery treatment programmes tend to involve perpetrators interacting in group situations. This may actually encourage batterers to continue engaging in domestic violence.[185] There is also a view that such programmes may dilute the response of the criminal justice system to domestic violence.[186] It is likely that if the government continues to take steps to combat domestic violence, it will be more focused on implementing measures that will be more widely supported than would the further development of battery treatment programmes.

Could the statements of international human rights bodies be used more effectively?

Overall it seems that the UK is complying with the recommendations of the international human rights bodies to only a limited extent. Even in areas in which the state does seem to be acting in accordance with the recommendations, at least to a certain degree, such as in relation to improving the criminal justice system, it seems very likely that the UK is acting in such a way due to factors other than the recommendations themselves. Nevertheless, it appears that the recommendations have had an impact on policy as regards developing an inter-agency approach. However, could the statements of the international human rights bodies be used more effectively?

In strict theoretical terms, the CEDAW Convention is the only international document discussed in this section of the book that is actually binding on states. However, if a state does not comply with its duties even under CEDAW in the area of domestic violence, there is little that can be done to enforce compliance. For example, the CEDAW Committee cannot impose sanctions. Nonetheless, the statements of international human rights bodies can be used by domestic violence groups and NGOs to put pressure on the government to fulfil its obligations.

As Merry comments, the impact of CEDAW 'depends on its cultural legitmacy and its embodiment in local cultures and legal consciousness'.[187] National NGOs can play a substantial role in ensuring that the Convention is firmly embedded in local cultures. Essentially, NGOs can publicise the fact that the state has obligations under CEDAW and that it is failing to comply with these duties. The government may then be shamed into fulfilling its obligations.

Women in Asia and Africa use CEDAW as a powerful tool much more frequently than women do in western states. In 1995 Zimbabwe reported to the CEDAW Committee that it had passed the Legal Age of Majority Act, which would give women equality as regards the right to vote, property rights and inheritance rights. Two weeks later the Parliament of Zimbabwe was on the point of repealing the legislation. However, a range of NGOs took action through the media and were successful in shaming the government into allowing the legislation to proceed. This is a classic example of CEDAW being used to promote the rights of women. In South Africa, an international human rights law strategy has been used by women to advocate reform.[188] Likewise, women's groups in Asia frequently use CEDAW as a tool to educate society in the values of equality and non-discrimination. For example, women's groups in Japan rally around CEDAW. In Iran and Zambia, the UN treaties provide focal points for lobbying activities in the areas of women's and children's rights.[189] In Nepal, women have used CEDAW to strengthen arguments in favour of a bill that would give property rights to women, raise the marriageable age and ensure harsher sanctions for sexual assault and rape.[190]

In Bangladesh, the use of CEDAW by NGOs resulted in a substantial improvement in the attitude of the government. Bangladesh ratified CEDAW in 1984. For several years the state failed to fulfil its obligations under the Treaty. In 1993, Bangladesh presented its second periodic report to the CEDAW Committee. This report contained a multitude of mistakes and was very short. However, the combined third and fourth periodic report, presented in 1997, showed a great improvement. This transformation was due largely to the work of NGOs in Bangladesh. In November 1993, women's organisations in Bangladesh set up an NGO forum to prepare for the Beijing Conference. This forum had three primary activities. First, workshops on CEDAW were held at both local and national levels. Second, newsletters on the subject of women's rights were distributed. Third, a media campaign was implemented. Essentially NGOs were able to assert influence over the government in its preparation for Beijing. Following the Conference, the government of Bangladesh formulated a National Action Plan to implement its obligations under CEDAW. Its third and fourth periodic report, written in accordance with the CEDAW guidelines, was evidence of the changes that had taken place in the attitude of the Bangladesh government. The report was informative and expressed the intention of the state to comply fully with CEDAW. It also recognised the efforts made by NGOs. As evidence of its commitment, the Bangladesh government withdrew two of its reservations to CEDAW. It would certainly seem that the work of NGOs played a major role in the change in attitude of the Bangladesh government.[191]

In China, a women's NGO called Domestic Violence Network directly links the issue of domestic violence to international human rights law. In so doing, the NGO 'underlines domestic violence as a high profile international public policy issue and gains legitimacy in its call for institutional action'.[192] Zhang comments that the argument that domestic violence constitutes a breach of human rights law 'powerfully counters the institutional tendency to relegate domestic violence to the realm of personal privacy'.[193]

By contrast, many women's groups in the UK are unaware of the existence of CEDAW or of the ways in which it can be used to make a difference in the lives of women. However, domestic violence groups may benefit from a recognition of the potential held by international human rights treaties to contribute to the fight to combat violence against women in the home. If such groups were to publicise the fact that the government is not fulfilling its international duties under CEDAW, this may place more pressure on the government to take further steps to address the issue of domestic violence.[194] Nevertheless, it must be remembered that domestic violence is not actually mentioned explicitly in CEDAW and was only brought within the ambit of the Treaty by General Recommendation No. 19 of the CEDAW Committee. Essentially, using CEDAW to promote women's rights is one thing, using it to deal with domestic violence may be quite another.

Conclusion

The international human rights bodies have certainly made a fairly comprehensive set of recommendations to states in relation to domestic violence. If these recommendations were implemented it seems that beneficial results would occur. All of the measures outlined in the second chapter of this book have been included by the human rights bodies. However, the recommendations have not been uniformly implemented in the UK. It seems that the main reason for this may be a simple lack of will on the part of the state, combined with a lack of enforcement mechanisms. The achievement of the measures outlined in the international human rights documents requires the expenditure of financial resources. It is therefore unlikely that the government would be very willing to implement the recommendations. It is noteworthy that the most problematic area in relation to the government's response to domestic violence is the provision of social support measures to victims. This is the category of recommendations that requires the greatest amount of money to be spent. The reluctance of the government to accord large amounts of finance to the fight to combat domestic violence may be indicative of an attitude whereby domestic violence is still viewed as being a 'women's issue' and therefore less worthy of resources than other issues. The fact that CEDAW suffers from a lack of enforcement measures means that there is very little that the CEDAW Committee can do when faced by a state that lacks the will to implement its duties under the treaty.[195]

Even in areas in which the UK does seem to be fulfilling the recommendations of the international human rights bodies, at least to some extent, such as in relation to improving the criminal justice system and implementing public awareness campaigns, it appears that changes in government policy are more likely to have been due to other factors, such as pressure from domestic violence groups and academic commentators. The UK Government has stated to the CEDAW Committee that there is a 'very high level of commitment throughout all aspects of government to the principles of the Convention'[196] and that 'Continued compliance with the Convention and a determination to eliminate all forms of discrimination against women are themes running through UK Government policy'.[197] However, it seems likely that pressure emanating from within a state itself will have a greater impact than pressure emanating from external bodies that can impose no sanctions.

This argument is reinforced by the example of child contact in cases of domestic violence. In 1996 the Special Rapporteur on Violence against Women made recommendations discouraging the granting of contact to perpetrators of domestic violence. However, these recommendations were entirely ignored. It was only in 2000, following the issuing of two reports emanating from within the UK itself, that attitudes began to alter in this area. It certainly seems that the Special Rapporteur's comments played no part in this change. It also appears that the preferred position of the Special Rapporteur – that contact should never take place in cases with a background of domestic violence – will not be implemented in the UK.[198] It seems that the state would simply not enter the private sphere of family life to such an extent as to lay down a rule whereby a perpetrator of domestic violence should not have contact with his children.

It appears therefore that the statements of the international human rights bodies on domestic violence have had little impact to date on policy in the UK. However, could these statements be used more effectively? Many women's groups in the UK are unaware of the existence of CEDAW and the fact that under this treaty the UK has international obligations to take steps to prevent domestic violence. If such groups were to publicise the fact that the government is not fulfilling its international duties, this may serve to place more pressure on the government to make greater efforts to address the issue of domestic violence. In this way the statements of the international human rights bodies may be able to contribute in an indirect manner to the struggle to combat domestic violence.

7 Conclusion

In this book the effectiveness of human rights law is assessed through the medium of a case study of domestic violence. This is an issue that affects very large numbers of women around the globe. It thus appears that an examination of the potential of human rights law to make a contribution in this area casts new light on the effectiveness of the discourse of rights. Domestic violence would certainly not have been regarded as a human rights violation by those who drafted the main human rights treaties. Can international human rights law only be effective in a 'traditional' case of human rights abuse, or may it also be used beneficially in relation to such an issue as domestic violence?

Various commentators have claimed that domestic violence constitutes a human rights violation. For example, Copelon argues that domestic violence breaches the right to be free from torture.[1] Roth comments that violence against women in the home belongs 'to the realm of human rights'.[2] Grdinic argues that domestic violence breaches the rights to be free from torture and inhuman and degrading treatment and punishment.[3] However, prior to this study, the question of whether human rights law can actually be used in an effective manner to assist in the fight to combat domestic violence had not been considered to any great extent.

A litigation approach

The first way in which international human rights law could be used in relation to the issue of violence against women in the United Kingdom is through a litigation approach. The European Convention on Human Rights has been incorporated into UK law, and the European Court has certainly taken a very dynamic approach in interpreting the fundamentally negative provisions of the Convention in such a manner as to impose positive obligations on states to protect the rights of individuals from threats posed by other private individuals, in certain circumstances. Domestic violence constitutes a clear violation of articles 2, 3 and 8 of the Convention, as has now been recognised by the Court in its recent jurisprudence. It has now been firmly established that states have positive obligations to ensure that their criminal justice systems are of a sufficient standard in dealing with domestic violence.

It does appear that the jurisprudence of the European Court has potential to be used effectively in relation to domestic violence. However, it seems that this potential may at present be limited to the amelioration of the criminal justice system, for example, ensuring that the police respond effectively to cases of domestic violence. Nevertheless, it is not inconceivable that the Court may in the future place obligations on the state to provide social support measures for victims or to take measures to raise awareness of domestic violence (see Chapter 3).

Could the judiciary of the UK rise to the challenge and use the Convention rights under the Human Rights Act 1998 to assist victims of domestic violence? In 2000, McColgan claimed that the Act would not be effective in protecting the rights of women.[4] Under the legislation it falls to the judiciary to balance the rights of parties against each other and McColgan argued that 'judges have not, by and large, served women's interests'.[5] She commented that, 'this has, in part, resulted from sexist assumptions embedded within the common law'[6] and that, 'the legal strides which have been made by women over the last decades are, by and large, thanks to the efforts of the legislature rather than the judiciary'.[7] Also in 2000, Temkin remarked that 'the European Convention on Human Rights, with its emphasis on the rights of defendants, poses a possible threat to women'.[8] This book reinforces the views of both these commentators, to a certain extent. By examining the case law under the Human Rights Act after 2000, the book argues that in cases where the rights of victims of domestic violence come into conflict with those of alleged perpetrators, it appears that the judiciary may be predisposed to protecting the fair trial rights of alleged perpetrators.

The study of how human rights law could be used through a litigation strategy in relation to domestic violence also sheds light on the theoretical issues highlighted in Chapter 1. A great deal has been written on the public/private dichotomy in human rights law and the difficulties that it causes for the protection of the rights of women. For example, Ewing comments that, 'the public/private distinction in international law ... places many forms of violence against women beyond the protective scope of human rights instruments'.[9] Likewise, Charlesworth states that the primary effect of the public/private dichotomy is 'to muffle, and often completely silence, the voices of women'.[10] However, does the public/private divide still pose as great a problem for international human rights law as these statements would suggest?

This study shows that the public/private divide is not insurmountable. The European Court has certainly used the concept of state responsibility to transcend the public/private dichotomy, at least to some extent (see Chapter 3). The Court has shown itself to be willing to enter the private sphere and deal with cases in which the rights of one individual have been breached by another. However, it seems that the public/private divide may still cause difficulties for the effectiveness of human rights law. It appears from the *Stubbings*[11] case that states may be granted a wider margin of appreciation in cases involving their positive obligations to protect the rights of individuals from being violated by the actions of other private entities, although this could of course change. Nevertheless, the fact that the Human Rights Act 1998 has a horizontal effect demonstrates that the UK judges are willing to transcend the public/private dichotomy in cases involving human rights (see Chapter 4). Overall, it seems that the public/private divide may not now pose as great a problem for the effectiveness of human rights law as was once the case.

The fact that rights will conflict, and will therefore have to be balanced against each other, is an unavoidable problem in international human rights law. For example, the rights of a victim of domestic violence may conflict with the rights of the alleged perpetrator. In carrying out the necessary balancing exercise, it appears that judges in the UK may be predisposed to protecting the fair trial rights of alleged perpetrators. As McColgan comments,

> When it comes to the 'balance' between the 'right to a fair trial' and the complainant's interests in privacy, security of the person or the equal protection of the law, the accused's 'right to a fair trial', understood decontextualised from the rights of the complainant, can operate to trump any other considerations.[12]

This study reinforces the point that major difficulties surround the enforcement of international human rights law. For example, the implementation of socio-economic rights has always been controversial. Various commentators argue that states should not be obliged to take expensive measures to ensure an individual's rights. For example, Beetham remarks that, while states may be reasonably required to refrain from torturing their citizens, it is not clear that they can equally be required to guarantee them a livelihood.[13] Oloka-Onyango comments that,

> Despite the statement in the Vienna Declaration of 1993 that proclaims all human rights as ' . . . universal, indivisible and interdependent and interrelated,' certain categories of rights within the international corpus are marginalized. Civil and political rights are considered to belong to a first category, or 'generation' of rights, while economic, social, and cultural rights have been relegated to a lower less important sphere. The marginalization of the latter category can be discerned not only from the level of international attention paid to them, but also with respect to the approach of governments, judges, non-governmental actors, and even academics to the subject.[14]

What does this study indicate concerning the current status of socio-economic rights?

The European Court in *Airey*[15] did envisage cases in which the state may be obliged to expend monetary resources in order to ensure access to particular forms of protection. However, it seems that one cannot argue on the basis of this case that the state has an obligation to provide victims of domestic violence with social support measures such as financial resources, refuge accommodation and permanent housing. Nevertheless, it is not inconceivable that the European Court could order that steps should be taken to re-house victims of abuse. The Court does seem to be prepared to move with the times and it has repeatedly stated that the Convention is a 'living instrument which . . . must be interpreted in the light of present-day conditions'.[16]

The UK case of *Oxfordshire County Council v R (on the application of Khan) and another*[17] certainly indicated that the national courts may be reluctant to place duties on the state to provide resources for victims of domestic violence. This is a major drawback to the effectiveness of a litigation strategy as it has been argued that the most pressing needs of victims of domestic violence are for adequate measures of social support. One criticism of socio-economic rights is that judges are not equipped to take decisions about the allocation of resources, and that such a task should be left to politicians. It was certainly stated in *R (on the application of Douglas) v North Tyneside Metropolitan Borough Council and another* that the courts must take care 'not to trespass into the discretionary area of resource allocation'.[18] It certainly seems that the judiciary in the UK would be reluctant to take steps to ensure the socio-economic rights of victims of domestic violence.

The case of *R (on the application of Limbuela) v Secretary of State for the Home Department; R (on the application of Tesema) v Secretary of State for the Home Department; R (on the application of Adam) v Secretary of State for the Home Department*[19] does give some hope that the Supreme Court could potentially hold that the state has a duty to provide support to victims of domestic violence. Nevertheless, it must be remembered that the House of Lords was making its decision based on very extreme circumstances and it seems that the case does not therefore automatically indicate that the courts would be willing to place obligations on the state to provide social support measures to victims of domestic violence.

This study also demonstrates that relying on a litigation strategy as a vehicle for the implementation of human rights law may be problematic. Various commentators have expressed grave concerns about the effectiveness of litigation as a strategy for achieving change. For example, Epp comments that 'the judicial process is costly and slow and produces changes in the law only in small increments'.[20] Van Schaack states that, 'an overreliance on adversarial litigation . . . raises . . . concerns . . . about the efficacy of resorting to law and the judicial process to promote durable social change and the ability of the judicial process to address major social . . . problems'.[21] This book reinforces the views of such commentators, to some extent. The study has found many factors that cause difficulties for the use of human rights law through a litigation strategy in relation to domestic violence.

For example, judges generally must confine themselves to dealing with the precise matter in the actual case that is before them. They cannot make sweeping statements on societal issues. For instance, in relation to domestic violence, it is unlikely that the European Court would order specifically that more refuges be built. However, courts can set general standards and one should not entirely discount the possibility that the Court may in the future place an obligation on states to take steps to re-house victims. Nevertheless, at present it seems that the potential of the case law of the European Court to be used effectively in relation to domestic violence is limited to the amelioration of the criminal justice system, for example, ensuring that the police respond effectively to cases of domestic violence (see Chapter 3).

Another problem with the litigation strategy is that it relies greatly on the attitudes of individual judges. Palmer expresses concern that,

> rights are capable of being given a wide range of interpretations, [and thus] there are times when consequential choices need to be made. Inevitably, these broad and open-textured guarantees can lead to uncertainty when these general rights are applied in specific contexts.[22]

If judges are unwilling to use human rights instruments in a dynamic way, this will create difficulties for the effectiveness of human rights law. It seems that the judiciary in the UK displays a deferential attitude when dealing with certain types of cases under the Human Rights Act, such as those concerning the allocation of resources and policing. This is problematic as these are areas that are of particular relevance to the issue of domestic violence (see Chapter 4).

Epp states that, 'there are limits to the social changes produced by judicial rulings, and those rulings depend on support from government officials'.[23] This book certainly supports Epp's assertion. Even with a very activist judiciary, a litigation strategy will not result in transformation unless such change is supported by the legislature and by the general public. As discussed in Chapter 3, the case of *A v United Kingdom*[24] illustrates this point clearly – if a court makes a dynamic judgment upholding human rights standards, such a judgment may yet not be fully effective if bodies such as the legislature do not also have a commitment to human rights norms.

Epp also comments that, 'judges . . . cannot make rights-supportive law unless they have . . . cases to decide'.[25] Using litigation in relation to the issue of domestic violence raises a further problem. Domestic violence is an 'unseen' crime which victims are often too frightened or too ashamed to report. The British Crime Survey found that the police come to know of less than one in four of the worst cases of domestic violence.[26] Many victims may not want to take cases to court. This study found that to date there have been very few cases dealing with the issue of domestic violence before the European Court. This fact may be indicative of the limitations of human rights law when dealing with crime in the private sphere. By definition, a case before the European Court needs an applicant – someone who is a victim for the purposes of the Convention. Victims of domestic violence simply may not wish to bring human rights cases.

Overall, it certainly seems that a strategy of using international human rights law through a litigation approach suffers from limitations in relation to the issue of domestic violence.

Using the statements of the international human rights bodies

An alternative strategy is to use the statements of international human rights bodies on the issue of domestic violence. The UN human rights bodies have made a wide variety of recommendations to states in the area of domestic violence. Indeed, these statements encompass all of the types of measures identified in Chapter 2 as being of potential benefit in the area of domestic violence.

Various commentators have described the recommendations made by the international human rights bodies concerning the issue of domestic violence. For example, Cook discusses the idea of state accountability under CEDAW.[27] Fitzpatrick examines the way in which CEDAW has been interpreted to prohibit domestic violence.[28] Thomas describes the statements that have been made by the international bodies[29] and comments that, 'Now, when officials ignore domestic violence, they ignore their concrete obligations as members of the international community'.[30] At first glance it seems that using the statements of international human rights bodies in this field may have advantages over the use of a litigation approach. It appears that such bodies, through statements, declarations and resolutions can make a fuller set of recommendations in relation to domestic violence than can courts. Also, one is not dependent on the attitudes of individual members of the judiciary. In addition, the strategy of using the statements of international human rights bodies is much better suited to dealing with an 'unseen' crime such as domestic violence than is a litigation strategy. Essentially there is no reliance on victims taking cases to court.[31]

This study found that the UN human rights bodies have used the concept of state responsibility to great effect to transcend the public/private divide that has posed substantial difficulties for the effectiveness of human rights law in relation to issues such as domestic violence (see Chapter 5). Indeed, the ease with which they have done so again seems to indicate that the public/private divide does not pose as great an obstacle to the effectiveness of human rights law as was once the case. For example, in its General Recommendation 19 the CEDAW Committee stated,

> that discrimination under the Convention is not restricted to action by or on behalf of Governments . . . Under general international law and specific human rights covenants, States may be responsible for private acts if they fail to act with due diligence to prevent violations of rights or to investigate and punish acts of violence, and for providing compensation.[32]

However, the major difficulty with relying on the statements of the UN human rights bodies lies in the question of implementation. As highlighted in Chapter 1, the enforcement of human rights law can be very problematic. Ulrich comments that, 'a long-standing debate among international legal scholars exists about whether international law constitutes law at all, or whether such law is little more than grandiose policymaking'.[33] Merry remarks that 'CEDAW is law without sanctions'.[34] Ritz states that 'CEDAW . . . has proven ineffective in ending gender discrimination'.[35] Afsharipour comments that 'due to a lack of effective enforcement mechanisms, the Convention's success in improving the lives of women has been limited'.[36]

This book provides further strong evidence, through a case study of the United Kingdom, for the proposition that the recommendations made by the international bodies suffer from great difficulties in relation to their effectiveness. The recommendations have not been uniformly implemented in the UK. It seems that the main reason for this is a simple lack of will on the part of the state, combined with a lack of enforcement mechanisms. The achievement of the measures outlined in the international human rights documents requires the expenditure of financial resources. It is therefore unlikely that the government would be very willing to implement the recommendations. It is noteworthy that the most problematic area in relation to the government's response to domestic violence is the provision of social support measures to victims. This is the category of recommendations that requires the greatest amount of money to be spent. The fact that CEDAW suffers from a lack of enforcement measures means that there is very little that the CEDAW Committee can do when faced by a state that lacks the will to implement its duties under the treaty.

This study has found that even in areas in which the UK does seem to be fulfilling the recommendations of the international human rights bodies, at least to some extent, such as in relation to improving the criminal justice system, it appears that changes in government policy are more likely to have been due to other factors, such as pressure from domestic violence groups and academic commentators (see Chapter 6).

However, could the statements of the international human rights bodies on the issue of domestic violence be used more effectively? Many women's groups in the UK are unaware of the existence of CEDAW and of the fact that under this treaty the UK has international obligations to take steps to prevent domestic violence. If such groups were to publicise the fact that the government is not fulfilling its international duties, this may serve to place more pressure on the government to make greater efforts to address the issue of domestic violence. In this way the statements of the international human rights bodies may be able to contribute in an indirect manner to the struggle to combat domestic violence.

Final points

On the whole it seems that international human rights law could be used with only a limited degree of effectiveness in relation to the issue of domestic violence. This body of law usually depends on a litigation approach. In a situation involving a 'traditional' human rights violation, for example, a man being wrongfully imprisoned and tortured by agents of the state, such a litigation approach can be very effective. If the case were taken before the European Court of Human Rights, the Court would have no hesitation in holding the state to be in violation of the European Convention and would award the applicant substantial damages. However, such a strategy would not be as effective in relation to the issue of domestic violence. In a 'traditional' human rights case, the court would simply order the state to desist from its conduct. However, in the case of domestic violence, one would wish the court to place comprehensive duties on the state to take positive steps to protect and assist victims. Also, the victims of 'traditional' human rights abuses would usually have no hesitation in engaging in litigation. Indeed, often they desire a public disclosure of the wrongs they have suffered. However, many victims of domestic violence are too frightened or too humiliated to go to court. Although there are some signs of hope, nevertheless overall it appears that using human rights law through a litigation strategy is unlikely to prove very effective in relation to domestic violence in the UK.

It seems that an alternative strategy of using the statements of the international human rights bodies on domestic violence is also unlikely to be greatly effective, as evidenced by the finding that these statements do not appear to have had a major impact on UK Government policy to date. Nevertheless, if domestic violence groups were to publicise the fact that the UK is failing to fulfil its international duties under CEDAW this may result in greater pressure being placed on the government to take further steps to combat domestic violence. In this way human rights law could possibly be effective indirectly in relation to the issue of domestic violence.

This case study of domestic violence illustrates the point that even though a practice constitutes a clear violation of human rights law, it will not necessarily be the case that human rights law, whether in the form of 'hard law' or 'soft law', can be used in an effective manner to combat that practice. Domestic violence certainly violates the right to life, the right to be free from inhuman and degrading treatment, the right to bodily integrity and also arguably the right to be free from torture. These are all well-established internationally recognised rights. Yet it appears that human rights law may not have a great deal of potential to be used effectively in relation to domestic violence. International human rights law has certainly been extremely successful in a large number of situations. In cases involving 'traditional' human rights violations, human rights law can be used very effectively. However, domestic violence is not such a situation. At the inception of the human rights movement domestic violence would certainly not have been regarded as a human rights violation. Although the human rights movement has now evolved to such an extent as to allow domestic violence to be seen as a violation, it still may be the case that human rights law cannot be used in a very effective manner in relation to this issue. It seems that in a situation involving a 'non-traditional' human rights violation in relation to which a litigation strategy is problematic, international human rights law may only have a limited degree of effectiveness.

Notes

Introduction

1 Kelly L and Radford J, ' "Nothing really happened": the invalidation of women's experiences of sexual violence', in Hester M, Kelly L and Radford J (eds), *Women, Violence and Male Power*, 2002, 19–33 at 20.
2 Dobash RE and Dobash RP, *Women, Violence & Social Change*, 1996, at pp.39–40.
3 Dobash and Dobash, op. cit., at pp.39–40.
4 Diduck A and Kaganas F, *Family Law, Gender and the State*, 1999, at p.316.
5 Walker A, Flatley J, Kershaw C and Moon D, 'Crime in England and Wales 2008/09: Home Office Statistical Bulletin', 2009.
6 Hester M, *Who Does What to Whom? Gender and Domestic Violence Perpetrators*, 2009, University of Bristol in association with the Northern Rock Foundation, Bristol, at p.19.
7 Mullender and Morley, op. cit., at p.5.
8 Mullender A, *Rethinking Domestic Violence*, 1996, at p.31.

1 Potential problems for the effectiveness of international human rights law as regards domestic violence

1 Baxi U, *The Future of Human Rights*, 2002, at 1.
2 Wallace RMM, *International Human Rights*, 2001, at 589.
3 Black D, 'The long and winding road: international norms and domestic political change in South Africa', in Risse T, Ropp SC and Sikkink K (eds), *The Power of Human Rights – International Norms and Domestic Change*, 1999, 78–108 at 78.
4 Robinson M, 'Making Human Rights Matter: Eleanor Roosevelt's Time Has Come', (2003) 16 *Harvard Human Rights Journal*, 1–11 at 1.
5 Cassel D, 'Does International Human Rights Law Make a Difference?', (2001) 2 *Chicago Journal of International Law*, 121–135 at 122.
6 Robinson, op. cit., at 3.
7 Heyns C and Viljoen F, *The Impact of the United Nations Human Rights Treaties on the Domestic Level*, 2002, at 19.
8 Robinson, op. cit., at 4.
9 Cassel, op. cit., at 132.
10 Cassel, op. cit., at 133–134.
11 Robinson, op. cit., at 4.
12 Risse T and Ropp SC, 'International human rights norms and domestic change: conclusions', in Risse T, Ropp SC and Sikkink K (eds), *The Power of Human Rights – International Norms and Domestic Change*, 1999, 234–178 at 275.
13 Wallace, op. cit., at 589.

14 Heyns and Viljoen, op. cit., at 20.
15 Heyns and Viljoen, op. cit., at 23.
16 Heyns and Viljoen, op. cit., at 25.
17 Heyns and Viljoen, op. cit., at 31. For example, at the start of a case dealing with the treaty system in Jamaica, the judges involved did not have copies of the treaties in question.
18 Cassel, op. cit., at 122.
19 Thomas DQ and Beasley ME, 'Symposium on Reconceptualizing Violence Against Women By Intimate Partners', (1995) 58 *Albany Law Review*, 1119–1147 at 1121.
20 Romany C, 'Women as Aliens: A Feminist Critique of the Public/Private Distinction in International Human Rights Law', (1993) 6 *Harvard Human Rights Journal*, 87–125 at 90.
21 Romany (1993), op. cit., at 89–98.
22 For historical arguments on rights, see Harvey C, 'Talking about Human Rights', [2004] *European Human Rights Law Review*, 500–516.
23 Cook RJ, 'State Responsibility For Violations of Women's Human Rights', (1994) 7 *Harvard Human Rights Journal*, 125–175 at 151.
24 Thomas and Beasley, op. cit., at 121.
25 Hirschl R, ' "Negative" Rights vs. "Positive" Entitlements: A Comparative Study of Judicial Interpretations of Rights in an Emerging Neo-Liberal Economic Order', (2000) 22 *Human Rights Quarterly*, 1060–1097 at 1063.
26 Romany C, 'State Responsibility Goes Private: A Feminist Critique of the Public/Private Distinction in International Human Rights Law', in Cook RJ, *Human Rights of Women – National and International Perspectives*, 1994, 85–115 at 89.
27 Mall LL, 'The Right to Privacy in Great Britain: Will Renewed Anti-Media Sentiment Compel Great Britain to Create a Right to Be Let Alone?', (1998) 4 *ILSA Journal of International and Comparative Law*, 785–815 at 805.
28 Schriver T, 'Establishing an Affirmative Governmental Duty to Protect Children's Rights: The European Court of Human Rights as a Model for the United States Supreme Court', (2000) 34 *University of San Francisco Law Review*, 379–408 at 400. Article 8(2) states that, 'There shall be no interference with this right except as is in accordance with the law and is necessary in a democratic society in the interests of national security, public safety or the economic well-being of the country, for the prevention of disorder or crime, for the protection of health or morals, or for the protection of the rights and freedoms of others'.
29 Cook RJ, 'Women's International Human Rights Law: The Way Forward', in Cook RJ (ed), *Human Rights of Women – National and International Perspectives*, 1994, 3–36 at 6.
30 Charlesworth H and Chinkin C, *The Boundaries of International Law – A Feminist Analysis*, 2000, at 30.
31 Charlesworth and Chinkin, op. cit., at 30.
32 Binion G, 'Human Rights: A Feminist Perspective', (1995) 17 *Human Rights Quarterly*, 509–526 at 516.
33 Charlesworth and Chinkin, op. cit., at 31.
34 Charlesworth H, 'What are 'Women's International Human Rights'?', in Cook RJ (ed), *Human Rights of Women – National and International Perspectives*, 1994, 58–84 at 69, quoting from Scottish Home Department, Report of the Committee on Homosexual Offences and Prostitution, 1957, Cmnd 247 at para. 61.
35 Rabinowitz CB, 'Proposals for Progress: Sodomy Laws and the European Convention on Human Rights', (1995) 21 *Brooklyn Journal of International Law*, 425–469 at 431, referring to the Wolfenden Report at para. 14.
36 Hirschl, op. cit., at 1095.

37 Hirschl, op. cit., at 1095.
38 Charlesworth, op. cit., at 68.
39 Ewing AP, 'Establishing State Responsibility For Private Acts of Violence Against Women Under the American Convention on Human Rights', (1995) 26 *Columbia Human Rights Law Review*, 751–800 at 753.
40 Rishmawi M, 'The Developing Approaches of the International Commission of Jurists to Women's Human Rights', in Cook RJ (ed), *Human Rights of Women – National and International Perspectives*, 1994, 340–348 at 341.
41 Rishmawi, op. cit., at 341.
42 Cook, 'State Responsibility For Violations of Women's Human Rights', op. cit., at 151.
43 Van Leeuwen F, *Women's Rights Are Human Rights*, 2010, at 9.
44 Charlesworth, op. cit., at 72. It should however be noted that in *Venables and another v News Group Newspapers Ltd and others* [2001] 1 All ER 908, it was held that a private party could breach article 3 of the European Convention on Human Rights (the right to be free from torture and inhuman or degrading treatment and punishment) under the Human Rights Act 1998.
45 For example, Copelon R, 'Intimate Terror: Understanding Domestic Violence as Torture', in Cook RJ, *Human Rights of Women – National and International Perspectives*, 1994, 116–152; Grdinic E, 'Application of the Elements of Torture and Other Forms of Ill-Treatment, as Defined by the European Court and Commission of Human Rights, to the Incidents of Domestic Violence', (2000) 23 *Hastings International and Comparative Law Review*, 217–260.
46 Section 8(2) of the Constitution states that, 'A provision of the Bill of Rights binds a natural or a juristic person if, and to the extent that, it is applicable, taking into account the nature of the right and the nature of any duty imposed by the right'.
47 For an example of the use of section 3 by the House of Lords, see *Ghaidan v Godin-Mendoza* [2004] 3 All ER 411.
48 U.N. Doc A/47/38 (1992) at para. 9.
49 Case No. IT-96-23T, 22 February 2001.
50 Dixon R, 'Rape as a Crime in International Humanitarian Law: Where to from Here?' (2002) 13 *European Journal of International Law*, 697–719 at 700.
51 ICTR-96-4-T, 2 September 1998.
52 ICTR-96-13-T, 27 January 2000.
53 Buss D, 'Prosecuting Mass Rape: *Prosecutor v Dragoljub Kunarac, Radomir Kovac and Zoran Vukovic*' (2002) 10 *Feminist Legal Studies*, 91–99 at 97.
54 Article 43(6).
55 Article 36(8)(b).
56 McColgan A, 'Women and the Human Rights Act', (2000) 51 *Northern Ireland Legal Quarterly*, 417–444 at 444.
57 It should also be noted that some rights have built-in limitations, for example, articles 2, 5 and 6 of the European Convention on Human Rights.
58 See Blake N, 'Importing Proportionality: Clarification or Confusion', [2002] *European Human Rights Law Review*, 19–27.
59 [2004] 2 All ER 995.
60 [2001] 2 WLR 1038.
61 At para. 44.
62 At para. 83.
63 [2004] 4 All ER 683.
64 Fenwick H, 'Clashing Rights, the Welfare of the Child and the Human Rights Act', (2004) 67 *Modern Law Review*, 889–927 at 890.
65 For an example of the rights of a victim of violence coming into conflict with those of an alleged perpetrator, see *R v A* [2001] 3 All ER 1.

66 McColgan, op. cit., at 429.
67 Kennedy D, *The Dark Sides of Virtue – Reassessing International Humanitarianism*, 2004, at 25.
68 Wallace, op. cit., at 589.
69 Wallace, op. cit., at 589.
70 Wallace, op. cit., at 590.
71 Robinson, op. cit., at 1.
72 Copelon R, 'International Human Rights Dimensions of Intimate Violence: Another Strand in the Dialectic of Feminist Lawmaking', (2003) 11 *American University Journal of Gender, Social Policy and the Law*, 865–876 at 875.
73 Robinson, op. cit., at 4.
74 Ulrich JL, 'Confronting Gender-Based Violence With International Instruments: Is a Solution to the Pandemic Within Reach?', (2000) 7 *Indiana Journal of Global Legal Studies,* 629–654 at 637.
75 Byrnes A, 'Enforcement Through International Law and Procedures', in Cook RJ (ed), *Human Rights of Women – National and International Perspectives*, 1994, 189–227 at 191–192.
76 Ulrich, op. cit., at 637.
77 Ulrich, op. cit., at 638–639.
78 Ulrich, op. cit., at 638.
79 Risse T and Sikkink K, 'The socialization of international human rights norms into domestic practices: introduction', in Risse T, Ropp SC and Sikkink K (eds), *The Power of Human Rights – International Norms and Domestic Change*, 1999, 1–38 at 37–38.
80 Cassel, op. cit., at 135.
81 Merry SE, 'Constructing a Global Law – Violence against Women and the Human Rights System', (2003) 28 *Law and Social Inquiry,* 941–974 at 959.
82 Evatt E, 'Finding a Voice for Women's Rights: The Early Days of CEDAW', (2002) 34 *George Washington International Law Review,* 515–553 at 519–520.
83 Ulrich, op. cit., at 638.
84 Article 24(u).
85 Article 24(v).
86 Byrnes, op. cit., at 207.
87 Schopp-Schilling HB, 'Treaty Body Reform: The Case of the Committee on the Elimination of Discrimination Against Women', (2007) 7 *Human Rights Law Review* 201–224 at 204.
88 Merry, op. cit., at 958.
89 Fortin J, *Children's Rights and the Developing Law*, 2003, at 46.
90 Ulrich, op. cit., at 647.
91 Vesa A, 'International and Regional Standards for Protecting Victims of Domestic Violence', (2004) 12 *American University Journal of Gender, Social Policy and the Law*, 309–360 at 360.
92 See also McQuigg R, 'The Responses of States to the Comments of the CEDAW Committee on Domestic Violence', (2007) 11 *International Journal of Human Rights*, 461–479.
93 Schneider EM, *Battered Women & Feminist Lawmaking*, 2000, at 196–197.
94 Oloka-Onyango J, 'Reinforcing Marginalized Rights in an Age of Globalization: International Mechanisms, Non-State Actors, and the Struggle for Peoples' Rights in Africa', (2003) 18 *American University International Law Review*, 851–913 at 852, citing article 5 of the Vienna Declaration, A/CONF.157/23, 12 July, 1993.
95 Johnstone RL, 'Feminist Influences on the United Nations Human Rights Treaty Bodies', (2006) 28 *Human Rights Quarterly* 148–185 at 149–150.

96 Lyon B, 'Postcolonial Law: Theory and Law Reform Conference: Discourse in Development: A Post-Colonial "Agenda" for the United Nations Committee on Economic, Social and Cultural Rights', (2002) 10 *American University Journal of Gender, Social Policy and the Law*, 535–579 at 536.

97 Lyon, op. cit., at 539.

98 McGregor G, 'The International Covenant on Social, Economic, and Cultural Rights: Will it Get its Day in Court?', (2002) 28 *The Manitoba Law Journal*, 321–345 at 323–324.

99 Steiner HJ and Alston P, *International Human Rights in Context – Law, Politics, Morals*, 2000, at 235.

100 Steiner and Alston, op. cit., at 235.

101 Woods JM, 'Justiciable Social Rights as a Critique of the Liberal Paradigm', (2003) 38 *Texas International Law Journal*, 763–793 at 764–765.

102 Dennis MJ and Stewart DP, 'Justiciability of Economic, Social, and Cultural Rights: Should There be an International Complaints Mechanism to Adjudicate the Rights to Food, Water, Housing, and Health?', (2004) 98 *American Journal of International Law*, 462–515 at 465.

103 Hirschl, op. cit., at 1073.

104 Oloka-Onyango, op. cit., at 853.

105 Steiner and Alston, op. cit., at 275.

106 Robinson M, 'From Rhetoric to Reality: Making Human Rights Work', (2003) *European Human Rights Law Review*, 1–8 at 2–4.

107 Steiner and Alston, op. cit., at 249.

108 Steiner and Alston, op. cit., at 250.

109 Dennis and Stewart, op. cit., at 514.

110 Epp CR, *The Rights Revolution*, 1998, at 3.

111 Van Schaack B, 'With All Deliberate Speed: Civil Human Rights Litigation as a Tool For Social Change', (2004) 57 *Vanderbilt Law Review*, 2305–2348 at 2307.

112 Scheingold SA, *The Politics of Rights: Lawyers, Public Policy, and Political Change*, 2004, at 5.

113 Chayes A, 'The Role of the Judge in Public Law Litigation', (1976) 89 *Harvard Law Review*, 1281–1316 at 1295–1296.

114 Chayes, op. cit., at 1309.

115 Rosenberg GN, *The Hollow Hope: Can Courts Bring About Social Change?*, 1991, at 339.

116 Epp, op. cit., at 15.

117 Palmer S, 'Feminism and the Promise of Human Rights: Possibilities and Paradoxes', in James S and Palmer S (eds), *Visible Women*, 2002, 91–115 at 101.

118 Palmer, op. cit., at 101–102.

119 See her dissents in *R v J* [2005] 1 AC 562 and *R (Kehoe) v Secretary of State for Work and Pensions* [2006] 1 AC 42.

120 Rosenberg, op. cit., at 337.

121 (1999) 27 EHRR 611.

122 Fortin, op. cit., at 279.

123 Department of Health, 'Protecting Children, Supporting Parents: A Consultation Document on the Physical Punishment of Children', 2000, at para. 2.4.

124 Department of Health, op. cit., at para. 5.1.

125 Fortin, op. cit., at 280.

126 Epp, op. cit., at 9.

127 Rosenberg, op. cit., at 336.

128 Walby S and Allen J, 'Domestic violence, sexual assault and stalking: Findings from the British Crime Survey', 2004, Home Office Research Study 276, at 97.

129 Epp, op. cit., at 15.

2 What measures may it be beneficial for human rights law to achieve in relation to domestic violence?

1 Freedman AE, 'Symposium: Fact-Finding in Civil Domestic Violence Cases: Secondary Traumatic Stress and the Need for Compassionate Witnesses', (2003) 11 *American University Journal of Gender, Social Policy & the Law*, 567–656 at 588.
2 Freedman, op. cit., at 588.
3 Merry SE, 'Rights Talk and the Experience of Law: Implementing Women's Human Rights to Protection from Violence', (2003) 25 *Human Rights Quarterly*, 343–381 at 354–355.
4 [1992] 4 All ER 889.
5 [1992] 1 All ER 306.
6 Rollinson M, 'Re-Reading Criminal Law: Gendering the Mental Element', in Nicolson D and Bibbings L (eds), *Feminist Perspectives On Criminal Law*, 2000, 101–122 at 114–115.
7 Nicolson D, 'What the Law Giveth, it also Taketh Away: Female-Specific Defences to Criminal Liability', in Nicolson D and Bibbings L (eds), *Feminist Perspectives On Criminal Law*, 2000, 159–180 at 172.
8 Merry, op. cit., at 354–355.
9 Freedman, op. cit., at 589.
10 Diduck A and Kaganas F, *Family Law, Gender and the State*, 1999, at 329.
11 James A, 'In Practice: Prosecutiong Domestic Violence', [2008] *Family Law*, 456.
12 Freedman, op. cit., at 589–590.
13 Freedman, op. cit., at 590–591.
14 Maguigan H, 'Wading into Professor Schneider's "Murky Middle Ground" Between Acceptance and Rejection of Criminal Justice Responses to Domestic Violence', (2003) 11 *American University Journal of Gender, Social Policy and the Law*, 427–445 at 431.
15 Merry, op. cit., at 378.
16 Hague G and Malos E, *Domestic Violence: Action for Change*, 2005, at 108.
17 Zedner L, 'Victims', in Maguire M, Morgan R and Reiner R (eds), *The Oxford Handbook of Criminology*, 2002, 419–456 at 435.
18 Shapland J, 'Victims, the Criminal Justice System and Compensation'=, (1984) 24 *British Journal of Criminology*, 131–149 at 131.
19 Shapland, op. cit., at 136.
20 Elias R, *The Politics of Victimization*, 1986, at 133.
21 Elias, op. cit., at 160.
22 Zedner, op. cit., at 439.
23 Zedner, op. cit., at 436–437.
24 Mawby RI and Walklate S, *Critical Victimology*, 1998, at 97.
25 Elias, op. cit., at 142.
26 Shapland, op. cit., at 134.
27 Mawby and Walklate, op. cit., at 129.
28 Elias, op. cit., at 170.
29 Zedner, op. cit., at 443.
30 Zedner, op. cit., at 443.
31 Elias, op. cit., at 140.
32 Roach K, *Due Process and Victims' Rights*, 1999, at 310.
33 For further literature on victimology, see Crawford A and Goodey J (eds), *Integrating a Victim Perspective within Criminal Justice*, 2000; Ashworth A, 'Restorative Justice and Victims' Rights', (2000) *New Zealand Law Journal*, 84–88; Crawford A and Enterkin J, 'Victim Contact Work in the Probation Service: Paradigm Shift or Pandora's Box?', (2001) 41 *British Journal of Criminology*, 707–725; Dignan J and

Cavadino M, 'Towards a Framework for Conceptualising and Evaluating Models of Criminal Justice from a Victim's Perspective', (1996) 4 *International Review of Victimology*, 153–182; Edwards I, 'Victim Participation in Sentencing; The Problem of Incoherence', (2001) 40 *Howard Journal of Criminal Justice*, 39–54; Fenwick H, 'Procedural "Rights" of Victims of Crime: Public or Private Ordering of the Criminal Justice Process?', (1997) 60 *Modern Law Review*, 317–333.

34 Jones D and Brown J, 'The Relationship between Victims and Prosecutors: Defending Victims' Rights? A CPS Response', (2010) *Criminal Law Review*, 212–225 at 225.

35 Mullender A and Hague G, 'Women survivors' views', in Taylor-Browne J (ed), *What Works in Reducing Domestic Violence? A comprehensive guide for professionals*, 2001, 1–33 at 20.

36 Mullender and Hague (2001), op. cit., at 21.

37 Mullender and Hague (2001), op. cit., at 21.

38 Armatta J, 'Getting Beyond the Law's Complicity in Intimate Violence Against Women', (1997) 33 *Willamette Law Review*, 774–845 at 812.

39 Sullivan CM, 'Using the ESID Model to Reduce Intimate Male Violence Against Women', (2003) 32 *American Journal of Community Psychology*, 295–303 at 296.

40 Stanko, EA, *Intimate Intrusions*, 1985, at 10.

41 Thomas C, 'Domestic Violence', in Askin KD and Koenig DM (eds), *Women and International Human Rights Law* (Vol.1), 1999, 219–256 at 221.

42 Thomas, op. cit., at 21.

43 Thomas, op. cit., at 21.

44 Armatta, op. cit., at 812.

45 Hague and Malos, op. cit., at 177.

46 Hughes B, 'Can Domestic Violence be considered a Violation of Human Rights Law?', (2006) 14 *British Journal of Midwifery*, 192.

47 Bruce E, 'Attitudes of Social Workers and Police in the Select Committee Report on Violence to Women and Children', in University of Bradford, *Battered Women and Abused Children – Intricacies of Legal and Administrative Intervention*, 1979, 50–61 at 53.

48 Smith LJF, 'Domestic Violence: an overview of the literature', 1989, Home Office Research Study 107, at 47.

49 Smith, op. cit., at 47.

50 Smith, op. cit., at 47.

51 Smith, op. cit., at 55.

52 Goodmark L, 'Symposium: Domestic Violence & the Law: Theory, Policy, and Practice: Law is the Answer? Do We Know that for Sure?: Questioning the Efficacy of Legal Interventions for Battered Women', (2004) 23 *Saint Louis University Public Law Review*, 7–48 at 13.

53 Diduck and Kaganas, op. cit., at 329.

54 Hester M and Radford L, 'Contradictions and compromises: the impact of the Children Act on women and children's safety', in Hester M, Kelly L and Radford J (eds), *Women, Violence and Male Power*, 2002, 81–98 at 84.

55 Diduck and Kaganas, op. cit., at 331.

56 Home Office Circular 60/90.

57 Hague G, 'Domestic violence policy in the 1990s', in Watson S and Doyal L (eds), *Engendering Social Policy*, 1999, 131–147 at 134.

58 Circular 60/90, at para. 11.

59 Hale B, Pearl D, Cooke E and Bates P, *The Family, Law & Society*, 2002, at 401.

60 'Domestic Violence: Revised Circular to Police', Home Office Circular 19/2000.

61 'Guidance on Investigating Domestic Abuse', National Policing Improvement Agency, 2008, at 26.

62 Diduck and Kaganas, op. cit., at 332.
63 Mullender and Hague (2001), op. cit., at 21.
64 Mullender and Hague (2001), op. cit., at 21.
65 Hanmer J and Griffiths S, 'Effective policing', in Taylor-Browne J (ed), *What Works in Reducing Domestic Violence? A comprehensive guide for professionals*, 2001, 123–150 at 142.
66 Mullender A and Hague G, 'Reducing Domestic Violence . . . What Works? Women Survivors' Views', 2000, Crime Reduction Research Series, available at http://www.homeoffice.gov.uk.
67 Mullender and Hague (2000), op. cit.
68 Hanmer and Griffiths, op. cit., at 143.
69 Hanmer and Griffiths, op. cit., at 140.
70 Hester M and Westmarland N, 'Tackling Domestic Violence: effective interventions and approaches', 2005, Home Office Research Study 290, at 42.
71 Hanmer and Griffiths, op. cit., at 147.
72 Mullender and Hague (2000), op. cit.
73 Mullender and Hague (2001), op. cit., at 20.
74 Hanmer and Griffiths, op. cit., at 146.
75 Hanmer and Griffiths, op. cit., at 147.
76 Mullender and Hague (2001), op. cit., at 20.
77 Connelly C and Cavanagh K, 'Domestic Abuse, Civil Protection Orders and the "New Criminologies": Is there any Value in Engaging with the Law?', (2007) 15 *Feminist Legal Studies*, 259–287 at 275.
78 Hague and Malos, op. cit., at 77.
79 Mullender and Hague (2001), op. cit., at 20.
80 Mullender and Hague (2001), op. cit., at 20.
81 Hester and Westmarland, op. cit., at x.
82 Hague G, Mullender A, Aris R and Dear W, 'Abused Women's Perspectives: Responsiveness and Accountability of Domestic Violence and Inter-Agency Initiatives', 2001, Report to the ESRC, at 11.
83 United Nations Centre for Social Development and Humanitarian Affairs, Strategies for Confronting Domestic Violence: A Resource Manual 7 (1993) U.N.Doc.ST/CSDHA/20 (1993) at 38, as quoted by Thomas, op. cit., at 227.
84 Thomas, op. cit., at 227.
85 Stanko, op. cit., at 129.
86 Hopkins CQ, Koss MP and Bachar KJ, 'Symposium: Domestic Violence & the Law: Theory, Policy, and Practice: Applying Restorative Justice to Ongoing Intimate Violence: Problems and Possibilities', (2004) 23 *Saint Louis University Public Law Review*, 289–311.
87 Hopkins, Koss and Bachar, op. cit., at 290.
88 Cretney A and Davis G, 'Prosecuting "Domestic" Assault', [1996] *Criminal Law Review*, 162–174 at 166.
89 Stanko, op. cit., at 130.
90 Stanko, op. cit., at 130.
91 Hall M, 'The Relationship between Victims and Prosecutors: Defending Victims' Rights?', (2010) *Criminal Law Review*, 31–45 at 40.
92 Edwards S, 'New directions in prosecution', in Taylor-Browne J (ed), *What Works in Reducing Domestic Violence? A comprehensive guide for professionals*, 2001, 211–238 at 223.
93 Cretney A and Davis G, 'Prosecuting Domestic Assault: Victims Failing Courts, or Courts Failing Victims?', (1997) 36 *The Howard Journal*, 146–157 at 147–149.
94 Home Affairs Select Committee on Domestic Violence, 'Domestic Violence, Volume I and II', 1993, HMSO, London, Vol. II, 20, para. 4.6.

95 Hester M, Hanmer J, Coulson S, Morahan M and Razak A, *Domestic Violence: Making it Through the Criminal Justice System*, 2003, at 13.
96 Cretney and Davis (1997), op. cit., at 154.
97 Cretney and Davis (1997), op. cit., at 147.
98 Hester and Westmarland, op. cit., at 43.
99 Hester and Westmarland, op. cit., at 56.
100 Edwards, op. cit., at 212.
101 Edwards, op. cit., at 212.
102 Edwards, op. cit., at 212.
103 Hague and Malos, op. cit., at 102.
104 Smith, op. cit., at p.94.
105 Smith, op. cit., at p.95.
106 Edwards, op. cit., at 221.
107 Hester, Hanmer, Coulson, Morahan and Razak, op. cit., at 9.
108 Miles J, 'Domestic violence', in Herring J (ed), *Family Law – Issues, Debates, Policy*, 2001, 78–124 at 92.
109 Section 23(3)(b) states that a statement made by a person in a document shall be admissible in criminal proceedings as evidence of any fact of which direct oral evidence by him would be admissible if 'the person who made it does not give oral evidence through fear or because he is kept out of the way'.
110 Edwards, op. cit., at 219.
111 Thomas, op. cit., at 219.
112 Thomas, op. cit., at 228–230.
113 Berry DB, *The Domestic Violence Sourcebook*, 1998, at 154–155.
114 Berry, op. cit., at 154–155.
115 Diduck and Kaganas, op. cit., at 333.
116 Miles, op. cit., at 93.
117 Edwards, op. cit., at 212.
118 Mullender, Hague, Aris and Dear, op. cit., at 13.
119 Hester, Hanmer, Coulson, Morahan and Razak, op. cit., at 13.
120 Hester, Hanmer, Coulson, Morahan and Razak, op. cit., at 13.
121 Hester and Westmarland, op. cit., at 56.
122 Edwards, op. cit., at 237.
123 Office of Law Reform, 'Review of the Family Homes and Domestic Violence (Northern Ireland) Order 1998', October 2003, at 2.
124 Office of Law Reform, op. cit., at 2.
125 Mullender A, *Re-thinking Domestic Violence*, 1996, at 57–58.
126 Hester and Westmarland, op. cit., at 56.
127 Edwards S, 'Domestic violence and harassment: An assessment of the civil remedies', in Taylor-Browne J (ed), *What Works in Reducing Domestic Violence? A comprehensive guide for professionals*, 2001, 187–210 at 188.
128 Edwards S, 'Domestic violence and harassment: An assessment of the civil remedies', op. cit., at 188.
129 Edwards S, 'Domestic violence and harassment: An assessment of the civil remedies', op. cit., at 188.
130 Edwards S, 'Domestic violence and harassment: An assessment of the civil remedies', op. cit., at 188.
131 Connelly and Cavanagh, op. cit., at 261.
132 Schneider EM, *Battered Women & Feminist Lawmaking*, 2000, at 52.
133 Randall M, 'Symposium: Domestic Violence & the Law: Theory, Policy, and Practice: Domestic Violence and the Construction of "Ideal Victims": Assaulted Women's "Image Problems" in Law', (2004) 23 *Saint Louis University Public Law Review*, 107–154 at 144.
134 Schneider, op. cit., at 196–197.

135 Balos B, 'Symposium: Domestic Violence & the Law: Theory, Policy, and Practice: A Man's Home is his Castle: How the Law Shelters Domestic Violence and Sexual Harassment', (2004) 23 *Saint Louis University Public Law Review*, 77–105 at 99.
136 Mullender and Hague (2001), op. cit., at 14.
137 Hague (1999), op. cit., at 133.
138 Hague (1999), op. cit., at 133.
139 Mullender, op. cit., at 59.
140 Smith, op. cit., at 78.
141 Dobash RE and Dobash RP, *Women, Violence & Social Change*, 1996, at 60.
142 Mullender and Hague (2001), op. cit., at 8.
143 Becker M, 'Access to Justice: The Social Responsibility of Lawyers: Access to Justice for Battered Women', (2003) 12 *Washington University Journal of Law & Policy*, 63–98 at 83.
144 Becker, op. cit., at 83.
145 Smith, op. cit., at 88.
146 Levison D and Harwin N, 'Accommodation provision', in Taylor-Browne J (ed), *What Works in Reducing Domestic Violence? A comprehensive guide for professionals,* 2001, 151–185 at 167.
147 Levison and Harwin, op. cit., at 152.
148 Mullender, op. cit., at 56.
149 Dobash and Dobash, op. cit., at 93.
150 Mullender and Hague (2001), op. cit., at 17.
151 Hague (1999), op. cit., at 143–144.
152 Hague (1999), op. cit., at 144.
153 Hague and Malos, op. cit., at 115.
154 Hague and Malos, op. cit., at 117.
155 Hague and Malos, op. cit., at 122.
156 Smith, op. cit., at 88.
157 Hague (1999), op. cit., at 143.
158 Sullivan, op. cit., at 297.
159 Randall, op. cit., at 151.
160 Stanko, op. cit., at 50.
161 Mullender, op. cit., at 45–46.
162 Mullender, op. cit., at 46.
163 Dobash and Dobash, op. cit., at 4.
164 Stanko, op. cit., at 53.
165 Mirrlees-Black C, 'Domestic Violence: Findings from a new British Crime Survey self-completion questionnaire', 1999, Home Office Research Study 191, at 40.
166 Walby S and Allen J, 'Domestic violence, sexual assault and stalking: Findings from the British Crime Survey', 2004, Home Office Research Study 276, at 45.
167 Kelly L and Radford J, 'Nothing really happened': the invalidation of women's experiences of sexual violence', in Hester M, Kelly L and Radford J, *Women, Violence and Male Power*, 2002, 19–33 at 19.
168 Mullender, op. cit., at 60–61.
169 Mirrlees-Black, op. cit., at 44–45.
170 Schneider, op. cit., at 77.
171 Bennett LW and Williams OJ, 'Men Who Batter', in Hampton RL (ed), *Family Violence – Prevention and Treatment*, 1999, 227–259 at 228.
172 Bennett and Williams, op. cit., at 228.
173 Bennett and Williams, op. cit., at 228.
174 Walker LE, *The Battered Woman*, 1979, Harper & Row, New York, as cited by Hampton RL, Jenkins P and Vandergriff-Avery M, 'Physical and Sexual

Violence in Marriage', in Hampton RL (ed), *Family Violence – Prevention and Treatment*, 1999, 168–197 at 182–183.

175 Mullender A and Morley R, 'Context and Content of a New Agenda', in Mullender A and Morley R (eds), *Children Living With Domestic Violence*, 1994, 2–16 at 8.

176 Dobash and Dobash, op. cit., at 231.

177 Dobash and Dobash, op. cit., at 231.

178 Dobash and Dobash, op. cit., at 232.

179 Stanko, op. cit., at 57.

180 Stanko, op. cit., at 57.

181 Diduck and Kaganas, op. cit., at 339.

182 Mullender, op. cit., at 60–61.

183 Berry, op. cit., at 193.

184 Garvey LE, 'Symposium: The Race Card: Dealing With Domestic Violence in the Courts', (2003) 11 *American University Journal of Gender, Social Policy & the Law,* 287–307 at 288.

185 Garvey, op. cit., at 288–289.

186 Hester and Westmarland, op. cit., at xiii.

187 Hester and Westmarland, op. cit., at xiii.

188 Connelly and Cavanagh, op.cit., at p.283.

189 Schneider, op. cit., at 210.

190 Hester and Westmarland, op. cit., at viii.

191 Hague and Malos, op. cit., at 131.

192 Mullender and Morley, op. cit., at 9.

193 Mullender, op. cit., at 62.

194 Dobash and Dobash, op. cit., at 232.

195 Burman JM, 'Lawyers and Domestic Violence: Raising the Standard of Practice', (2003) 9 *Michigan Journal of Gender & Law,* 207–259 at 209.

196 Mullender and Hague, op. cit., at 5.

197 Mullender and Hague, op. cit., at 4.

198 Hague (1999), op. cit., at 135.

199 Hague (1999), op. cit., at 136.

200 Hague and Malos, op. cit., at 151.

201 Hague, Mullender, Aris and Dear, op. cit., at 13.

202 Davidson LL, King V, Garcia J and Marchant S, 'What role can the health services play?', in Taylor-Browne J (ed), *What Works in Reducing Domestic Violence? A comprehensive guide for professionals,* 2001, 95–122 at 117.

203 Davidson, King, Garcia and Marchant, op. cit., at 122.

204 Mullender and Hague (2001), op. cit., at 15.

205 Mullender and Hague (2001), op. cit., at 16.

206 Levison and Harwin, op. cit., at 164.

207 Mullender, op. cit., at 61.

208 Smith, op. cit., at 97–98.

209 Berry, op. cit., at 195.

210 Smith, op. cit., at 99.

211 Prasad, op. cit.

212 Hague (1999), op. cit., at 142.

213 Hague (1999), op. cit., at 143.

214 Hague (1999), op. cit., at 143.

215 Hague and Malos, op. cit., at 174.

216 Hague G, 'Multi-agency initiatives', in Taylor–Browne J (ed), *What Works in Reducing Domestic Violence? A comprehensive guide for professionals,* 2001, 275–305 at 304.

217 Burman, op. cit., at 212.

218 Carter J, *Domestic Violence, Child Abuse, and Youth Violence: Strategies for Prevention and Early Intervention*, 2000, available at http://mincava.umn.edu/link/documents/fvpf2/fvpf2.shtml (Minnesota Center Against Violence and Abuse).
219 Mullender, op. cit., at 42.
220 Banks HD and Randolph SM, 'Substance Abuse and Family Violence', in Hampton RL (ed), *Family Violence – Prevention and Treatment*, 1999, 288–308 at 291.
221 Banks and Randolph, op. cit., at 293.
222 Mirrlees-Black, op. cit., at 45.
223 Mullender, op. cit., at 43.
224 Mirrlees-Black, op. cit., at 46.
225 Mirrlees-Black, op. cit., at 33.
226 Hester M, *Who Does What to Whom? Gender and Domestic Violence Perpetrators*, 2009, University of Bristol in association with the Northern Rock Foundation, Bristol.
227 Walby and Allen, op. cit., at 79.
228 Kelly and Radford, op. cit., at 27–28.
229 Bennett and Williams, op. cit., at 240.
230 Bennett and Williams, op. cit., at 240–241.
231 Hague and Malos, op. cit., at 194.
232 Bennett and Williams, op. cit., at 241.
233 Hague and Malos, op. cit., at 194.
234 Becker, op. cit., at 86.
235 Mullender M and Burton S, 'Dealing with perpetrators', in Taylor-Browne J (ed), *What Works in Reducing Domestic Violence? A comprehensive guide for professionals*, 2001, 59–93 at 75.
236 Mullender and Burton, op. cit., at 75.

3 The jurisprudence of the European Court of Human Rights

1 (1998) 29 EHRR 245.
2 Schriver T, 'Establishing an Affirmative Governmental Duty to Protect Children's Rights: The European Court of Human Rights as a Model for the United States Supreme Court', (2000) 34 *University of San Francisco Law Review*, 379–408 at 400.
3 Thomas DQ and Beasley ME, 'Symposium on Reconceptualizing Violence Against Women By Intimate Partners', (1995) 58 *Albany Law Review*, 1119–1147 at 1121.
4 Starmer K, *European Human Rights Law, the Human Rights Act 1998 and the European Convention on Human Rights*, 1999, at 194.
5 Clapham A, *Human Rights in the Private Sphere*, 1993, at 178.
6 Mowbray AR, *The Development of Positive Obligations under the European Convention on Human Rights by the European Court of Human Rights*, 2004, at 221.
7 Starmer, op. cit., at 194.
8 Schriver, op. cit., at 399.
9 Schriver, op. cit., at 401.
10 Clapham, op. cit., at 178.
11 Schriver, op. cit., at 402.
12 (1990) 12 EHRR 355, at para. 41.
13 (1998) 29 EHRR 245.
14 At para. 115.
15 At para. 116.

16 At para. 116.
17 Starmer, op. cit., at 196.
18 (1998) 29 EHRR 245, at para. 115.
19 At para. 115.
20 Choudhry S and Herring J, 'Domestic Violence and the Human Rights Act 1998: A New Means of Legal Intervention?', (2006) *Public Law*, 752–784 at 759.
21 Nguyen AM, 'The Torture Convention: A Gap Filler For the Holes in U.S. Asylum Policy Towards Victims of Domestic Violence', (2000) 30 *Southwestern University Law Review*, 171–195 at 195.
22 Copelon R, 'Intimate Terror: Understanding Domestic Violence as Torture', in Cook RJ (ed), *Human Rights of Women – National and International Perspectives*, 1994, 116–152 at 117.
23 Grdinic, op. cit.
24 (1979–80) 2 EHRR 25.
25 Grdinic, op. cit., at 226.
26 Copelon, op. cit., at 128.
27 Nguyen, op. cit., at 187.
28 Copelon, op. cit, at 123.
29 Selden, op. cit., at 17.
30 Copelon, op. cit., at 123–125.
31 Grdinic, op. cit., at 240.
32 (1979–80) 2 EHRR 25, Dissenting Opinion of Judge Sir Gerald Fitzmaurice at footnote 19, p.138.
33 Grdinic, op. cit., at 242.
34 Grdinic, op. cit., at 259.
35 Hopkins CQ, 'Rescripting Relationships: Towards a Nuanced Theory of Intimate Violence As Sex Discrimination', (2001) 9 *Virginia Journal of Social Policy & the Law*, 411–469 at 435.
36 (1998) 25 EHRR 251.
37 At para. 86.
38 Grdinic, op. cit., at 236.
39 (1998) 25 EHRR 251, at para. 83.
40 At para. 83.
41 (2004) 39 EHRR 34, at para. 33.
42 The findings of the British Crime Survey support this submission. Among those questioned who had been subjected to at least four incidents of domestic violence from the perpetrator of the worst incident, 89 per cent were women. Injuries were more often sustained by women. During the worst incident of domestic violence experienced in the last year, 46 per cent of women suffered a minor injury, 20 per cent a moderate injury and 6 per cent a severe injury. For 31 per cent of women the incident resulted in mental or emotional difficulties. Among male victims, 41 per cent sustained a minor injury, 14 per cent a moderate injury and 1 per cent a severe injury. The incident resulted in mental or emotional problems for 9 per cent of men. These findings give credence to the assertion that domestic violence is primarily carried out against women. (Walby S and Allen J, 'Domestic violence, sexual assault and stalking: Findings from the British Crime Survey', 2004, Home Office Research Study 276, at vii–viii.)
   In 2009, it was found that 77 per cent of all victims of domestic violence in the UK are women. (Walker A, Flatley J, Kershaw C and Moon D, 'Crime in England and Wales 2008/09: Home Office Statistical Bulletin', 2009.)
43 Application No. 28244/95, 1 July 1998.
44 (1986) 8 EHRR 235, at para. 23.
45 Application No. 7510/04, 24 September 2007.

46 Application No. 71127/01, 12 September 2008.
47 Application No. 33401/02, 9 September 2009.
48 Application No. 8227/04, 15 December 2009.
49 Application No. 55164/08, 14 October 2010.
50 Application No. 2660/03, 30 November 2010.
51 Note 45, at para. 49.
52 Note 46, at para. 83.
53 Note 47, at para. 153.
54 At para. 176.
55 At para. 200.
56 McColgan A, 'Women and the Human Rights Act', (2000) 51 *Northern Ireland Legal Quarterly*, 417–444 at 433–434.
57 Breaches of article 8 were also found in *A v Croatia* and *Hajduova v Slovakia*, both of which involved domestic violence.
58 Note 13, at para. 116.
59 At para. 116.
60 At para. 121.
61 Walby and Allen, op. cit., at 97.
62 It should also be noted that in *Z v UK* it was commented that the Court's reasoning in *Osman* 'was based on an understanding of the law of negligence . . . which has to be reviewed in the light of the clarifications subsequently made by the domestic courts'. (2002) 34 EHRR 3 at para. 100. At the time of the *Osman* case, public authorities were effectively immune from being sued for negligence.
63 (1999) 27 EHRR 611.
64 At para. 21.
65 At para. 23.
66 For example, Schneider EM, *Battered Women & Feminist Lawmaking*, 2000, at 52.
67 (1981) 3 EHRR 592.
68 At para. 25.
69 At para. 32.
70 Dissenting Opinion of Judge Thor Vilhjalmsson.
71 Dissenting Opinion of Judge Thor Vilhjalmsson.
72 Oloka-Onyango J, 'Reinforcing Marginalized Rights in an Age of Globalization: International Mechanisms, Non-State Actors, and the Struggle for Peoples' Rights in Africa', (2003) 18 *American University International Law Review*, 851–913 at 852.
73 Dissenting Opinion of Judge Thor Vilhjalmsson.
74 Chayes A, 'The Role of the Judge in Public Law Litigation', (1976) 89 *Harvard Law Review*, 1281–1316 at 1295–1296.
75 Application No. 25801/94, 30 January, 2001.
76 Paglione G, 'Domestic Violence and Housing Rights: A Reinterpretation of the Right to Housing', (2006) 28 *Human Rights Quarterly*, 120–147 at 139.
77 The Court first stated this principle in *Tyrer v United Kingdom* (1979–80) 2 EHRR 1, at para. 31.
78 Mowbray A, 'The Creativity of the European Court of Human Rights', [2005] 5 *Human Rights Law Review*, 57–79 at 79. See also Kay RS, 'The European Convention on Human Rights and the Control of Private Law', [2005] *European Human Rights Law Review*, 466–479.
79 (1997) 23 EHRR 213.
80 At para. 50.
81 At para. 62.
82 At para. 66.
83 Partly Dissenting Opinion of Judge MacDonald, at para. 2.
84 Partly Dissenting Opinion of Judge Foighel, at para. 10.
85 (1998) 29 EHRR 245.

86 Mowbray (2004), op. cit., at 230–231.
87 *Stubbings and Others v United Kingdom* (1997) 23 EHRR 213.
88 (1999) 27 EHRR 611.
89 *Airey v Ireland* (1981) 3 EHRR 592.

4 The Human Rights Act 1998: Could the United Kingdom courts rise to the challenge?

1 For literature on the impact of the Human Rights Act on the courts, see Lester A, 'The Human Rights Act 1998 – Five Years On', [2004] *European Human Rights Law Review*, 258–271; Lord Steyn, '2000–2005: Laying the Foundations of Human Rights Law in the United Kingdom', [2005] *European Human Rights Law Review*, 349–362; Sedley S, 'The Rocks or the Open Sea: Where is the Human Rights Act Heading?', (2005) 32 *Journal of Law and Society*, 3–17; Ewing KD, 'The Futility of the Human Rights Act', [2004] *Public Law*, 829–852; Lord Irvine of Lairg, 'The Impact of the Human Rights Act: Parliament, the Courts and the Executive', [2003] *Public Law*, 308–325; Klug F and Starmer K, 'Standing Back from the Human Rights Act: how effective is it five years on?', [2005] *Public Law*, 716–728; Gearty C, *Principles of Human Rights Adjudication*, 2004.
2 For example, Buxton R, 'The Human Rights Act and Private Law', (2000) 116 *Law Quarterly Review*, 48–65; Wade W, 'Opinion: Human Rights and the Judiciary', [1998] *European Human Rights Law Review*, 520–533; Wade HRW, 'Horizons of Horizontality', (2000) 116 *Law Quarterly Review*, 217–224; Bamforth N, 'The True "Horizontal Effect" of the Human Rights Act 1998', (2001) 117 *Law Quarterly Review*, 34–41; Hunt M, 'The "Horizontal Effect" of the Human Rights Act', [1998] *Public Law*, 423–443.
3 [2001] 2 All ER 289.
4 [2001] 2 WLR 1038.
5 [2004] 2 All ER 995.
6 This was an interlocutory hearing to decide whether an injunction restraining publication should be continued in force until trial.
7 The case returned to an Appeal Committee of the House of Lords as *Campbell v MGN Ltd (No. 2)* [2005] 4 All ER 793. The claimant's appeal to the House of Lords had been conducted under a conditional fee agreement as allowed under the Access to Justice Act 1999. The House of Lords had ordered the defendant to pay costs. The defendant argued that the success fees were an interference with the right to freedom of expression contained in article 10 of the European Convention as an award of costs increased by a success fee was disproportionate. The House of Lords held that there was no violation of article 10.
8 [2001] EWCA Civ 1955.
9 At para. 38.
10 [1999] 1 FLR 193 at 222.
11 (1986) 8 EHRR 235 at 241.
12 (2001) EWCA Civ 1955, at para. 38.
13 [1999] 2 All ER 545.
14 At 562.
15 At 562.
16 At 564–565.
17 At 565.
18 Palmer S, 'Feminism and the Promise of Human Rights: Possibilities and Paradoxes', in James S and Palmer S (eds), *Visible Women*, 2002, 91–115 at 101.
19 On the issue of deference, see Klug F, 'Judicial Deference Under the Human Rights Act 1998', [2003] *European Human Rights Law Review*, 125–133; Clayton R, 'Judicial deference and "democratic dialogue": the legitimacy of judicial inter-

vention under the Human Rights Act 1998', [2004] *Public Law,* 33–47; Jowell J, 'Judicial deference: servility, civility or institutional capacity?', [2003] *Public Law,* 592–601; Lord Steyn, 'Deference: a Tangled Story', [2005] *Public Law,* 346–359.

20 *Regina (Alconbury Developments Ltd and others) v Secretary of State for the Environment, Transport and the Regions; Regina (Holding & Barnes plc) v Same; Secretary of State for the Environment, Transport and the Regions v Legal and General Assurance Society Ltd* [2003] 2 AC 295, at para. 60.

21 *R v Secretary of State for the Home Department, ex p. Isiko* (2001) 1 FLR 930, at para. 31.

22 Edwards RA, 'Judicial Deference under the Human Rights Act', (2002) 65 *Modern Law Review,* 859–882 at 859.

23 [2004] 1 All ER 709.

24 At para. 62.

25 Schneider EM, *Battered Women & Feminist Lawmaking,* 2000, at 196–197.

26 (2000) EHRR 245, at para. 116.

27 [2004] NIQB 35.

28 At para. 46.

29 [2004] EWCA Civ 309.

30 At para. 52.

31 At para. 52.

32 [2004] 1 All ER 709.

33 At para. 62.

34 *Anufrijeva v Southwark London Borough Council; R (N) v Secretary of State for the Home Department; R (M) v Secretary of State for the Home Department* [2004] QB 1124.

35 At para. 43.

36 [2005] UKHL 66.

37 At para. 80.

38 Steiner HJ and Alston P, *International Human Rights in Context – Law, Politics, Morals,* 2000, at 235.

39 Beetham D, 'What Future for Economic and Social Rights?', (1995) 43 *Political Studies,* 41, as cited by Steiner and Alston, op. cit., at 255.

40 *R (on the application of Limbuela) v Secretary of State for the Home Department; R (on the application of Tesema) v Secretary of State for the Home Department; R (on the application of Adam) v Secretary of State for the Home Department* [2005] UKHL 66.

41 Palmer E, 'Courts, Resources and the HRA: Reading section 17 of the Children Act 1989 Compatibly with Article 8 ECHR', [2003] *European Human Rights Law Review,* 308–324 at 310.

42 Chayes A, 'The Role of the Judge in Public Law Litigation', (1976) 89 *Harvard Law Review,* 1281–1316 at 1309.

43 (1981) 3 EHRR 592, at para. 26.

44 Notably, McKeever and Ni Aolain argue that enforcement of socio-economic rights must be viewed in an imaginative manner. McKeever G and Ni Aolain F, 'Thinking Globally, Acting Locally: Enforcing Socio-Economic Rights in Northern Ireland' [2004] *European Human Rights Law Review,* 158–180. See also Van Bueren G, 'Including the Excluded: the Case for an Economic, Social and Cultural Human Rights Act', [2002] *Public Law,* 456–472.

45 Fredman S, 'Social, Economic and Cultural Rights', in Feldman D (ed), *English Public Law,* 2004, 529–579 at 530.

46 Temkin J, 'Rape and Criminal Justice at the Millennium', in Nicolson D and Bibbings L (eds), *Feminist Perspectives On Criminal Law,* 2000, 183–203 at 203.

47 [2001] 3 All ER 1.

48 McColgan A, 'Women and the Human Rights Act', (2000) 51 *Northern Ireland Legal Quarterly,* 417–444 at 441.
49 McColgan, op. cit., at 441.
50 Criminal Evidence (Northern Ireland) Order 1999, article 28.
51 Birch D, 'A Better Deal for Vulnerable Witnesses', [2000] *Criminal Law Review,* 223–249 at 226.
52 Lord Williams, House of Lords Hansard Debates for 1 February 1999, at Column 1376.
53 Birch, op. cit., at 226.
54 McColgan, op. cit., at 441.
55 McColgan, op. cit., at 441–442.
56 Lord Bingham of Cornhill, House of Lords Hansard Debates for 8 February 1999, at Column 55.
57 Lord Williams, House of Lords Hansard Debates for 8 February 1999, at Column 58.
58 [2001] 3 All ER 1.
59 At 18.
60 At 18.
61 Sandy D, '*R v A*: the death of the declaration of incompatibility?', (2001) *New Law Journal,* 1615.
62 Sandy, op. cit.
63 At 17.
64 Ekins R, 'A Critique of Radical Approaches to Rights-Consistent Statutory Interpretation', [2003] *European Human Rights Law Review,* 641–650 at 650.
65 [2004] 3 All ER 411.
66 At para. 67.
67 At para. 33.
68 Clare A, 'Statutory Interpretation Post-Human Rights Act 1998; Youth Justice and Criminal Evidence Act 1999 must be read so as to be compatible with the European Convention on Human Rights', (2001) 65 *Journal of Criminal Law,* 411–413 at 413.
69 For further discussion on the section 3 interpretative obligation, see Kavanagh A, 'Unlocking the Human Rights Act: The "Radical" Approach to Section 3(1) Revisited', [2005] *European Human Rights Law Review,* 259–275; Gearty CA, 'Reconciling Parliamentary Democracy and Human Rights', (2002) 118 *Law Quarterly Review,* 248–269.
70 Kavanagh A, 'Statutory interpretation and human rights after *Anderson*: a more contextual approach', [2004] *Public Law,* 537–545 at 543.
71 [2002] EWCA Civ 86.
72 (1999) 28 EHRR 603.
73 [2001] 2 FLR 1017.
74 At para. 67.
75 At para. 88.
76 *R v Seaboyer; R v Gayme* [1991] 2 SCR 577.
77 Mullender A, *Rethinking Domestic Violence,* 1996, at 33–34.
78 Walby S and Allen J, 'Domestic violence, sexual assault and stalking: Findings from the British Crime Survey', 2004, Home Office Research Study 276, at 97.
79 Crown Prosecution Service, 'Policy on Prosecuting Cases of Domestic Violence', 2001, at paras. 4–5.
80 At para. 4.12.
81 Crown Prosecution Service, 'Policy on Prosecuting Cases of Domestic Violence', 2005.
82 Crown Prosecution Service, 'Policy for Prosecuting Cases of Domestic Violence', 2009.

83 Section 7(3). This is in contrast to, for example, the Indian approach, which allows cases brought by groups on behalf of others and cases brought by publicly interested individuals – see Epp CR, *The Rights Revolution,* 1998, at 86. For criticism of the test of standing under the Human Rights Act, see Marriott J and Nicol D, 'The Human Rights Act, Representative Standing and the Victim Culture', [1998] *European Human Rights Law Review,* 730–741. See also Miles J, 'Standing Under the Human Rights Act 1998: Theories of Rights Enforcement & the Nature of Public Law Adjudication', (2000) 59 *Cambridge Law Journal,* 133–167.
84 Schneider, op. cit., at 196–197.
85 *R (on the application of Limbuela) v Secretary of State for the Home Department; R (on the application of Tesema) v Secretary of State for the Home Department; R (on the application of Adam) v Secretary of State for the Home Department* [2005] UKHL 66.
86 [2004] 2 All ER 409.
87 At para. 52.
88 [2005] UKHL 71. See also the First Belmarsh case – *A v Secretary of State for the Home Department* [2005] 2 AC 68.
89 For example, General Recommendation No.19 of the Committee on the Elimination of Discrimination Against Women (U.N. Doc A/47/38 (1992)), reports of the Second, Third and Fourth World Conferences on Women, resolutions of the General Assembly, the UN Declaration on the Elimination of Violence against Women (General Assembly Resolution 48/104 (1993)), reports of the Special Rapporteur on Violence against Women and resolutions of the Commission on Human Rights.

5 The approach of the international human rights bodies to domestic violence

1   General Assembly Resolution 48/104 (1993) article 3.
2   General Recommendation No.19, Committee on the Elimination of Discrimination Against Women, U.N. Doc A/47/38 (1992).
3   General Assembly Resolution 48/104 (1993).
4   Article 1.
5   General Recommendation No.19, Committee on the Elimination of Discrimination Against Women, U.N. Doc A/47/38 (1992) at para. 4.
6   At para. 6.
7   At para. 7.
8   At para. 9.
9   At para. 23.
10 At para. 24(r)(i).
11 At para. 24(b).
12 U.N. C.H.R. Res 1994/45 (ESCOR 1994) paras. 7(a) and (b).
13 Stark B, 'Symposium on Integrating Responses to Domestic Violence', (2001) 47 *Loyola Law Review,* 255–282 at 265.
14 Report of the Special Rapporteur on violence against women, its causes and consequences – A framework for model legislation on domestic violence, E/CN.4/1996/53/Add.2, 2 February 1996, at para. 12.
15 At para. 13.
16 At para. 14.
17 At para. 16.
18 At para. 17(a).
19 At para. 17(b).
20 At para. 17(c).

21 At para. 17(e).
22 At para. 17(f).
23 At para. 17(h).
24 At para. 21(e).
25 At para. 21(d).
26 At para. 23.
27 At para. 24.
28 At para. 45.
29 At para. 49.
30 At para. 55.
31 At para. 54.
32 For other UN documents dealing with the question of how the criminal justice system should respond to cases of domestic violence, see Report of the World Conference of the United Nations Decade for Women: Equality, Development and Peace, Copenhagen, July 1980, U.N. Doc A/CONF. 94/35 (80.IV.3) at para. 65; General Assembly Resolution 40/36 (1985) at paras. 3 and 7; Report of the World Conference to Review and Appraise the Achievements of the United Nations Decade for Women: Equality, Development and Peace, held in Nairobi, July 1985, including Nairobi Forward-Looking Strategies for the Advancement of Women, U.N. Doc A/CONF.116/28/Rev.1 (85.IV.10) at para. 76; General Assembly Resolution 45/114 (1990) at para. 2; General Assembly Resolution 48/104 (1993) articles 4(d) and (f); Beijing Platform for Action, U.N. Doc.A/CONF.177/20 (1995) at paras. 112, 113 and 124; Commission on Human Rights Resolution 2001/49, at para. 10(c); Commission on Human Rights Resolution 2004/46, at para. 15; General Assembly Resolution 60/143 (2007) at paras. 7 and 8(i).
33 At para. 24(t)(i).
34 At paras. 26–43.
35 For other UN documents dealing with the necessity for adequate civil law measures in relation to domestic violence, see General Assembly Resolution 40/36 (1985) at para. 7; General Assembly Resolution 48/104 (1993) article 4(d); Commission on Human Rights Resolution 2004/46, at para. 15(h).
36 Report of the Special Rapporteur on violence against women, its causes and consequences, E/CN.4/1996/53, 5 February 1996, at para. 142(k).
37 Schneider EM, *Battered Women & Feminist Lawmaking*, 2000, at 196–197.
38 At para. 24(t)(iii).
39 At para. 60.
40 At para. 61(a).
41 At para. 61(c).
42 Report of the Special Rapporteur on violence against women, its causes and consequences, E/CN.4/1996/53, 5 February 1996, at para. 142(m).
43 For other UN documents dealing with the need for social support measures for victims of domestic violence, see General Assembly Resolution 40/36 (1985) at paras. 7(e) and 7(f); Report of the World Conference to Review and Appraise the Achievements of the United Nations Decade for Women: Equality, Development and Peace, held in Nairobi, July 1985, including Nairobi Forward-Looking Strategies for the Advancement of Women, U.N. Doc A/CONF.116/28/Rev.1 (85.IV.10) at para. 231; General Assembly Resolution 48/104 (1993) article 4(g); Beijing Platform for Action, U.N. Doc.A/CONF.177/20 (1995) at para. 125(a); Commission on Human Rights Resolution 2001/49, at para. 2; Commission on Human Rights Resolution 2004/46, at para. 15(g).
44 Interim report of the Ad Hoc Committee on Preventing and Combating Violence Against Women and Domestic Violence, CM(2009)84, at para. 25.

45 At para. 24(t)(ii).
46 At para. 2(i)(iv).
47 Report of the Special Rapporteur on violence against women, its causes and consequences, E/CN.4/1996/53, 5 February 1996, at para. 141.
48 Report of the Special Rapporteur on violence against women, its causes and consequences, E/CN.4/2004/66, 26 December 2003, at para. 58.
49 Beijing Platform for Action, U.N. Doc.A/CONF.177/20 (1995) at para. 125(d).
50 At para. 125(e).
51 At para. 125(g).
52 At para. 125(j).
53 For other UN documents dealing with the need to raise societal awareness of domestic violence, see General Assembly Resolution 45/114 (1990) at para. 1(c); General Assembly Resolution 48/104 (1993) article 4(j); Commission on Human Rights Resolution 2001/49, at paras. 10(e) and (g); Commission on Human Rights Resolution 2004/46, at paras. 15(k) and (m); General Assembly Resolution 61/143 (2007) at para. 8(n).
54 Council of Europe, Committee of Ministers, Recommendation Rec(2002)5, Appendix, para. 7.
55 Interim report of the Ad Hoc Committee on Preventing and Combating Violence Against Women and Domestic Violence, CM(2009)84, at para. 18.
56 Smith LJF, 'Domestic Violence: an Overview of the Literature', 1989, Home Office Research Study 107, at 97–98.
57 At para. 24(b).
58 At para. 2(k).
59 At paras. 66–68.
60 At para. 62(a).
61 At paras. 62(b) and (c).
62 At para. 62(e).
63 At para. 65.
64 Report of the Special Rapporteur on violence against women, its causes and consequences, E/CN.4/2002/83, 31 January 2002, at para. 128.
65 For other UN documents dealing with the need to educate professionals in the issues involved in domestic violence, see General Assembly Resolution 40/36 (1985) at para. 7(g); General Assembly Resolution 45/114 (1990) at para. 1(c); General Assembly Resolution 48/104 (1993) article 4(i); Beijing Platform for Action, U.N. Doc.A/CONF.177/20 (1995) at para. 124(g); Commission on Human Rights Resolution 2001/49, at para. 10(f); Commission on Human Rights Resolution 2004/46, at para. 15(g).
66 Resolution 40/36 (1985) at para. 7(j).
67 Resolution 45/114 (1990) at para. 1.
68 Resolution 48/104 (1993) article 4(e).
69 Commission on Human Rights Resolution 2001/49, at para. 10(d).
70 Commission on Human Rights Resolution 2004/46, at para. 15(j).
71 Interim report of the Ad Hoc Committee on Preventing and Combating Violence Against Women and Domestic Violence, CM(2009)84, at para. 35.
72 The 1999 British Crime Survey found that a third of attacks took place while the assailant was under the influence of alcohol. 8 per cent of female chronic victims said their last assault had taken place while their assailant was under the influence of drugs. It was found that victims of domestic assault had far higher levels of alcohol consumption than non-victims. Victims were also far more likely to say they had recently used illegal drugs. Mirlees-Black C, 'Domestic Violence: Findings from a new British Crime Survey self-completion questionnaire', 1999, Home Office Research Study 191, at 33 and 45–46.

73 Kelly L and Radford J, ' "Nothing really happened": the invalidation of women's experiences of sexual violence', in Hester M, Kelly L and Radford J (eds), *Women, Violence and Male Power*, 2002, 19–33 at 27–28.
74 Resolution 40/36 (1985) Preamble.
75 Resolution 45/114 (1990) Preamble.
76 At para. 21.
77 At para. 24(o).
78 Resolution 48/104 (1993) Preamble.
79 Report of the Special Rapporteur on violence against women, its causes and consequences, E/CN.4/1996/53, 5 February 1996, at para. 142(n).
80 At para. 126(d).
81 At para. 124(m).
82 At para. 125(b).
83 Preamble.
84 At para. 24(r)(iv).
85 At para. 61(b).
86 At para. 70.
87 At para. 71(i).
88 At para. 71(ii).
89 At para. 72.
90 For other UN documents dealing with the development of rehabilitation programmes for perpetrators of domestic violence, see General Assembly Resolution 40/36 (1985) at para. 7(a); Report of the World Conference to Review and Appraise the Achievements of the United Nations Decade for Women: Equality, Development and Peace, held in Nairobi, July 1985, including Nairobi Forward-Looking Strategies for the Advancement of Women, U.N. Doc A/CONF.116/28/Rev.1 (85.IV.10) at para. 123; General Assembly Resolution 45/114 (1990) at para. 1(d); Beijing Platform for Action, U.N. Doc.A/CONF.177/20 (1995) at para. 125(i); Commission on Human Rights Resolution 2001/49, at para. 10(g); Commission on Human Rights Resolution 2004/46, at para. 15(k).
91 Becker M, 'Access to Justice: The Social Responsibility of Lawyers: Access to Justice for Battered Women', (2003) 12 *Washington University Journal of Law & Policy*, 63–98 at 86.
92 Bennett LW and Williams OJ, 'Men who Batter', in Hampton RL (ed), *Family Violence – Prevention and Treatment*, 1999, 227–259 at 241.
93 At para. 24(c).
94 At para. 120.
95 Strategic objective D.2.
96 At para. 129(b). For other UN documents on the need to carry out research in relation to domestic violence, see General Assembly Resolution 40/36 (1985) at para. 7(h); General Assembly Resolution 48/104 (1993) article 4(k); Commission on Human Rights Resolution 2001/49, at para. 22; Commission on Human Rights Resolution 2004/46, at para. 15(n).
97 The Organisation of American States created the Inter-American Convention on the Prevention, Punishment and Eradication of Violence Against Women 'Convention of Belem Do Para'. The African Union has adopted the Protocol on the Rights of Women.
98 (1999) 27 EHRR 611.
99 10 December 1999.
100 10 December 1999.
101 Byrnes A, 'Enforcement Through International Law and Procedures', in Cook RJ (ed), *Human Rights of Women – National and International Perspectives*, 1994, 189–227 at 203.

102 Article 8.
103 'The Convention on the Elimination of All Forms of Discrimination against Women and its Optional Protocol', United Nations, 2003, at 77.
104 At 77.
105 22 December 2000.
106 Ritz KL, 'Soft Enforcement: Inadequacies of Optional Protocol as a Remedy for the Convention on the Elimination of All Forms of Discrimination Against Women', (2001) 25 *Suffolk Transnational Law Review*, 191–216 at 211.
107 Communication No. 2/2003, views adopted 26 January 2005.
108 At para 9.6(II)(b).
109 Communication No. 5/2005, views adopted 6 August 2007.
110 At para. 12.1.5.
111 At para. 12.3(b).
112 Communication No. 6/2005, views adopted 6 August 2007.
113 At para. 12.1.5.
114 Byrnes A and Bath E, 'Violence against women, the obligation of due diligence, and the Optional Protocol to the Convention on the Elimination of All Forms of Discrimination Against Women – recent developments', (2008) 8 *Human Rights Law Review*, 517–533 at 533.
115 Murdoch J, 'Unfulfilled expectations: the Optional Protocol to the Convention on the Elimination of All Forms of Discrimination against Women', (2010) *European Human Rights Law Review* 26–46 at 45.
116 At para. 9.
117 Hopkins CQ, 'Rescripting Relationships: Towards a Nuanced Theory of Intimate Violence As Sex Discrimination', (2001) 9 *Virginia Journal of Social Policy & the Law*, 411–469 at 435.
118 Hernandez-Truyol BE, 'Conceptualizing Violence: Present and Future Developments in International Law', (1997) 60 *Albany Law Review*, 607–634 at 630.
119 Vienna Declaration and Programme of Action, sec. II, B para. 38, U.N. Doc A/CONF. 157/24 (October 1993).
120 General Assembly Resolution 48/104 (1993) article 4(c).
121 Preliminary Report of the Special Rapporteur on Violence Against Women to the Commission on Human Rights E/CN.4/1995/42 (1994), at para. 107.
122 At para. 124(b).

6 Implementation of the statements of the international human rights bodies in the United Kingdom

1 General Recommendation No.19, Committee on the Elimination of Discrimination against Women, U.N. Doc A/47/38 (1992) at para. 24(r)(i).
2 Offences Against the Person Act 1861, s.42.
3 s.43.
4 s.47.
5 s.18.
6 s.20.
7 See Diduck A and Kaganas F, *Family Law, Gender and the State*, 1999, at 369–370.
8 Declaration on the Elimination of Violence Against Women, General Assembly Resolution 48/104 (1993) at para. 4(f).
9 Home Office Circular 60/90, at para. 11.
10 'Domestic Violence: Revised Circular to Police', Home Office Circular 19/2000.

11 'Guidance on Investigating Domestic Abuse', National Policing Improvement Agency, 2008, at 26.
12 Miles J, 'Domestic Violence', in Herring J (ed), *Family Law – Issues, Debates, Policy*, 2001, 78–124 at 92.
13 Miles, op. cit., at 92.
14 Grace S, 'Policing Domestic Violence in the 1990s', 1995, Home Office Research Study 139.
15 Grace, op. cit., at 53.
16 Miles, op. cit., at 92.
17 Hester M and Westmarland N, 'Tackling Domestic Violence: effective interventions and approaches', 2005, Home Office Research Study 290, at 54.
18 'Together we can end Violence against Women and Girls: A Strategy', Home Office, 2009, at 61.
19 Walklate S, 'What is to be done about violence against women? Gender, v iolence, cosmopolitanism and the law', (2008) 48 *British Journal of Criminology*, 39–54 at 42.
20 Burton M, *Legal Responses to Domestic Violence*, 2008, at 96.
21 Crown Prosecution Service, 'Policy On Prosecuting Cases of Domestic Violence', 2001, at paras. 4–5.
22 At para. 4.5.
23 At para. 4.12.
24 At para. 5.7.
25 Crown Prosecution Service, 'Policy On Prosecuting Cases of Domestic Violence', 2005.
26 At para. 1.15.
27 Crown Prosecution Service, 'CPS Policy for Prosecuting Cases of Domestic Violence', 2009, at para. 4.6.
28 Choudhry S and Herring J, 'Righting Domestic Violence', (2006) *International Journal of Law, Policy and the Family*, 95–119 at 99.
29 'Women 2000: Report from the UK Women's National Commission on the implementation of the Beijing Platform for Action in the UK'.
30 At 41–42.
31 At 42.
32 At 42.
33 Beijing Platform for Action, U.N. Doc.A/CONF.177/20 (1995) at para. 124(d).
34 At 42–43.
35 Herring J, *Family Law*, 2009, at 310.
36 Connelly C and Cavanagh K, 'Domestic Abuse, Civil Protection Orders and the "New Criminologies": Is there any Value in Engaging with the Law?', (2007) 15 *Feminist Legal Studies*, 259–287 at 282.
37 General Recommendation No.19, Committee on the Elimination of Discrimination against Women, U.N. Doc A/47/38 (1992) at para. 24(t)(i).
38 Humphries M, 'Occupation Orders Revisited', [2001] *Family Law Review*, 542–544. See also Choudhry S and Herring H, 'Domestic Violence and the Human Rights Act 1998: A New Means of Legal Intervention?', (2006) *Public Law*, 752–784 at 754–757.
39 [2000] 2 FLR 36 at 41.
40 Humphries, op. cit., at 544.
41 Edwards S, 'Domestic violence and harassment: An assessment of the civil remedies', in Taylor-Browne J (ed), *What Works in Reducing Domestic Violence? A comprehensive guide for professionals*, 2001, 187–210 at 202.
42 Office of Law Reform, 'Review of the Family Homes and Domestic Violence (Northern Ireland) Order 1998', October 2003, at 19.
43 At 19.

44 Edwards, op. cit., at 202.
45 Fifth periodic report of the UK to the CEDAW Committee, at 63.
46 s.1.
47 s.3.
48 s.8.
49 s.8.
50 Hester M, Westmarland N, Pearce J and Williamson E, 'Early Evaluation of the Domestic Violence, Crime and Victims Act 2004', 2008, Ministry of Justice Research Series 14/08.
51 Report of the Special Rapporteur on violence against women, its causes and consequences, E/CN.4/1996/53, 5 February 1996, at para. 142(k).
52 Report of the Special Rapporteur on violence against women, its causes and consequences, E/CN.4/1996/53, 5 February 1996, at para. 142(k).
53 [2000] 2 FLR 334.
54 At 341–342.
55 At 356.
56 At 358.
57 'Women 2000: Report from the UK Women's National Commission on the implementation of the Beijing Platform for Action in the UK', at 42.
58 At 42.
59 Bell C, 'In Practice: Domestic Violence and Contact', [2008] *Family Law* 1139.
60 Burton, op. cit., at 32.
61 General Recommendation No.19, Committee on the Elimination of Discrimination against Women, U.N. Doc A/47/38 (1992) at para. 24(t)(iii).
62 Fourth periodic report of the UK to the CEDAW Committee, at 177.
63 Concluding Observations of the Committee on the Elimination of Discrimination Against Women: United Kingdom of Great Britain and Northern Ireland, 01/07/99, at para. 311.
64 'Women 2000: Report from the UK Women's National Commission on the implementation of the Beijing Platform for Action in the UK', at 39.
65 At 40.
66 At 40.
67 At 41.
68 At 41.
69 At 41.
70 Sixth periodic report of the UK to the CEDAW Committee, at para. 596.
71 At paras. 597–598.
72 Concluding Observations of the Committee on the Elimination of Discrimination Against Women: United Kingdom of Great Britain and Northern Ireland, 10 July 2008, at para. 280.
73 At para. 272.
74 At para. 280.
75 At para. 273.
76 At para. 281.
77 'Submission to the United Nations Convention on the Elimination of All Forms of Discrimination Against Women from the Women's National Commission of the United Kingdom of Great Britain and Northern Ireland', March 2005, at 20, available at http://www.thewnc.org.uk.
78 Soteri A, *Funding in London Women's Organisations – A First Report*, 2002, Centre for Institutional Studies, University of East London, at 17.
79 Soteri, op. cit., at 2.
80 Soteri, op. cit., at 17.

81 'Submission to the United Nations Committee on the Convention on the Elimination of All Forms of Discrimination Against Women', July 2007, at 75, available at http://www.thewnc.org.uk.

82 Levison D and Harwin N, 'Accommodation provision', in Taylor-Browne J (ed), *What Works in Reducing Domestic Violence? A comprehensive guide for professionals*, 2001, 151–185 at 168–169.

83 Barran D, 'Developments in Protecting Victims of Domestic Abuse', [2009] *Family Law* 416.

84 General Recommendation No.19, Committee on the Elimination of Discrimination against Women, U.N. Doc A/47/38 (1992) at para. 24(t)(iii).

85 Report of the Special Rapporteur on violence against women, its causes and consequences, E/CN.4/2002/83, 31 January 2002, at para. 128.

86 Fourth periodic report of the UK to the CEDAW Committee, at 174.

87 Concluding Observations of the Committee on the Elimination of Discrimination Against Women: United Kingdom of Great Britain and Northern Ireland, 01/07/99, at para. 280.

88 Hague G and Malos E, *Domestic Violence: Action for Change*, 2005, at 203.

89 'Together we can end Violence against Women and Girls: A Strategy', Home Office, 2009, at 21.

90 Hague G, 'Domestic violence policy in the 1990s', in Watson S and Doyal L (eds), *Engendering Social Policy*, 1999, 131–147 at 132.

91 'National Domestic Violence Delivery Plan: Annual Progress Report 2008–09', 2009, at 4.

92 Hague and Malos, op. cit., at 136.

93 Davidson LL, King V, Garcia J and Marchant S, 'What role can the health services play?', in Taylor-Browne J (ed), *What Works in Reducing Domestic Violence? A comprehensive guide for professionals,* 2001, 95–122 at 97.

94 Davidson, King, Garcia and Marchant, op. cit., at 106.

95 Hague and Malos, op. cit., at 152.

96 Davidson, King, Garcia and Marchant, op. cit., at 106–107.

97 Davidson, King, Garcia and Marchant, op. cit., at 107.

98 Sixth periodic report of the UK to the CEDAW Committee, at para. 587.

99 'Together we can end Violence against Women and Girls: A Strategy', Home Office, 2009, at 57.

100 General Assembly Resolution 45/114 (1990) at para. 1.

101 Fourth periodic report of the UK to the CEDAW Committee, at 175.

102 At 177.

103 At 39–40.

104 'National Domestic Violence Delivery Plan: Annual Progress Report 2008–09', 2009, at 32–33.

105 Beijing Platform for Action, U.N. Doc.A/CONF.177/20 (1995) at para. 126(d).

106 'Safety and Justice: The Government's Proposals on Domestic Violence', June 2003, at 18.

107 'Safety and Justice', op. cit., at 18.

108 'Safety and Justice', op. cit., at 19.

109 Home Office, 'Alcohol-Related Crime'.

110 'Safety and Justice', op. cit., at 19.

111 Home Office, 'Drug Strategy', available at http://drugs.homeoffice.gov.uk/drug-strategy/

112 'Safety and Justice', op. cit., at 55.

113 Home Office Development and Practice Report 35, 2005, available at http://www.homeoffice.gov.uk.

114 'National Domestic Violence Delivery Plan: Annual Progress Report 2008–09', 2009, at 26.
115 General Recommendation No.19, Committee on the Elimination of Discrimination against Women, U.N. Doc A/47/38 (1992) at para. 24(r)(iv).
116 Mullender A and Burton S, 'Reducing Domestic Violence . . . What Works? Perpetrator Programmes', 2000, Crime Reduction Research Series, available at http://www.homeoffice.gov.uk.
117 Hague and Malos, op. cit., at 191–192.
118 Mullender M and Burton S, 'Dealing with perpetrators', in Taylor-Browne J (ed), *What Works in Reducing Domestic Violence? A comprehensive guide for professionals*, 2001, 59–93 at 62.
119 Hague and Malos, op. cit., at 179.
120 Hague and Malos, op. cit., at 188.
121 Mullender and Burton (2001), op. cit., at 92.
122 General Recommendation No.19, Committee on the Elimination of Discrimination Against Women, U.N. Doc A/47/38 (1992) at para. 24(c).
123 For example, Morley R and Mullender A, 'Preventing Domestic Violence to Women', 1994, Home Office Police Department, London; Grace S, 'Policing domestic violence in the 1990s', 1995, Home Office Research Study 139; Plotnikoff J and Woolfson R, 'Policing Domestic Violence: Effective Organisational Structures', 1998, Police Research Series Paper 100, available at http://www.homeoffice.gov.uk; Kelly L, 'Domestic Violence Matters: an evaluation of a development project', 1999, Home Office Research Study 193; The 'Reducing Domestic Violence . . . What Works?' research, 2000, Crime Reduction Research Series, available at http://www.homeoffice.gov.uk; Walby S, 'The Cost of Domestic Violence', 2004, available at http://www.equalities.gov.uk; Hester M and Westmarland N, 'Tackling Domestic Violence: effective interventions and approaches', 2005, Home Office Research Study 290; 'Domestic Violence – A National Report', March 2005, available at http://www.crimereduction.gov.uk.
124 Diane Maddock, House of Commons Hansard Debates for 17 December 1996, at Column 802. There was certainly no mention of international human rights law.
125 Smith LJF, 'Domestic Violence: an overview of the literature', 1989, Home Office Research Study 107.
126 Smith, op. cit., at 47.
127 Home Office Circular 60/90.
128 Morley R and Mullender A, 'Preventing Domestic Violence to Women', 1994, Home Office Police Department, London.
129 Grace, op. cit.
130 Plotnikoff J and Woolfson R, 'Policing Domestic Violence: Effective Organisational Structures', 1998, Police Research Series Paper 100, available at http://www.homeoffice.gov.uk; and Hanmer J, Griffiths S and Jerwood D, 'Arresting Evidence: Domestic Violence and Repeat Victimisation', 1999, Police Research Series Paper 104, available at http://www.homeoffice.gov.uk.
131 Hanmer J and Griffiths S, 'Reducing Domestic Violence . . . What Works? Policing Domestic Violence', 2000, Crime Reduction Research Series, available at http://www.homeoffice.gov.uk.
132 'Domestic Violence: Revised Circular to Police', Home Office Circular No 19/2000.
133 Hanmer J and Griffiths S, 'Reducing Domestic Violence . . . What Works? Policing Domestic Violence', 2000, Crime Reduction Research Series, available at http://www.homeoffice.gov.uk.
134 Hanmer and Griffiths, op. cit.

135 Circular No 19/2000, at part 2.
136 At part 5.
137 Hanmer and Griffiths, op. cit.
138 At part 15.
139 Hanmer and Griffiths, op. cit.
140 At part 14.
141 Hanmer and Griffiths, op. cit.
142 At part 12.
143 Hanmer and Griffiths, op. cit.
144 At part 15.
145 Plotnikoff J and Woolfson R, 'Policing Domestic Violence: Effective Organisational Structures', 1998, Police Research Series Paper 100, available at http://www.homeoffice.gov.uk.
146 Plotnikoff and Woolfson, op. cit., at v.
147 At part 5.
148 Plotnikoff and Woolfson, op. cit., at vi.
149 At part 15.
150 Plotnikoff and Woolfson, op. cit., at vi.
151 At part 15.
152 It should also be noted that international human rights law was not mentioned in any of the research discussed in this section.
153 At part 1.
154 'Guidance on Investigating Domestic Abuse', National Policing Improvement Agency, 2008, 26.
155 Ibid., at 34.
156 Cretney SM, Masson JM and Bailey-Harris R, *Principles of Family Law*, 2002, at 235.
157 Law Commission No.207 (1992).
158 At para. 1.2.
159 At para. 2.48.
160 Lord Mackay of Clashfern, House of Lords Hansard Debates for 11 December 1996, at Column 1092.
161 John Bercow, House of Commons Hansard Debates for 18 June 2003, at Column 389.
162 John Bercow, House of Commons Hansard Debates for 18 June 2003, at Column 389.
163 Report of the Special Rapporteur on violence against women, its causes and consequences, E/CN.4/1996/53, 5 February 1996, at para. 142(k).
164 [2000] 2 FLR 334.
165 Advisory Board on Family Law: Children Act Sub-committee (2000).
166 Sturge C in consultation with Glaser D, 'Contact and Domestic Violence – The Experts' Court Report', [2000] *Law Review,* 615.
167 [2000] 2 FLR 865.
168 Bridge C, '*Re G (Domestic Violence: Direct Contact)* – Comment', [2000] *Family Law Review,* 789–790 at 790.
169 Davidson L, King V, Garcia J and Marchant S, 'Reducing Domestic Violence . . . What Works? Health Services', 2000, Crime Reduction Research Series, available at http://www.homeoffice.gov.uk.
170 Taket A, 'Tackling Domestic Violence: the role of health professionals', Home Office Development and Practice Report 32, 2004, available at http://www.homeoffice.gov.uk, at 3.
171 Concluding Observations of the Committee on the Elimination of Discrimination Against Women: United Kingdom of Great Britain and Northern Ireland, 01/07/99, at para. 311.

172 Fifth periodic report of the UK to the CEDAW Committee, at 63.
173 'Domestic Violence: Break the Chain Multi-Agency Guidance for Addressing Domestic Violence', March 2000, available at http://www.homeoffice.gov.uk.
174 Fifth periodic report of the UK to the CEDAW Committee, at 63.
175 At para. 365.
176 Sixth periodic report of the UK to the CEDAW Committee, at para. 590.
177 At para. 366.
178 Hague G, 'Reducing Domestic Violence ... What Works? Multi-Agency Fora', 2000, Crime Reduction Research Series, available at http://www.homeoffice.gov.uk.
179 Hague, 2000, op. cit.
180 Concluding Observations of the Committee on the Elimination of Discrimination Against Women: United Kingdom of Great Britain and Northern Ireland, 10 July 2008, at para. 280.
181 'Tackling Domestic Violence: providing advocacy and support to survivors from Black and other minority ethnic communities', Home Office Development and Practice Report 35, 2005, available at http://www.homeoffice.gov.uk.
182 At 1.
183 For example, Douglas N, Lilley SJ, Kooper L and Diamond A, 'Safety and justice: sharing personal information in the context of domestic violence – an overview', 2004, Home Office Development and Practice Report No. 30, Home Office, London; Hester M and Westmarland N, 'Tackling Domestic Violence: effective interventions and approaches', 2005, Home Office Research Study No. 290.
184 Mullender and Burton (2000), op. cit.
185 Bennett LW and Williams OJ, 'Men who Batter', in Hampton RL (ed), *Family Violence – Prevention and Treatment*, 1999, 227–259 at 241.
186 Mullender and Burton (2000), op. cit.
187 Merry SE, 'Constructing a Global Law – Violence against Women and the Human Rights System', (2003) 28 *Law and Social Inquiry*, 941–974 at 941.
188 Schneider EM, 'Anna Hirsch Lecture: Transnational Law as a Domestic Resource: Thoughts on the Case of Women's Rights', (2004) 38 *New England Law Review*, 689–723 at 690.
189 Heyns C and Viljoen F, *The Impact of the United Nations Human Rights Treaties on the Domestic Level*, 2002, at 19.
190 Ulrich JL, 'Confronting Gender-Based Violence With International Instruments: Is a Solution to the Pandemic Within Reach?', (2000) 7 *Indiana Journal of Global Legal Studies*, 629–654 at 644.
191 Afsharipour A, 'Empowering Ourselves: The Role of Women's NGOs in the Enforcement of the Women's Convention', (1999) 99 *Columbia Law Review*, 129–172 at 146–161.
192 Zhang L, 'Domestic violence network in China: Translating the transnational concept of violence against women into local action', (2009) 32 *Women's Studies International Forum*, 227–239 at 230.
193 Ibid., at 231.
194 See also McQuigg R, 'The Responses of States to the Comments of the CEDAW Committee on Domestic Violence', (2007) 11 *International Journal of Human Rights*, 461–479.
195 It should be noted that a communications procedure has been established under the Optional Protocol to CEDAW, whereby individuals can submit communications to the CEDAW Committee. However, the Committee has no effective means of enforcing its decisions under this Protocol.
196 Fourth periodic report of the UK to the CEDAW Committee, at 10.

197 At 11.
198 Although in *Re L (a child) (contact: domestic violence); Re V (a child) (contact: domestic violence); Re M (a child) (contact; domestic violence); Re H (children) (contact: domestic violence)* [2000] 2 FLR 334, the court did seem to recognise that domestic violence is relevant when assessing parental ability, this is a long way from saying that contact should never take place in cases with a background of domestic violence.

7 Conclusion

1 Copelon R, 'Intimate Terror: Understanding Domestic Violence as Torture', in Cook RJ, *Human Rights of Women – National and International Perspectives*, 1994, 116–152.
2 Roth K, 'Domestic Violence as an International Human Rights Issue', in Cook RJ (ed), *Human Rights of Women – National and International Perspectives*, 1994, 326–339 at 339.
3 Grdinic E, 'Application of the Elements of Torture and Other Forms of Ill-Treatment, as Defined by the European Court and Commission of Human Rights, to the Incidents of Domestic Violence', (2000) 23 *Hastings International and Comparative Law Review,* 217–260.
4 McColgan A, 'Women and the Human Rights Act', (2000) 51 *Northern Ireland Legal Quarterly*, 417–444.
5 McColgan, op. cit., at 417.
6 McColgan, op. cit., at 417.
7 McColgan, op. cit., at 444.
8 Temkin J, 'Rape and Criminal Justice at the Millennium', in Nicolson D and Bibbings L (eds), *Feminist Perspectives on Criminal Law*, 2000, 183–203 at 203.
9 Ewing AP, 'Establishing State Responsibility For Private Acts of Violence Against Women Under the American Convention on Human Rights', (1995) 26 *Columbia Human Rights Law Review,* 751–800 at 753.
10 Charlesworth H, 'What are "Women's International Human Rights"?', in Cook RJ (ed), *Human Rights of Women – National and International Perspectives*, 1994, 58–84 at 68.
11 *Stubbings and Others v United Kingdom* (1997) 23 EHRR 213.
12 McColgan, op. cit., at 429.
13 Beetham D, 'What Future for Economic and Social Rights?', (1995) 43 *Political Studies,* 41, as cited by Steiner HJ and Alston P, *International Human Rights in Context – Law, Politics, Morals,* 2000, at 255.
14 Oloka-Onyango J, 'Reinforcing Marginalized Rights in an Age of Globalization: International Mechanisms, Non-State Actors, and the Struggle for Peoples' Rights in Africa', (2003) 18 *American University International Law Review,* 851–913 at 852.
15 *Airey v Ireland* (1981) 3 EHRR 592.
16 The Court first stated this principle in *Tyrer v United Kingdom* (1979–80) 2 EHRR 1, at para. 31.
17 [2004] EWCA Civ 309.
18 [2004] 1 All ER 709, at para. 62.
19 [2005] UKHL 66.
20 Epp CR, *The Rights Revolution*, 1998, at 3.
21 Van Schaack B, 'With All Deliberate Speed: Civil Human Rights Litigation as a Tool For Social Change', (2004) 57 *Vanderbilt Law Review*, 2305–2348 at 2307.

22 Palmer S, 'Feminism and the Promise of Human Rights: Possibilities and Paradoxes', in James S and Palmer S (eds), *Visible Women,* 2002, 91–115 at 101.

23 Epp, op. cit., at 9.

24 (1999) 27 EHRR 611.

25 Epp, op. cit., at 15.

26 Walby S and Allen J, 'Domestic violence, sexual assault and stalking: Findings from the British Crime Survey', 2004, Home Office Research Study 276, at 97.

27 Cook RJ, 'State Accountability Under the Convention on the Elimination of All Forms of Discrimination Against Women', in Cook RJ (ed), *Human Rights of Women – National and International Perspectives*, 1994, 228–256.

28 Fitzpatrick J, 'The Use of International Human Rights Norms to Combat Violence Against Women', in Cook RJ (ed), *Human Rights of Women – National and International Perspectives*, 1994, 532–571 at 534–535.

29 Thomas C, 'Domestic Violence', in Askin KD and Koenig DM (eds), *Women and International Human Rights Law*, Vol. 1, 1999, 219–256 at 244–252.

30 Thomas, op. cit., at 256.

31 Another alternative may be the Indian/US concept of public interest litigation.

32 U.N. Doc A/47/38 (1992) at para. 9.

33 Ulrich JL, 'Confronting Gender-Based Violence With International Instruments: Is a Solution to the Pandemic Within Reach?', (2000) 7 *Indiana Journal of Global Legal Studies*, 629–654 at 637.

34 Merry SE, 'Constructing a Global Law – Violence against Women and the Human Rights System', (2003) 28 *Law and Social Inquiry*, 941–974 at 943.

35 Ritz KL, 'Soft Enforcement: Inadequacies of Optional Protocol as a Remedy for the Convention on the Elimination of All Forms of Discrimination Against Women', (2001) 25 *Suffolk Transnational Law Review*, 191–216 at 193.

36 Afsharipour A, 'Empowering Ourselves: The Role of Women's NGOs in the Enforcement of the Women's Convention', (1999) 99 *Columbia Law Review*, 129–172 at 129.

Bibliography

Afsharipour A, 'Empowering Ourselves: The Role of Women's NGOs in the Enforcement of the Women's Convention', (1999) 99 *Columbia Law Review*, 129–172.

Armatta J, 'Getting Beyond the Law's Complicity in Intimate Violence Against Women', (1997) 33 *Willamette Law Review*, 774–845.

Ashworth A, 'Restorative Justice and Victims' Rights', (2000) *New Zealand Law Journal*, 84–88.

Balos B, 'Symposium: Domestic Violence & the Law: Theory, Policy, and Practice: A Man's Home is his Castle: How the Law Shelters Domestic Violence and Sexual Harassment', (2004) 23 *Saint Louis University Public Law Review*, 77–105.

Bamforth N, 'The True "Horizontal Effect" of the Human Rights Act 1998', (2001) 117 *Law Quarterly Review*, 34–41.

Banks HD and Randolph SM, 'Substance Abuse and Family Violence', in Hampton RL (ed), *Family Violence – Prevention and Treatment*, 1999, Sage Publications, Thousand Oaks, 288–308.

Barran D, 'Developments in Protecting Victims of Domestic Abuse', [2009] *Family Law* 416.

Becker M, 'Access to Justice: The Social Responsibility of Lawyers: Access to Justice for Battered Women', (2003) 12 *Washington University Journal of Law & Policy*, 63–98.

Bell C, 'In Practice: Domestic Violence and Contact', [2008] *Family Law* 1139.

Bennett LW and Williams OJ, 'Men Who Batter', in Hampton RL (ed), *Family Violence – Prevention and Treatment*, 1999, Sage Publications, Thousand Oaks, 227–259.

Berry DB, *The Domestic Violence Sourcebook*, 1998, Lowell House, Los Angeles.

Binion G, 'Human Rights: A Feminist Perspective', (1995) 17 *Human Rights Quarterly*, 509–526.

Birch D, 'A Better Deal for Vulnerable Witnesses', [2000] *Criminal Law Review*, 223–249.

Black D, 'The long and winding road: international norms and domestic political change in South Africa', in Risse T, Ropp SC and Sikkink K (eds), *The Power of Human Rights – International Norms and Domestic Change*, 1999, Cambridge University Press, 78–108.

Blake N, 'Importing Proportionality: Clarification or Confusion', [2002] *European Human Rights Law Review*, 19–27.

Bridge C, 'Re G (Domestic Violence: Direct Contact) Comment', [2000] *Family Law Review*, 789–790.

Bruce E, 'Attitudes of Social Workers and Police in the Select Committee Report on Violence to Women and Children', in University of Bradford, *Battered Women and Abused Children – Intricacies of Legal and Administrative Intervention*, 1979, Issues Publications, University of Bradford, 50–61.

Burman JM, 'Lawyers and Domestic Violence: Raising the Standard of Practice', (2003) 9 *Michigan Journal of Gender & Law*, 207–259.

Burton M, *Legal Responses to Domestic Violence*, 2008, Routledge-Cavendish, Abingdon.

Buss D, 'Prosecuting Mass Rape: *Prosecutor v Dragoljub Kunarac, Radomir Kovac and Zoran Vukovic*' (2002) 10 *Feminist Legal Studies*, 91–99.

Bustelo MR, 'The Committee on the Elimination of Discrimination Against Women at the Crossroads', in Alston P and Crawford J (eds), *The Future of UN Human Rights Treaty Monitoring*, 2000, Cambridge University Press, 79–111.

Buxton R, 'The Human Rights Act and Private Law', (2000) 116 *Law Quarterly Review*, 48–65.

Byrnes A, 'Enforcement Through International Law and Procedures', in Cook RJ (ed), *Human Rights of Women – National and International Perspectives*, 1994, University of Pennsylvania Press, Philadelphia, 189–227.

Byrnes A and Bath E, 'Violence against women, the obligation of due diligence, and the Optional Protocol to the Convention on the Elimination of All Forms of Discrimination Against Women – recent developments', (2008) 8 *Human Rights Law Review*, 517–533.

Carter J, *Domestic Violence, Child Abuse, and Youth Violence: Strategies for Prevention and Early Intervention*, 2000, available at http://mincava.umn.edu/link/documents/fvpf2/fvpf2.shtml (Minnesota Center Against Violence and Abuse).

Cassel D, 'Does International Human Rights Law Make a Difference?', (2001) 2 *Chicago Journal of International Law*, 121–135.

Charlesworth H, 'What are "Women's International Human Rights"?', in Cook RJ (ed), *Human Rights of Women – National and International Perspectives*, 1994, University of Pennsylvania Press, Philadelphia, 58–84.

Charlesworth H and Chinkin C, *The Boundaries of International Law – A Feminist Analysis*, 2000, Manchester University Press.

Chayes A, 'The Role of the Judge in Public Law Litigation', (1976) 89 *Harvard Law Review*, 1281–1316.

Choudhry S and Herring J, 'Domestic Violence and the Human Rights Act 1998: A New Means of Legal Intervention?', (2006) *Public Law*, 752–784.

Choudhry S and Herring J, 'Righting Domestic Violence', (2006) *International Journal of Law, Policy and the Family*, 95–119.

Clapham A, *Human Rights in the Private Sphere*, 1993, Clarendon, Oxford.

Clare A, 'Statutory Interpretation Post-Human Rights Act 1998; Youth Justice and Criminal Evidence Act 1999 Must Be Read So As to Be Compatible with the European Convention on Human Rights', (2001) 65 *Journal of Criminal Law*, 411–413.

Clayton R, 'Judicial deference and "democratic dialogue": the legitimacy of judicial intervention under the Human Rights Act 1998', [2004] *Public Law*, 33–47.

Connelly C and Cavanagh K, 'Domestic Abuse, Civil Protection Orders and the "New Criminologies": Is there any Value in Engaging with the Law?', (2007) 15 *Feminist Legal Studies*, 259–287.

Cook RJ, 'State Accountability Under the Convention on the Elimination of All Forms of Discrimination Against Women', in Cook RJ (ed), *Human Rights of Women – National and International Perspectives*, 1994, University of Pennsylvania Press, Philadelphia, 228–256.

Cook RJ, 'Women's International Human Rights Law: The Way Forward', in Cook RJ (ed), *Human Rights of Women – National and International Perspectives*, 1994, University of Pennsylvania Press, Philadelphia, 1–36.

Cook RJ, 'State Responsibility For Violations of Women's Human Rights', (1994) 7 *Harvard Human Rights Journal*, 125–175.

Copelon R, 'Intimate Terror: Understanding Domestic Violence as Torture', in Cook RJ, *Human Rights of Women – National and International Perspectives*, 1994, University of Pennsylvania Press, Philadelphia, 116–152.

Copelon R, 'International Human Rights Dimensions of Intimate Violence: Another Strand in the Dialectic of Feminist Lawmaking', (2003) 11 *American University Journal of Gender, Social Policy and the Law*, 865–876.

Crawford A and Enterkin J, 'Victim Contact Work in the Probation Service: Paradigm Shift or Pandora's Box?', (2001) 41 *British Journal of Criminology*, 707–725.

Crawford A and Goodey J (eds), *Integrating a Victim Perspective within Criminal Justice*, 2000, Ashgate Dartmouth, Aldershot.

Cretney A and Davis G, 'Prosecuting "Domestic" Assault', [1996] *Criminal Law Review*, 162–174.

Cretney A and Davis G, 'Prosecuting Domestic Assault: Victims Failing Courts, or Courts Failing Victims?', (1997) 36 *The Howard Journal*, 146–157.

Cretney SM, Masson JM and Bailey-Harris R, *Principles of Family Law*, 2002, Sweet & Maxwell, London.

Davidson L, King V, Garcia J and Marchant S, 'Reducing Domestic Violence . . . What Works? Health Services', 2000, Crime Reduction Research Series, available at http://www.homeoffice.gov.uk.

Davidson LL, King V, Garcia J and Marchant S, 'What role can the health services play?', in Taylor-Browne J (ed), *What Works in Reducing Domestic Violence? A comprehensive guide for professionals*, 2001, Whiting & Birch Ltd, London, 95–122.

Dennis MJ and Stewart DP, 'Justiciability of Economic, Social, and Cultural Rights: Should There be an International Complaints Mechanism to Adjudicate the Rights to Food, Water, Housing, and Health?', (2004) 98 *American Journal of International Law*, 462–515.

Diduck A and Kaganas F, *Family Law, Gender and the State*, 1999, Hart Publishing, Oxford.

Dignan J and Cavadino M, 'Towards a Framework for Conceptualising and Evaluating Models of Criminal Justice from a Victim's Perspective', (1996) 4 *International Review of Victimology*, 153–182.

Dixon R, 'Rape as a Crime in International Humanitarian Law: Where to from Here?' (2002) 13 *European Journal of International Law*, 697–719.

Dobash RE and Dobash RP, *Women, Violence & Social Change*, 1996, Routledge, London.

Douglas N, Lilley SJ, Kooper L and Diamond A, 'Safety and justice: sharing personal information in the context of domestic violence – an overview', 2004, Home Office Development and Practice Report No. 30, Home Office, London.

Edwards I, 'Victim Participation in Sentencing; The Problem of Incoherence', (2001) 40 *Howard Journal of Criminal Justice*, 39–54.

Edwards RA, 'Judicial Deference under the Human Rights Act', (2002) 65 *Modern Law Review*, 859–882.

Edwards S, 'Domestic violence and harassment: An assessment of the civil remedies', in Taylor-Browne J (ed), *What Works in Reducing Domestic Violence? A comprehensive guide for professionals*, 2001, Whiting & Birch Ltd, London, 187–210.

Edwards S, 'New directions in prosecution', in Taylor-Browne J (ed), *What Works in Reducing Domestic Violence? A comprehensive guide for professionals*, 2001, Whiting & Birch Ltd, London, 211–238.

Ekins R, 'A Critique of Radical Approaches to Rights-Consistent Statutory Interpretation', [2003] *European Human Rights Law Review*, 641–650.

Elias R, *The Politics of Victimization*, 1986, Oxford University Press.

Epp CR, *The Rights Revolution*, 1998, University of Chicago Press, Chicago and London.

Evatt E, 'Finding a Voice for Women's Rights: The Early Days of CEDAW', (2002) 34 *George Washington International Law Review*, 515–553.

Ewing AP, 'Establishing State Responsibility For Private Acts of Violence Against Women Under the American Convention on Human Rights', (1995) 26 *Columbia Human Rights Law Review*, 751–800.

Ewing KD, 'The Futility of the Human Rights Act', [2004] *Public Law*, 829–852.

Fenwick H, 'Clashing Rights, the Welfare of the Child and the Human Rights Act', (2004) 67 *Modern Law Review*, 889–927.

Fenwick H, 'Procedural "Rights" of Victims of Crime: Public or Private Ordering of the Criminal Justice Process?', (1997) 60 *Modern Law Review*, 317–333.

Fitzpatrick J, 'The Use of International Human Rights Norms to Combat Violence Against Women', in Cook RJ (ed), *Human Rights of Women – National and International Perspectives*, 1994, University of Pennsylvania Press, Philadelphia, 532–571.

Fortin J, *Children's Rights and the Developing Law*, 2003, Butterworths, London.

Fredman S, 'Social, Economic and Cultural Rights', in Feldman D (ed), *English Public Law*, 2004, Oxford University Press, 529–579.

Freedman AE, 'Symposium: Fact-Finding in Civil Domestic Violence Cases: Secondary Traumatic Stress and the Need for Compassionate Witnesses', (2003) 11 *American University Journal of Gender, Social Policy & the Law*, 567–656.

Garvey LE, 'Symposium: The Race Card: Dealing With Domestic Violence in the Courts', (2003) 11 *American University Journal of Gender, Social Policy & the Law*, 287–307.

Gearty CA, 'Reconciling Parliamentary Democracy and Human Rights', (2002) 118 *Law Quarterly Review*, 248–269.

Gearty C, *Principles of Human Rights Adjudication*, 2004, Oxford University Press.

Goodmark L, 'Symposium: Domestic Violence & the Law: Theory, Policy, and Practice: Law is the Answer? Do we Know that for Sure?: Questioning the Efficacy of Legal Interventions for Battered Women', (2004) 23 *Saint Louis University Public Law Review*, 7–48.

Grace S, 'Policing Domestic Violence in the 1990s', 1995, Home Office Research Study 139, HMSO, London.

Grdinic E, 'Application of the Elements of Torture and Other Forms of Ill-Treatment, as Defined by the European Court and Commission of Human

Rights, to the Incidents of Domestic Violence', (2000) 23 *Hastings International and Comparative Law Review*, 217–260.

Hague G, 'Domestic violence policy in the 1990s', in Watson S and Doyal L (eds), *Engendering Social Policy*, 1999, Open University Press, Buckingham, 131–147.

Hague G, 'Reducing Domestic Violence . . . What Works? Multi-Agency Fora', 2000, Crime Reduction Research Series, available at http://www.homeoffice. gov.uk.

Hague G, 'Multi-agency initiatives', in Taylor-Browne J (ed), *What Works in Reducing Domestic Violence? A comprehensive guide for professionals*, 2001, Whiting & Birch Ltd, London, 275–305.

Hague G and Malos E, *Domestic Violence: Action for Change*, 2005, New Clarion Press, Cheltenham.

Hague G, Mullender A, Aris R and Dear W, 'Abused Women's Perspectives: Responsiveness and Accountability of Domestic Violence and Inter-Agency Initiatives', 2001, Report to the ESRC.

Hale B, Pearl D, Cooke E and Bates P, *The Family, Law & Society*, 2002, Butterworths, London.

Hall M, 'The Relationship between Victims and Prosecutors: Defending Victims' Rights?', (2010) *Criminal Law Review*, 31–45.

Hampton RL, Jenkins P and Vandergriff-Avery M, 'Physical and Sexual Violence in Marriage', in Hampton RL (ed), *Family Violence – Prevention and Treatment*, 1999, Sage Publications, Thousand Oaks, 168–197.

Hanmer J and Griffiths S, 'Reducing Domestic Violence . . . What Works? Policing Domestic Violence', 2000, Crime Reduction Research Series, available at http:// www.homeoffice.gov.uk.

Hanmer J and Griffiths S, 'Effective policing', in Taylor-Browne J (ed), *What Works in Reducing Domestic Violence? A comprehensive guide for professionals*, 2001, Whiting & Birch Ltd, London, 123–150.

Hanmer J, Griffiths S and Jerwood D, 'Arresting Evidence: Domestic Violence and Repeat Victimisation', 1999, Police Research Series Paper 104, available at http://www.homeoffice.gov.uk.

Harvey C, 'Talking about Human Rights', [2004] *European Human Rights Law Review*, 500–516.

Hernandez-Truyol BE, 'Conceptualizing Violence: Present and Future Developments in International Law', (1997) 60 *Albany Law Review*, 607–634.

Herring J, *Family Law*, 2009, Pearson Education Limited, Harlow.

Hester M, *Who Does What to Whom? Gender and Domestic Violence Perpetrators*, 2009, University of Bristol in association with the Northern Rock Foundation, Bristol.

Hester M, Hanmer J, Coulson S, Morahan M and Razak A, *Domestic Violence: Making it Through the Criminal Justice System*, 2003, University of Sunderland and Northern Rock Foundation, Sunderland.

Hester M and Radford L, 'Contradictions and compromises: the impact of the Children Act on women and children's safety', in Hester M, Kelly L and Radford J (eds), *Women, Violence and Male Power*, 2002, Open University Press, Buckingham, 81–98.

Hester M and Westmarland N, 'Tackling Domestic Violence: effective interventions and approaches', 2005, Home Office Research Study 290, available at http:// www.homeoffice.gov.uk.

Hester M, Westmarland N, Pearce J and Williamson E, 'Early Evaluation of the Domestic Violence, Crime and Victims Act 2004', 2008, Ministry of Justice Research Series 14/08.

Heyns C and Viljoen F, *The Impact of the United Nations Human Rights Treaties on the Domestic Level*, 2002, Kluwer Law International, The Hague.

Hirschl R, ' "Negative" Rights vs. "Positive" Entitlements: A Comparative Study of Judicial Interpretations of Rights in an Emerging Neo-Liberal Economic Order', (2000) 22 *Human Rights Quarterly*, 1060–1097.

Hopkins CQ, 'Rescripting Relationships: Towards a Nuanced Theory of Intimate Violence as Sex Discrimination', (2001) 9 *Virginia Journal of Social Policy & the Law*, 411–469.

Hopkins CQ, Koss MP and Bachar KJ, 'Symposium: Domestic Violence & the Law: Theory, Policy, and Practice: Applying Restorative Justice to Ongoing Intimate Violence: Problems and Possibilities', (2004) 23 *Saint Louis University Public Law Review*, 289–311.

Hughes B, 'Can Domestic Violence be considered a Violation of Human Rights Law?', (2006) 14 *British Journal of Midwifery*, 192.

Humphries M, 'Occupation Orders Revisited', [2001] *Family Law Review*, 542–544.

Hunt M, 'The "Horizontal Effect" of the Human Rights Act', [1998] *Public Law*, 423–443.

Lord Irvine of Lairg, 'The Impact of the Human Rights Act: Parliament, the Courts and the Executive', [2003] *Public Law*, 308–325.

James A, 'In Practice: Prosecuting Domestic Violence', [2008] *Family Law*, 456.

Johnstone RL, 'Feminist Influences on the United Nations Human Rights Treaty Bodies', (2006) 28 *Human Rights Quarterly* 148–185.

Jones D and Brown J, 'The Relationship between Victims and Prosecutors: Defending Victims' Rights? A CPS Response', (2010) *Criminal Law Review*, 212–225.

Jowell J, 'Judicial deference: servility, civility or institutional capacity?', [2003] *Public Law*, 592–601.

Kavanagh A, 'Statutory interpretation and human rights after *Anderson*: a more contextual approach', [2004] *Public Law*, 537–545.

Kavanagh A, 'Unlocking the Human Rights Act: The "Radical" Approach to Section 3(1) Revisited', [2005] *European Human Rights Law Review*, 259–275.

Kay RS, 'The European Convention on Human Rights and the Control of Private Law', [2005] *European Human Rights Law Review*, 466–479.

Kelly L, 'Domestic Violence Matters: an evaluation of a development project', 1999, Home Office Research Study 193, Home Office, London.

Kelly L and Radford J, ' "Nothing really happened": the invalidation of women's experiences of sexual violence', in Hester M, Kelly L and Radford J, *Women, Violence and Male Power*, 2002, Open University Press, Buckingham, 19–33.

Kennedy D, *The Dark Sides of Virtue – Reassessing International Humanitarianism*, 2004, Princeton University Press, Princeton and Oxford.

Klug F, 'Judicial Deference Under the Human Rights Act 1998', [2003] *European Human Rights Law Review*, 125–133.

Klug F and Starmer K, 'Standing Back from the Human Rights Act: how effective is it five years on?', [2005] *Public Law*, 716–728.

Lester A, 'The Human Rights Act 1998 – Five Years On', [2004] *European Human Rights Law Review*, 258–271.

Levison D and Harwin N, 'Accommodation provision', in Taylor-Browne J (ed), *What Works in Reducing Domestic Violence? A comprehensive guide for professionals*, 2001, Whiting & Birch Ltd, London, 151–185.

Lyon B, 'Postcolonial Law: Theory and Law Reform Conference: Discourse in Development: A Post-Colonial "Agenda" for the United Nations Committee on Economic, Social and Cultural Rights', (2002) 10 *American University Journal of Gender, Social Policy and the Law*, 535–579.

McColgan A, 'Women and the Human Rights Act', (2000) 51 *Northern Ireland Legal Quarterly*, 417–444.

McGregor G, 'The International Covenant on Social, Economic, and Cultural Rights: Will it Get its Day in Court?', (2002) 28 *The Manitoba Law Journal*, 321–345.

McKeever G and Ni Aolain F, 'Thinking Globally, Acting Locally: Enforcing Socio-Economic Rights in Northern Ireland' [2004] *European Human Rights Law Review*, 158–180.

McQuigg R, 'The Responses of States to the Comments of the CEDAW Committee on Domestic Violence', (2007) 11 *International Journal of Human Rights*, 461–479.

Maguigan H, 'Wading into Professor Schneider's "Murky Middle Ground" Between Acceptance and Rejection of Criminal Justice Responses to Domestic Violence', (2003) 11 *American University Journal of Gender, Social Policy and the Law*, 427–445.

Mall LL, 'The Right to Privacy in Great Britain: Will Renewed Anti-Media Sentiment Compel Great Britain to Create a Right to Be Let Alone?', (1998) 4 *ILSA Journal of International and Comparative Law*, 785–815.

Marriott J and Nicol D, 'The Human Rights Act, Representative Standing and the Victim Culture', [1998] *European Human Rights Law Review*, 730–741.

Mawby RI and Walklate S, *Critical Victimology*, 1998, Sage, London.

Merry SE, 'Rights Talk and the Experience of Law: Implementing Women's Human Rights to Protection from Violence', (2003) 25 *Human Rights Quarterly*, 343–381.

Merry SE, 'Constructing a Global Law – Violence against Women and the Human Rights System', (2003) 28 *Law and Social Inquiry*, 941–974.

Miles J, 'Standing Under the Human Rights Act 1998: Theories of Rights Enforcement & the Nature of Public Law Adjudication', (2000) 59 *Cambridge Law Journal*, 133–167.

Miles J, 'Domestic Violence', in Herring J (ed), *Family Law – Issues, Debates, Policy*, 2001, Willan Publishing, Devon, 78–124.

Mirrlees-Black C, 'Domestic Violence: Findings from a new British Crime Survey self-completion questionnaire', 1999, Home Office Research Study 191, Home Office, London.

Morley R and Mullender A, 'Preventing Domestic Violence to Women', 1994, Home Office Police Department, London.

Mowbray AR, *The Development of Positive Obligations under the European Convention on Human Rights by the European Court of Human Rights*, 2004, Hart Publishing, Oxford.

Mowbray A, 'The Creativity of the European Court of Human Rights', [2005] 5 *Human Rights Law Review*, 57–79.

Mullally S, 'Feminism and Multicultural Dilemmas in India: Revisiting the *Shah Bano* Case', (2004) 24 *Oxford Journal of Legal Studies*, 671–692.

Mullender A, *Re-thinking Domestic Violence*, 1996, Routledge, London.

Mullender A and Burton S, 'Reducing Domestic Violence . . . What Works? Perpetrator Programmes', 2000, Crime Reduction Research Series, available at http://www.homeoffice.gov.uk.

Mullender M and Burton S, 'Dealing with perpetrators', in Taylor-Browne J (ed), *What Works in Reducing Domestic Violence? A comprehensive guide for professionals*, 2001, Whiting & Birch Ltd, London, 59–93.

Mullender A and Hague G, 'Reducing Domestic Violence . . . What Works? Women Survivors' Views', 2000, Crime Reduction Research Series, available at http://www.homeoffice.gov.uk.

Mullender A and Hague G, 'Women survivors' views', in Taylor-Browne J (ed), *What Works in Reducing Domestic Violence? A comprehensive guide for professionals*, 2001, Whiting & Birch Ltd, London, 1–33.

Mullender A and Morley R, 'Context and Content of a New Agenda', in Mullender A and Morley R (eds), *Children Living With Domestic Violence*, 1994, Whiting & Birch Ltd, London, 2–16.

Murdoch J, 'Unfulfilled expectations: the Optional Protocol to the Convention on the Elimination of All Forms of Discrimination against Women', (2010) *European Human Rights Law Review* 26–46.

Nicolson D, 'What the Law Giveth: it also Taketh Away: Female-Specific Defences to Criminal Liability', in Nicolson D and Bibbings L (eds), *Feminist Perspectives On Criminal Law*, 2000, Cavendish Publishing, London, 159–180.

Oloka-Onyango J, 'Reinforcing Marginalized Rights in an Age of Globalization: International Mechanisms, Non-State Actors, and the Struggle for Peoples' Rights in Africa', (2003) 18 *American University International Law Review*, 851–913.

Paglione G, 'Domestic Violence and Housing Rights: A Reinterpretation of the Right to Housing', (2006) 28 *Human Rights Quarterly*, 120–147.

Palmer E, 'Courts, Resources and the HRA: Reading section 17 of the Children Act 1989 Compatibly with Article 8 ECHR', [2003] *European Human Rights Law Review*, 308–324.

Palmer S, 'Feminism and the Promise of Human Rights: Possibilities and Paradoxes', in James S and Palmer S (eds), *Visible Women*, 2002, Hart Publishing, Oxford, 91–115.

Plotnikoff J and Woolfson R, 'Policing Domestic Violence: Effective Organisational Structures', 1998, Police Research Series Paper 100, available at http://www.homeoffice.gov.uk.

Rabinowitz CB, 'Proposals for Progress: Sodomy Laws and the European Convention on Human Rights', (1995) 21 *Brooklyn Journal of International Law*, 425–469.

Randall M, 'Symposium: Domestic Violence & the Law: Theory, Policy, and Practice: Domestic Violence and the Construction of "Ideal Victims": Assaulted Women's "Image Problems" in Law', (2004) 23 *Saint Louis University Public Law Review*, 107–154.

Rishmawi M, 'The Developing Approaches of the International Commission of Jurists to Women's Human Rights', in Cook RJ (ed), *Human Rights of Women – National and International Perspectives*, 1994, University of Pennsylvania Press, Philadelphia, 340–348.

Risse T and Roppe SC, 'International human rights norms and domestic change: conclusions', in Risse T, Roppe SC and Sikkink K (eds), *The Power of Human Rights – International Norms and Domestic Change*, 1999, Cambridge University Press, 234–278.

Risse T and Sikkink K, 'The socialization of international human rights norms into domestic practices: introduction', in Risse T, Ropp SC and Sikkink K (eds), *The Power of Human Rights – International Norms and Domestic Change*, 1999, Cambridge University Press, 1–38.

Ritz KL, 'Soft Enforcement: Inadequacies of Optional Protocol as a Remedy for the Convention on the Elimination of All Forms of Discrimination Against Women', (2001) 25 *Suffolk Transnational Law Review*, 191–216.

Robinson M, 'From Rhetoric to Reality Making Human Rights Work', (2003) *European Human Rights Law Review*, 1–8.

Robinson M, 'Making Human Rights Matter: Eleanor Roosevelt's Time Has Come', (2003) 16 *Harvard Human Rights Journal*, 1–11.

Rollinson M, 'Re-Reading Criminal Law: Gendering the Mental Element', in Nicolson D and Bibbings L (eds), *Feminist Perspectives On Criminal Law*, 2000, Cavendish Publishing, London, 101–122.

Romany C, 'State Responsibility Goes Private: A Feminist Critique of the Public/Private Distinction in International Human Rights Law', in Cook RJ (ed), *Human Rights of Women – National and International Perspectives*, 1994, University of Pennsylvania Press, Philadelphia, 85–115.

Romany C, 'Women as Aliens: A Feminist Critique of the Public/Private Distinction in International Human Rights Law', (1993) 6 *Harvard Human Rights Journal*, 87–125.

Rosenberg GN, *The Hollow Hope: Can Courts Bring About Social Change?*, 1991, University of Chicago Press.

Roth K, 'Domestic Violence as an International Human Rights Issue', in Cook RJ (ed), *Human Rights of Women – National and International Perspectives*, 1994, University of Pennsylvania Press, Philadelphia, 326–339.

Sandy D, '*R v A*; the death of the declaration of incompatibility?', (2001) *New Law Journal*, 1615.

Scheingold SA, *The Politics of Rights: Lawyers, Public Policy, and Political Change*, 2004, The University of Michigan Press.

Schneider EM, *Battered Women & Feminist Lawmaking*, 2000, Yale University Press.

Schneider EM, 'Anna Hirsch Lecture: Transnational Law as a Domestic Resource: Thoughts on the Case of Women's Rights', (2004) 38 *New England Law Review*, 689–723.

Schopp-Schilling HB, 'Treaty Body Reform: The Case of the Committee on the Elimination of Discrimination Against Women', (2007) 7 *Human Rights Law Review* 201–224.

Schriver T, 'Establishing an Affirmative Governmental Duty to Protect Children's Rights: The European Court of Human Rights as a Model for the United States Supreme Court', (2000) 34 *University of San Francisco Law Review*, 379–408.

Sedley S, 'The Rocks or the Open Sea: Where is the Human Rights Act Heading?', (2005) 32 *Journal of Law and Society*, 3–17.

Selden S, 'The Practice of Domestic Violence', (2001) 12 *UCLA Women's Law Journal*, 1–54.

Shapland J, 'Victims, the Criminal Justice System and Compensation', (1984) 24 *British Journal of Criminology*, 131–149.

Smith LJF, 'Domestic Violence: an Overview of the Literature', 1989, Home Office Research Study 107, HMSO, London.

Soteri A, *Funding in London Women's Organisations – A First Report*, 2002, Centre for Institutional Studies, University of East London.

Stanko EA, *Intimate Intrusions*, 1985, Routledge & Kegan Paul, London.

Stark B, 'Symposium on Integrating Responses to Domestic Violence', (2001) 47 *Loyola Law Review*, 255–282.

Starmer K, *European Human Rights Law, the Human Rights Act 1998 and the European Convention on Human Rights*, 1999, LAG, London.

Steiner HJ and Alston P, *International Human Rights in Context – Law, Politics, Morals*, 2000, Oxford University Press.

Lord Steyn, 'Deference: a Tangled Story', [2005] *Public Law*, 346–359.

Lord Steyn, '2000–2005: Laying the Foundations of Human Rights Law in the United Kingdom', [2005] *European Human Rights Law Review*, 349–362.

Strossen N, 'Recent U.S. and International Judicial Protection of Individual Rights: A Comparative Legal Process Analysis and Proposed Synthesis', (1990) 41 *Hastings Law Journal*, 805–904.

Sturge C in consultation with Glaser D, 'Contact and Domestic Violence – The Experts' Court Report', [2000] *Law Review*, 615.

Sullivan CM, 'Using the ESID Model to Reduce Intimate Male Violence Against Women', (2003) 32 *American Journal of Community Psychology*, 295–303.

Taket A, 'Tackling Domestic Violence: the role of health professionals', Home Office Development and Practice Report 32, 2004, available at http://www.homeoffice.gov.uk.

Temkin J, 'Rape and Criminal Justice at the Millennium', in Nicolson D and Bibbings L (eds), *Feminist Perspectives On Criminal Law*, 2000, Cavendish Publishing, London, 183–203.

Thomas C, 'Domestic Violence', in Askin KD and Koenig DM (eds), *Women and International Human Rights Law*, Vol. 1, 1999, Transnational Publishers, Inc., New York, 219–256.

Thomas DQ and Beasley ME, 'Symposium on Reconceptualizing Violence Against Women By Intimate Partners', (1995) 58 *Albany Law Review*, 1119–1147.

Ulrich JL, 'Confronting Gender-Based Violence With International Instruments: Is a Solution to the Pandemic Within Reach?', (2000) 7 *Indiana Journal of Global Legal Studies*, 629–654.

Van Bueren G, 'Including the Excluded: the Case for an Economic, Social and Cultural Human Rights Act', [2002] *Public Law*, 456–472.

Van Leeuwen F, *Women's Rights Are Human Rights*, 2010, Intersentia, Antwerp.

Van Schaack B, 'With All Deliberate Speed: Civil Human Rights Litigation as a Tool For Social Change', (2004) 57 *Vanderbilt Law Review*, 2305–2348.

Vesa A, 'International and Regional Standards for Protecting Victims of Domestic Violence', (2004) 12 *American University Journal of Gender, Social Policy and the Law*, 309–360.

Wade HRW, 'Horizons of Horizontality', (2000) 116 *Law Quarterly Review*, 217–224.

Wade W, 'Opinion: Human Rights and the Judiciary', [1998] *European Human Rights Law Review*, 520–533.

Walby S, 'The Cost of Domestic Violence', 2004, available at http://www.equalities.gov.uk.

Walby S and Allen J, 'Domestic violence, sexual assault and stalking: Findings from the British Crime Survey', 2004, Home Office Research Study 276, Home Office, London.

Walker A, Flatley J, Kershaw C and Moon D, 'Crime in England and Wales 2008/09: Home Office Statistical Bulletin', 2009.

Walklate S, 'What is to be done about violence against women? Gender, violence, cosmopolitanism and the law', (2008) 48 *British Journal of Criminology*, 39–54.

Wallace RMM, *International Human Rights*, 2001, Sweet & Maxwell, London.

Woods JM, 'Justiciable Social Rights as a Critique of the Liberal Paradigm', (2003) 38 *Texas International Law Journal*, 763–793.

Zedner L, 'Victims', in Maguire M, Morgan R and Reiner R (eds), *The Oxford Handbook of Criminology*, 2002, Oxford University Press, 419–456.

Zhang L, 'Domestic violence network in China: Translating the transnational concept of violence against women into local action', (2009) 32 *Women's Studies International Forum*, 227–239.

Index